1st Workshop on Formalisms and Methodology for Learning by Reading 2010

(FAM-LbR)

Held at NAACL HLT 2010

Los Angeles, California, USA
6 June 2010

ISBN: 978-1-61738-678-7

Printed from e-media with permission by:

Curran Associates, Inc.
57 Morehouse Lane
Red Hook, NY 12571

Some format issues inherent in the e-media version may also appear in this print version.

Printed by Curran Associates, Inc. (2010)

For permission requests, please contact the Association for Computational Linguistics
at the address below.

Association for Computational Linguistics
209 N. Eighth Street
Stroudsburg, Pennsylvania 18360

Phone: 1-570-476-8006
Fax: 1-570-476-0860

acl@aclweb.org

Additional copies of this publication are available from:

Curran Associates, Inc.
57 Morehouse Lane
Red Hook, NY 12571 USA
Phone: 845-758-0400
Fax: 845-758-2634
Email: curran@proceedings.com
Web: www.proceedings.com

Introduction

It has been a long term vision of Artificial Intelligence to develop Learning by Reading systems that can capture knowledge from naturally occurring texts, convert it into a deep logical notation and perform some inferences/reasoning on them. Such systems directly build on relatively mature areas of research, including Information Extraction (for picking out relevant information from the text), Commonsense and AI Reasoning (for deriving inferences from the knowledge acquired), Bootstrapped Learning (for using the learned knowledge to expand the knowledge base) and Question Answering (for providing evaluation mechanisms for Learning by Reading systems). In Natural Language Processing, statistical learning techniques have provided new solutions and breakthroughs in various areas over the last decade. In Knowledge Representation and Reasoning, systems have achieved impressive performance and scale in far more complex problems than the past.

Learning by Reading is a two-part process. One part deals with extracting interesting information from naturally occurring texts, and the other is to use this extracted knowledge to expand the knowledge base and consequently the system's inference capabilities. Previous systems have chosen either a "broad and shallow" or a "narrow and deep" knowledge acquisition and reasoning strategy. These techniques are constrained by either their limited reasoning ability or their extreme domain dependence.

The goal of this workshop is to draw together researchers to explore the nature and degree of integration possible between symbolic and statistical techniques for knowledge acquisition and reasoning. In particular, given these developments, what is the role of commonsense knowledge and reasoning in language understanding? What are the limitations of each style of processing, and how can they be overcome by complementary strengths of the other? What are appropriate evaluation metrics for Learning by Reading systems?

Organizers:

Rutu Mulkar-Mehta (University of Southern California)
James Allen (University of Rochester)
Jerry Hobbs (University of Southern California)
Eduard Hovy (University of Southern California)
Bernardo Magnini (Povo-Trento, Italy)
Chris Manning (Stanford University)

Program Committee:

Ken Barker (University of Texas, Austin)
Peter Clark (Boeing)
Ido Dagan (Bar Ilan University)
Oren Etzioni (University of Washington)
David Ferrucci (IBM)
Marjorie Freedman (BBN)
Tom Mitchell (Carnegie Mellon University)
Dan Moldovan (University of Texas at Dallas)
Alessandro Moschitti (University of Trento)
Sergei Nirenburg (University of Maryland, Baltimore County)
Tim Oates (University of Maryland, Baltimore County)
Dan Oblinger (DARPA)
Ellen Riloff (University of Utah)
Stuart Shapiro (SUNY Buffalo)
Len Schubert (Rochester University)
Ralph Weischedel (BBN)
Michael Witbrock (Cyc Corp.)

Table of Contents

Workshop Program

Sunday, June 6, 2010

9:00–9:10 **Opening**

Session 1

9:10–9:30 *Machine Reading as a Process of Partial Question-Answering*
Peter Clark and Phil Harrison

9:30–9:50 *Building an end-to-end text reading system based on a packed representation*
Doo Soon Kim, Ken Barker and Bruce Porter

9:50–10:10 *Semantic Enrichment of Text with Background Knowledge*
Anselmo Peñas and Eduard Hovy

10:10–10:30 Discussion

10:30–11:00 **Break**

Session 2

11:00–11:20 *Large Scale Relation Detection*
Chris Welty, James Fan, David Gondek and Andrew Schlaikjer

11:20–11:40 *Mining Script-Like Structures from the Web*
Niels Kasch and Tim Oates

11:40–12:00 *Open-domain Commonsense Reasoning Using Discourse Relations from a Corpus of Weblog Stories*
Matthew Gerber, Andrew Gordon and Kenji Sagae

12:00–12:20 Discussion

12:20–2:00 **Lunch**

Sunday, June 6, 2010 (continued)

Session 3

2:00–2:20 *Semantic Role Labeling for Open Information Extraction*
Janara Christensen, Mausam, Stephen Soderland and Oren Etzioni

2:20–2:40 *Empirical Studies in Learning to Read*
Marjorie Freedman, Edward Loper, Elizabeth Boschee and Ralph Weischedel

2:40–3:00 *Learning Rules from Incomplete Examples: A Pragmatic Approach*
Janardhan Rao Doppa, Mohammad NasrEsfahani, Mohammad Sorower, Thomas G. Dietterich, Xiaoli Fern and Prasad Tadepalli

3:00–3:30 **Break**

3:30–4:30 **Poster Session**

Unsupervised techniques for discovering ontology elements from Wikipedia article links
Zareen Syed and Tim Finin

Machine Reading at the University of Washington
Hoifung Poon, Janara Christensen, Pedro Domingos, Oren Etzioni, Raphael Hoffmann, Chloe Kiddon, Thomas Lin, Xiao Ling, Mausam, Alan Ritter, Stefan Schoenmackers, Stephen Soderland, Dan Weld, Fei Wu and Congle Zhang

Analogical Dialogue Acts: Supporting Learning by Reading Analogies
David Barbella and Kenneth Forbus

A Hybrid Approach to Unsupervised Relation Discovery Based on Linguistic Analysis and Semantic Typing
Zareen Syed and Evelyne Viegas

Supporting rule-based representations with corpus-derived lexical information.
Annie Zaenen, Cleo Condoravdi, Daniel Bobrow and Raphael Hoffmann

PRISMATIC: Inducing Knowledge from a Large Scale Lexicalized Relation Resource
James Fan, David Ferrucci, David Gondek and Aditya Kalyanpur

4:30–5:00 **Discussion**

Machine Reading as a Process of Partial Question-Answering

Peter Clark and Phil Harrison
Boeing Research & Technology
The Boeing Company, PO Box 3707, Seattle, WA 98124, USA
{peter.e.clark,philip.harrison}@boeing.com

Abstract

This paper explores the close relationship between question answering and machine reading, and how the active use of reasoning to answer (and in the process, disambiguate) questions can also be applied to reading declarative texts, where a substantial proportion of the text's contents is already known to (represented in) the system. In question answering, a question may be ambiguous, and it may only be in the process of trying to answer it that the "right" way to disambiguate it becomes apparent. Similarly in machine reading, a text may be ambiguous, and may require some process to relate it to what is already known. Our conjecture in this paper is that these two processes are similar, and that we can modify a question answering tool to help "read" new text that augments existing system knowledge. Specifically, interpreting a new text T can be recast as trying to answer, or partially answer, the question "Is it true that T?", resulting in both appropriate disambiguation and connection of T to existing knowledge. Some preliminary investigation suggests this might be useful for proposing knowledge base extensions, extracted from text, to a knowledge engineer.

1 Introduction

Machine reading is not just a task of language processing, but an active interplay between knowledge and language; Prior knowledge should guide interpretation of new text, and new interpretations should augment that prior knowledge. Such interaction is essential if ambiguities in language are to be resolved "correctly" (with respect to what is known), and if the resulting interpretations are to be integrated with existing knowledge. The main insight of this paper is that this interaction is similar to that required for knowledge-based question answering, which also requires searching a knowledge base (KB) for a valid interpretation of the question. In our earlier work on question answering (Clark and Harrison, 2010), we found that some disambiguation decisions for question interpretation could be deferred, to be resolved during question answering, guided by what was found in the KB. In this paper, we show how a similar approach can be applied to interpreting declarative text, so that a similar interplay between language and knowledge is achieved.

"Machine reading" itself is a loosely-defined notion, ranging from extracting selective facts to constructing complex, inference-supporting representations of text. One approach for selective extraction is the use of semantic templates ("scripts", "frames") to provide a set of roles (slots) and constraints on objects playing those roles (fillers) to be expected in text, and might be filled by methods ranging from simply skimming text, e.g., FRUMP (DeJong, 1979), to full language processing, e.g., (Dahlgren et al., 1991). Other work has looked at techniques for learning phrasal patterns likely to contain slot fillers (Riloff, 1996; Sekine, 2006) or contain information semantically similar to a set of seed examples (Carlson et al, 2009).

At the other end of the spectrum, some systems attempt a full understanding of text, i.e., have the ambitious goal of building a complete representation of the text's contents (e.g., Zadrozny 1991, Hobbs et al, 1993). A common thread of these approaches is to search a space of alternative disambiguations and elaborations and select the most

Proceedings of the NAACL HLT 2010 First International Workshop on Formalisms and Methodology for Learning by Reading, pages 1–9,
Los Angeles, California, June 2010.

"coherent", based on criteria such as maximizing coreference, minimizing redundancy, and avoiding contradictions. For example, Mulkar et al (2007) search for a set of abductive inferences on the (logical form of the) text that minimizes cost (maximizes coherence) of the result, where an abductive inference might be a word sense or coreference decision with an associated cost. Similarly, Zadrozny and Jensen (1991) search a space of disambiguations when interpreting paragraphs by elaborating each alternative (using dictionary definitions) and selecting the most coherent based on similar criteria. Work on model building is inspiring but also challenging due to the lack of constraint on the final models (even with substantial domain knowledge) and the difficulty of quantifying "coherence".

Our work falls somewhere between these two. We do not use templates for new knowledge, but rather use inference at run-time to identify what is known and thus what to expect that the text might be saying. However, unlike full model building approaches, we assume that the majority of what is being read is already known (represented) in the KB, and thus the reading task is primarily one of recognizing that knowledge in the text, and extending it with any new facts that are encountered. We might term this a "model extension" approach; it corresponds to Feigenbaum's (2003) challenge of, given the representation of a book, have a machine read a second book (about the same topic) and integrate the new knowledge contained in that text.

2 The Problem

Our work is in the context of cell biology, where we have a moderately sized[1], hand-built knowledge base available containing formal representations of biological structures and processes expressed in first-order logic. Our goal is to take paragraphs of text about a topic partially covered by the KB, and identify facts which are already known, facts which are new, and the connections between the two. An example of the system's output is shown in Figure 1. In the Output Axioms in that Figure, the normal font shows facts that the system has recognized as already known in the KB, while bold font shows new knowledge. It is important to note that the output facts are not just a simple recitation of the input, but have been interpreted in the context of the KB. For example in the input paragraph:

Topic: prophase
Input Paragraph:
In the cytoplasm, the mitotic spindle, consisting of microtubules and other proteins, forms between the two pairs of centrioles as they migrate to opposite poles of the cell.

Output Axioms: (expressed in English)
In all prophase events:
a. The mitotic spindle has parts the microtubule **and the protein.**
b. The mitotic spindle is created **between the centrioles in the cytoplasm**.
c. The centrioles move **to the poles.**

Figure 1: The system's behavior, showing known (normal font) and new (bold) facts identified from the text. Note that the output is not just a simple recitation of the input, but a mixture of known and new axioms for the KB.

"the mitotic spindle, consisting of microtubules"

has not been interpreted as describing some "consisting" event, but recognized (via use of paraphrases, described later) as referring to the has-part(mitotic-spindle01,microtubules01) element in the representation of prophase in the KB, i.e., denoting a "has part" relationship ((a) in Figure 1). Similarly,

"the spindle forms"

has not been interpreted as an organizing event ("form a team") nor as the spindle doing the forming ("the spindle forms something"), but instead been recognized as the result(create01,mitotic-spindle01) element in the representation of prophase in the KB, i.e., "forms" has been interpreted as this particular creation event in the representation of prophase (b in Figure 1). Doing this requires not just careful language processing; it requires querying the knowledge base to see/infer

[1] Specifically, it has detailed representations of entities and processes related to cell division, DNA replication, and protein synthesis, containing approximately 250 domain-specific concepts (built on top of a pre-existing library of approximately 500 domain-general concepts), 120 relations (binary predicates), and approximately 2000 axioms, built as part of Project Halo (Gunning et al., 2010).

what is already known, and using this to guide the interpretation.

This process is similar to that needed for question-answering. Consider giving a question form of (part of) the earlier paragraph to a question-answering system:

(1) Is it true that the mitotic spindle consists of microtubules?

Again, the phrase "consists of" is ambiguous, and may mean different things in different contexts. However, in the context of question-answering, there is a natural approach to disambiguating this: as the user is asking about what is in the KB, then a natural approach is to query the KB for relationships that hold between the mitotic spindle and microtubules, and see if any are a plausible interpretation of "consists of". If there is one, then it is likely to be the interpretation that the user intended (assuming the user is not being deliberately obscure; we call this a "benevolent user" assumption). If this happens, then the question-answering system can answer "yes"; but more importantly from a machine reading point of view, the system has also correctly disambiguated the original question and located the facts it mentions in the knowledge base as side-effects. It is this process that we want to apply to interpreting declarative texts, with the change that unproven parts should be treated as new assertions, rather than failed queries.

3 Approach

Based on these observations, our approach is to interpret a new text T by treating it as a question to the KB asking whether the facts in T are already known. By attempting to answer this question, the system resolves ambiguity for the known facts (namely, the resolution that leads to them being recognized is preferred). For new facts, the system falls back on more traditional NLP modules, filtered by coarser-grained type constraints. In addition, the identification of known facts in the KB and the connection between the old facts and the new facts provides anchor points for the new facts to be connected to.

To implement this approach, we have used three important features of our question-answering system, here reapplied to the task of text interpretation:

a. The use of a large database of paraphrases to explore alternative phrasings (hence alternative interpretations) of text;
b. Deferring word sense and semantic role commitment during initial language processing, to be resolved later based on what is found in the KB;
c. The use of standard disambiguation techniques to process new facts not located in the KB.

We now summarize these three features, then present the complete algorithm.

3.1 Paraphrases

A relatively recent advance in NLP has been the automatic construction of paraphrase databases (containing phrasal patterns with approximately equivalent meaning), built by finding phrases that occur in distributionally similar contexts (e.g., Dras et al, 2005). To date, paraphrase databases have primarily been exploited for recognizing textual entailment (e.g., Bentivogli et al., 2009). In our work, we take them in a new direction and exploit them for language interpretation.

We use the DIRT paraphrase database (Lin and Pantel, 2001a,b), containing approximately 12 million automatically learned rules of the form:

IF X *relation* Y THEN X *relation'* Y

where *relation* is a path in the dependency tree between constitutents X and Y, or equivalently (as we use later) a *chain of clauses*:

$$\{p_0(x_0,x_1), w_1(x_1), \ldots p_{n-1}(x_{n-1},x_n)\}$$

where p_i is the syntactic relation between (non-prepositional) constituents x_i and x_{i+1}, and w_i is the word used for x_i. An example from DIRT is:

IF X is found in Y THEN X is inside Y

The condition "X is found in Y" can be expressed as the clause chain:

{ object-of(x,f), "find"(f), "in"(f,y) }

We use DIRT to explore alternative interpretations of the text, singling out those that help identify the facts in the text that are already known in the KB.

3.2 Deferred Sense Commitment

Two common challenges for NLP are word sense disambiguation (WSD) and semantic role labeling

(SRL). While there are a number of existing tools for performing these tasks based on the linguistic context (e.g., Toutanova et al., 2008, Erk and Pado, 2006), their performance is only moderate (e.g., Agirre et al, 2007). The problem is accentuated when trying to disambiguate in a way consistent with a particular KB, because there is often a degree of subjectivity in how the knowledge engineer chose to represent the world in that KB (e.g., whether some object is the "agent" or "instrument" or "site" of an activity is to a degree a matter of viewpoint). Trying to create a WSD or SRL module that reliably mimics the knowledge engineer's decision procedure is difficult.

To address this, we defer WSD and SRL commitment during the initial text processing. Instead, these ambiguities are resolved during the subsequent stage of querying the KB to see if (some interpretion of) the text is already known. One can view this as a trivial form of preserving underspecification (eg. Pinkal, 1999) in the initial language processing, where the words themselves denote their possible meanings.

3.3 Interpretation of New Knowledge

Given some text, our system attempts to disambiguate it by searching for (some interpretation of) its statements in the KB. However, this will only disambiguate statements of facts that are already known. For new facts, we fall back on traditional disambiguation methods, using a set of approximately 100 hand-built rules for semantic role labelling, and word sense disambiguation preferences taken from WordNet sense frequency statistics and from the KB. In addition, we use a simple filter to discard apparently irrelevant/nonsensical assertions by discarding those that use concepts unrelated to the domain. These are defined as those with words whose preferred WordNet sense falls under one of a small number of hand-selected "non-biological" synsets (namely human_activity#n#1, mental_object#n#1, artifact#n#1, instrumentation#n#1, psychological_feature#n#1, device#n#1). One might also be able to use a KB-guided approach to disambiguation similar to that described for known facts, by (for example) looking for generalizations of (interpretations of) new facts in the knowledge base. This is a direction for future exploration.

4 Algorithm and Implementation

4.1 Topics and Participants

For now, we assume that all knowledge in the KB can be represented by "forall...exists..." statements, i.e., statements of the form:

$$\forall x \; isa(x,C) \rightarrow \exists y_1..y_n \; p_1(v_1,v_2), \ldots, p_q(v_r,v_s) \qquad [1]$$

(We will later discuss how this assumption can be relaxed). p_i are predicates in the KB's ontology and each v_i is either a variable $v \in \{x,y_1,\ldots,y_n\}$ or a symbol in the KB's ontology. We say clauses $p_i(v_j,v_k)$ are *about* concept C, and that C is the *topic* of the clauses. We also say that any instance y_i that is in some (possibly indirect) relationship to x is a *participant* in the representation of instance x of C. Thus all the y_i in [1] are participants, plus there may be additional participants implied by other axioms. For some given instance X0 of C, we can identify all the participants in the representation of X0 by forward chaining from isa(X0,C) and collecting all the instances connected via some chain of predicates to X0. We encode this using a participant(x,y_i) relation[2]. As this computation is potentially unbounded, we use a depth bound to heuristically limit this computation.

4.2 Initial Language Processing

Assume the system has a paragraph of text about a topic, and that it has identified what that topic is[3]. For example, consider that the topic is prophase (a step in cell division), and the paragraph is the single sentence:

T: The mitotic spindle consists of hollow microtubules.

Text is parsed using a broad coverage, phrase structure parser (Harrison and Maxwell, 1986), followed by coreference resolution, producing a "syntactic" logical form, here:

LF: "mitotic-spindle"(s), "consist"(c), "hollow"(h), "microtubule"(m), subject(c,s), "of"(c,m), modifier(m,h).

[2] We can formalize this by adding participant(x,y_i) to the conclusion in [1] for all y_i, plus an axiom that participant is transitive.

[3] E.g., via some topic classification algorithm. For our experiments here, we manually declare the topic.

4.3 Semantic Interpretation

To interpret T the system then tries to answer, or partially answer, the corresponding question:

T: Is it true that the mitotic spindle consists of hollow microtubules?

Note that this question is in the context of the topic (prophase), and thus the mentioned objects are implicitly participants in prophase. To do this, the system proceeds as follows, using a deductive reasoning engine operating over the KB:

(a) **setup:** create an instance X0 of the topic, i.e., assert isa(X0,*topic*) in the KB, then find its participants { y | participant(X0,y) }. Next, bind one of the variables in the LF to a participant that the variable's word might denote.

(b) **query:** for each clause in the LF with at least one bound variable, iteratively query the KB to see if some interpretation of those clauses are provable i.e., already known.

In this example, for setup (a) the system first creates an instance X0 of prophase, i.e., asserts isa(X0,Prophase) in the KB, then finds its participants Y0,...,Yn by querying for participant(X0,y). The participants Y0,Y1,… will be instances of objects and events known (in the KB) to be present in prophase, e.g., instances of Move, Centrosome, Elongate, Mitotic-Spindle, etc. The system then instantiates a variable in the LF, e.g., s in "mitotic-spindle"(s) with a participant that "mitotic spindle" might refer to, e.g., Y4, if Y4 is an instance of Mitotic-Spindle. The resulting LF looks:

LF:"mitotic-spindle"(Y4),"consist"(c),"hollow"(h), "microtubule"(m), subject(c,Y4), "of"(c,m), modifier(m,h).

For querying (b), the system uses the algorithm as follows (on the next page):

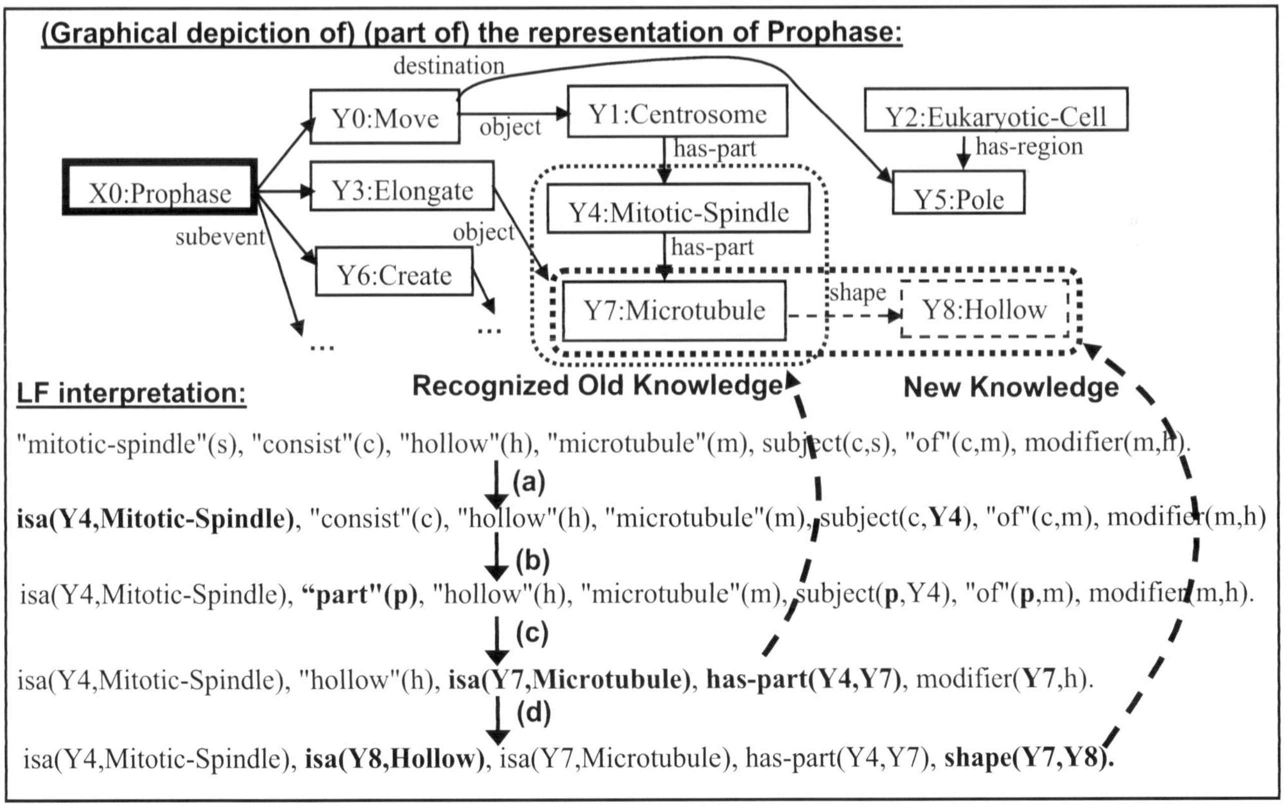

Figure 2: The path found through the search space for an interpretation of the example sentence. (a) setup (b) paraphrase substitution (c) interpretation of {subject-of(Y4,p),"part"(p),"of"(p,m)} as has-part(Y4,m), preferred as it is provable from the KB, resulting in m=Y7 (d) interpretation of new knowledge (standard WSD and SRL tools).

```
repeat
    select a clause chain C_u of "syntactic" clauses
            in the LF with at least 1 bound variable
        C_u = {p(x,y)} or {w(x)} or
                    {p_1(x,z), w(z), p_2(z,y)}
    select some interpretation C of C_u where:
        C is a possible interpretation of C_u
        or C'_u is a possible paraphrase for C_u and
            C is a possible interpretation of C'_u
    try prove C[bindings] → new-bindings
    If success:
      replace C_u with C
      add new-bindings to bindings
until
   as many clauses proved as possible
```

where:

- A *syntactic clause* is a clause whose predicate is a word or syntactic role (subject, object, modifier, etc.) All clauses in the initial LF are syntactic clauses.
- A *clause chain* is a set of "syntactic" clauses in the LF of the form {p(x,y)} or {w(x)} or $\{p_1(x,z), w(z), p_2(z,y)\}$, where p_i, w are words or syntactic roles (subject, modifier, etc).
- A *possible paraphrase* is a possible substitution of one syntactic clause chain with another, listed in the DIRT paraphrase database.
- A *possible interpretation* of the singleton syntactic clause chain {w(x)} is isa(x,*class*), where *class* is a possible sense of word w.
- A *possible interpretation* of a syntactic clause chain {p(x,y)} or {p1(x,z),w(z),p2(z,y)} is r(x,y), where r is a semantic relation corresponding to syntactic relation p (e.g., "in"(x,y) → is-inside(x,y)) or word w (e.g., {subject-of(e,h), "have"(h), "of"(h,n)} → has-part(e,n)).

Possible word-to-class and word-to-predicate mappings are specified in the KB.

As there are several points of non-determinism in the algorithm, including the setup (e.g., which clauses to select, which interpretation to explore), it is a search process. Our current implementation uses most-instantiated-first query ordering plus breadth-first search, although other implementations could traverse the space in other ways.

Figure 2 illustrates this procedure for the example sentence. The procedure iteratively replaces syntactic clauses with semantic clauses that correspond to an interpretation that is provable from the KB. If all the clauses are proved, then the original text T is redundant; there exists an interpretation under which it can be proved from the KB, and we assume under the benevolent user assumption that this is the interpretation that the user intended.

If some syntactic clauses remain unproved, then they correspond to new knowledge, and a standard NLP pipeline is then used to interpret them. In this example (Figure 2), the "hollow" modifier to the microtubule Y7 was unproved, and was subsequently interpreted by the NLP pipeline as the shape of the microtubule. This new clause is converted into a (potential) addition to the KB by identifying an axiom that concluded one of the known connected facts (here, has-part(Y4,Y7)), and then proposing the new clause as an additional conclusion of that axiom. If there are no connected clauses, it is instead proposed as a new axiom about prophase. The user can verify/reject that proposal as he/she desires.

5 Illustration

An illustration of the system's typical processing of a paragraph is shown in Figure 3. As in Figure 1, normal font shows facts recognized as already known, and bold shows new knowledge. Again note that the output facts are not a simple recitation of the input, but have been interpreted with respect to the KB. For example, in (e), Create is the preferred interpretation of "form", and in (d), has-part is the preferred interpretation of "consisting of", as these result in the interpretation being provable from the KB. Also note that new knowledge is anchored to old, e.g., in (d), proteins are posited as an additional part of the mitotic spindle participant of prophase.

There are several errors and meaningless statements in the output also. For example, "something signals" is not particularly helpful, and "the chromosome moves" is, although biologically correct, a misinterpretation of the original English "the chromosome is seen as...", with Move being a possible interpretation of "see" (as in "I'll see you to the door"). In addition some sentences were misparsed or unparsed, and some interpretations were discarded as they involved non-biological concepts. Many representational issues have been skirted also, discussed shortly.

Topic: prophase
Input Paragraph:[4]
During prophase, chromosomes become visible, the nucleolus disappears, the mitotic spindle forms, and the nuclear envelope disappears. Chromosomes become more coiled and can be viewed under a light microscope. Each duplicated chromosome is seen as a pair of sister chromatids joined by the duplicated but unseparated centromere. The nucleolus disappears during prophase. In the cytoplasm, the mitotic spindle, consisting of microtubules and other proteins, forms between the two pairs of centrioles as they migrate to opposite poles of the cell. The nuclear envelope disappears at the end of prophase. This signals the beginning of the substage called prometaphase.

Output Axioms: (expressed in English)
In all prophase events:
d. The chromosome moves**.**
e. The chromatids are attached **by the centromere.**
f. The nucleolus disappears during the prophase.
g. The mitotic spindle has parts the microtubule **and the protein.**
h. The mitotic spindle is created **between the centrioles in the cytoplasm**.
i. The centrioles move **to the poles**.
j. The nuclear envelope disappears at the end.
k. Something signals.

Figure 3: Illustration of the System's Behavior

6 Preliminary Evaluation

To make a preliminary assessment of how much useful information the system is producing, we conducted a small study. 10 paragraphs about prophase (from different Web sources) were run through the system (110 sentences in total). The system extracted 114 statements of which 23 (20%) were interpreted as fully known (i.e., already in the KB), 27 (24%) as partially new knowledge, and 64 (56%) as completely new knowledge. The extracted statements were then scored by a biologist as one of:

c = correct; useful knowledge that should be in the KB
q = questionable; not useful knowledge (meaningless, overly general, vague)
i = incorrect

The results are shown in Table 1.

	Statements that are:		
	Fully known	Mixture of known & new	Fully new
Correct	22	19	25
Questionable	1	8	38
Incorrect	0	0	1

Table 1: Correctness of axioms proposed by the system.

For the statements that mix old and new knowledge, 70% were judged correct, and for completely new statements, 39% were judged correct.[5] This suggests the system is at least producing some useful suggestions, and for the statements that mix old and new knowledge, has identified the connection points in the KB for the new facts. Although this level of accuracy is too low for automation, it suggests the system might be a useful tool for helping a knowledge engineer check that he/she has fully encoded the contents of a passage when building the KB, and performing those approved additions automatically.

7 Discussion and Conclusion

We have described a method for reading "at the fringe" of what is known, leveraging existing knowledge to help in the reading process by treating text interpretation as partial question answering. This approach is appropriate for situations in which a reasonable proportion of the text's content is already known to (represented in) the KB. Our evaluation suggests that the approach has merit, at least as an interactive knowledge acquisition tool.

As we have suggested, existing knowledge can help guide and anchor interpretation, but to what extent might it stifle the system from learning genuinely new knowledge? At present, our system is unable to extend its own ontology (it can only learns axioms expressed using its existing ontology), and thus will skim over unrecognized words

[4] From http://www.phschool.com/science/biology_place/ biocoach/mitosisisg/prophase.html

[5] For the 1 statement already fully known but judged as questionable, the score appears to be due to poor rendering in English, the axiom being rendered as "The membrane break down." rather than "The membrane breaks down.".

even if those words reflect something new (with respect to the KB) and important about the domain. The system is thus biased towards texts about concepts that it has at least heard of before (even if it knows little about them), expecting small, incremental additions of knowledge, rather than working hard to untangle information about completely novel topics. It can learn about concepts it has already heard of, but not, at present, learn new concepts. While it would be simple to modify the system to treat any new word as a new concept, this may potentially overwhelm the system, and so such extensions would need to be made carefully. This is an area for future work.

How large must the starting KB be? Although it can be missing (possibly many) axioms, we implicitly assume that at least the basic ontology and the mapping from words to concepts is reasonably complete (for the types of texts being considered), i.e., there is a good "skeleton" KB to add axioms to. Thus, methodologically, a first step for using our system would be to create the initial ontology and lexical mappings, e.g., via corpus analysis or using an ontology learning tool (Gomez-Perez and Manzano-Macho, 2003). Beyond that, the more axioms the starting KB has the better, as each axiom can potentially guide the interpretation of a new sentence. In the limiting case, where there are no axioms (only the ontology and lexical mappings), our system's behavior reverts to that of a normal, pipelined NLP interpreter (with the normal associated problems).

This work is still preliminary, and there are numerous other issues and limitations that need to be addressed also. Three notable issues are as follows:

- **Syntactic ambiguity:** While we defer WSD and SRL commitment, our system is eagerly committing to a single parse during initial language processing, and that parse may be wrong. An obvious extension is to similarly defer some syntactic commitments until semantic interpretation, for example using an underspecified or packed logical form (e.g., Bobrow et al, 2005) or exploring alternative parses.
- **Interpretation of new knowledge:** While our approach leverages the KB to interpret statements about known facts, and thus help find the anchor points for new facts, those statements of new facts are still interpreted using a traditional pipelined approach, with all its associated brittlenesses (as evidenced in the last column in Table 1). Creative ways for using the KB to similarly help guide new fact interpretation are needed, for example searching the KB for generalizations or variants of those facts, and then preferring the interpretations they suggest.
- **Representational adequacy:** Our work so far has assumed a simple, deductive representational framework of individual objects and events, and correspondingly assumes the same individuality in language. However the world, and language used to describe it, often goes beyond this to include a miriad of representationally difficult phenomena (sets, pairs, aggregates, conditionality, plausibility, constraints, etc.). Our system largely skips over such aspects, as it is unable to represent them.

Despite these limitations, the picture of text interpretation as partial question-answering appears to be a useful one, as it suggests a means by which language and knowledge can be connected. We are optimistic that it can be further developed and improved for better machine reading in the future.

Acknowledgements

We are grateful to Vulcan Inc. who partially supported this work through Project Halo.

References

Agirre, E., Marquez, L., Wicentowski, R., Eds., 2007. *Proceedings of the 4th International Workshop on Semantic Evaluations (SemEval),* ACL, Prague, Czech Republic.

Bentivogli, L., Dagan, I., Dang, Hoa, Giampiccolo, D., Magnini, B. 2009. The Fifth PASCAL Recognizing Textual Entailment Challenge. In *Proc Text Analysis Conference (TAC'09).*

Bobrow, D. G., Condoravdi, Crouch, R. Kaplan, R. Karttunen, L., King, L.T.H., de Paiva, V., Zaenen, A. 2005. A Basic Logic for Textual Inference. In *Proceedings of the AAAI Workshop on Inference for Textual Question Answering*, Pittsburgh, PA.

Carlson, A., Betteridge, J., Hruschka, E., Mitchell, T. 2009. Coupling Semi-Supervised Learning of Categories and Relations. *Proceedings of the NAACL HLT 2009 Workshop on Semi-supervised Learning for Natural Language Processing.*

Clark, P., Harrison, P. 2010. Exploiting Paraphraes and Deferred Sense Commitment to Interpret Questions more Reliably. (Submitted).

Dahlgren, K., Lord, C., Wada, H., McDowell, J., Sabler, E. 1991. ITP: Description of the interpretext system as used for MUC-*3. In Proc 3rd Message Understanding Conference (MUC-3)*, pp163-170.

DeJong, G. 1979. Prediction and Substantiation: Two processes that comprise understanding. *IJCAI'79,* pp217-222.

Dras, M., Yamamoto, K. (Eds). 2005. *Proc 3rd Internationl Workshop of Paraphrasing*. South Korea.

Erk, K., Pado, S. 2006. Shalmaneser – a flexible toolbox for semantic role assignment. *Proc LREC 2006*, Genoa, Italy.

Feigenbaum, E. 2003. Some Challenges and Grand Challenges for Computational Intelligence. Journal of ACM, 50 (1), pp 32-40.

Gomez-Perez, A., Manzano-Macho, D. 2003. "A Survey of Ontology Learning Methods and Techniques", Technical Report, Univ Politecnica de Madrid (OntoWeb Deliverable 1.5, http://www.sti-innsbruck.at/fileadmin/documents/deliverables/Ontoweb/D1.5.pdf)

Gunning, D., Greaves, M., Chaudhri, V. et al. 2010. *Project Halo Update – Progress Towards Digital Aristotle* (Submitted).

Harrison, P., Maxwell, M. 1986. A New Implementation of GPSG. In Proc. 6th Canadian Conf on AI.

Hobb, J., Stickel, M., Appelt, D., Martin, P. 1993. Interpretation as Abudction. In *Artificial Intelligence* 63 (1-2), pp 69-142.

Lin, D. and Pantel, P. 2001a. Discovery of Inference Rules for Question Answering. *Natural Language Engineering* 7 (4) pp 343-360.

Lin, D. and Pantel, P. 2001b. Discovery of Inference Rules in Text. *Proc ACM SIGKDD Conf on Knoweldge Discovery and Data Mining.*

Mulkar, R., Hobbs, J. Hovy, E. 2007. Learning to Read Syntactically Complex Biology Texts. In *Proc 8th International Symposium on Logical Formalizations of Commonsense Reasoning* (AAAI Spring Symposium).

Pinkal, M. 1999. On Semantic Underspecification. In Bunt, H./Muskens, R. (Eds.). *Proceedings of the 2nd International Workshop on Compuational Linguistics (IWCS 2).*

Riloff, E. 1996. Automatically Generating Extraction Patterns from Untagged Text. *Proc AAAI'96.*

Sekine, S. 2006. On-Demand Information Extraction. *Proc. COLING-ACL.*

Toutanova, K., Haghighi, A., Manning, C. 2008. A Global Joint Model for Semantic Role Labeling. *Computational Linguistics*, 34 (2).

Zadrozny, W., Jensen, K. 1991. Semantics of Paragraphs. in *Computational Linguistics* 17 (2) pp171-209.

Building an end-to-end text reading system based on a packed representation

Doo Soon Kim
Dept. of Computer Science
University of Texas
Austin, TX, 78712
onue5@cs.utexas.edu

Ken Barker
Dept. of Computer Science
University of Texas
Austin, TX, 78712
kbarker@cs.utexas.edu

Bruce Porter
Dept. of Computer Science
University of Texas
Austin, TX, 78712
porter@cs.utexas.edu

Abstract

We previously proposed a packed graphical representation to succinctly represent a huge number of alternative semantic representations of a given sentence. We also showed that this representation could improve text interpretation accuracy considerably because the system could postpone resolving ambiguity until more evidence accumulates. This paper discusses our plan to build an end-to-end text reading system based on our packed representation.

1 Introduction

Our goal is to build an end-to-end text understanding system by assembling together existing components for parsing, semantic interpretation, co-reference resolution and so on. Commonly, these components are combined in a pipeline in which each one passes forward a *single* best interpretation (see (a) in fig. 1). Although this approach is relatively straightforward, it can suffer from overly aggressive pruning; a component might prune those interpretations that downstream components might have been able to recognize as correct. Similarly, a component might prune an interpretation that would be validated by reading subsequent texts. The system's accuracy would almost certainly improve if it were able to delay pruning until sufficient evidence accumulates to make a principled commitment.

There is a naïve way of delaying pruning decisions in a pipelined architecture: each component passes forward not just a single interpretation, but *multiple* alternatives, thereby creating multiple interpretation paths (see (b) in fig 1). Then, the system might choose the best interpretation at the last step of the pipeline. However, this approach is intractable due to the combinatorial explosion in the number of interpretation paths.

In previous work (Kim et al., 2010), we proposed an alternative approach in which each component passes forward multiple interpretations which are compressed into an intensional representation that we call a *packed graphical (PG) representation* (see (c) in fig. 1). Our experiment showed that the approach could improve the interpretation accuracy considerably by delaying ambiguity resolution while avoiding combinatorial explosion.

In this paper, we discuss our plan to build an end-to-end text understanding system using the PG representation. We first introduce the language interpretation system we are currently building, which produces a PG representation from the parse of each sentence. Then, we propose an architecture for an end-to-end reading system that is based on the PG representation. The architecture allows the system to improve as it acquires knowledge from reading texts.

In the following sections, we briefly describe the PG representation and its disambiguation algorithm (see (Kim et al., 2010) for details). Then, we present the plan and the current status in the development of an end-to-end text understanding system.

2 Packed graphical representation

The PG representation compresses a huge number of alternative interpretations by locally represent-

Proceedings of the NAACL HLT 2010 First International Workshop on Formalisms and Methodology for Learning by Reading, pages 10–14,
Los Angeles, California, June 2010.

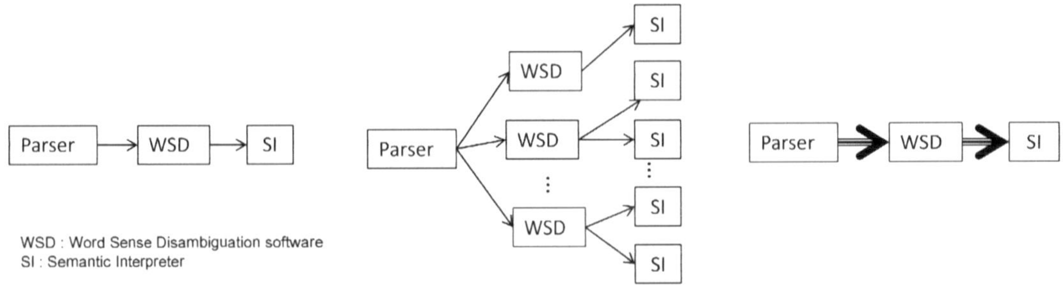

(a) single interpretation, single component *(b) single interpretation, multiple components* *(c) single PG representation, single component*

Figure 1: The three different architectures for text understanding system: In (a), each component passes forward a single interpretation. (b) can improve (a) by considering multiple interpretation paths, but suffers from combinatorial explosion. (c) is our approach in which the system considers multiple alternative interpretations (in contrast to (a)) while avoiding combinatorial explosion by packing the alternatives (in contrast to (b)).

ing common types of ambiguities and other types of constraints among the interpretations. Section 2.1 presents these ambiguity and constraint representations. Section 2.2 introduces an algorithm which aims to resolve the ambiguities captured in a PG representation.

2.1 Representation

Fig. 2 shows a PG representation produced from the interpretation of the following sentence:

S1 : The engine ignites the gasoline with its spark plug.

With this example, we will explain the ambiguity representations and the other types of constraints expressed in the PG representation.

Type ambiguity. Ambiguity in the assignment of a type for a word. In PG1, for example, the node engine-2a (corresponding to the word "engine") has type annotation [LIVING-ENTITY .3 | DEVICE .7]. It means that the two types are candidates for the type of engine-2a and their probabilities are respectively .3 (Living-Entity) and .7 (Device) .

Relational ambiguity. Ambiguity in the assignment of semantic relation between nodes. The edge from ignite-3 to engine-2a in PG1 has relation annotation <agent .6 | location .4>. It means that engine-2a is either *agent* (probability .6) or *location* (probability .4) of ignite-3.

Structural ambiguity. It represents structural alternatives in different interpretations. In PG1, for example, D and E represent an ambiguity of prepositional phrase attachment for "with its spark plug";

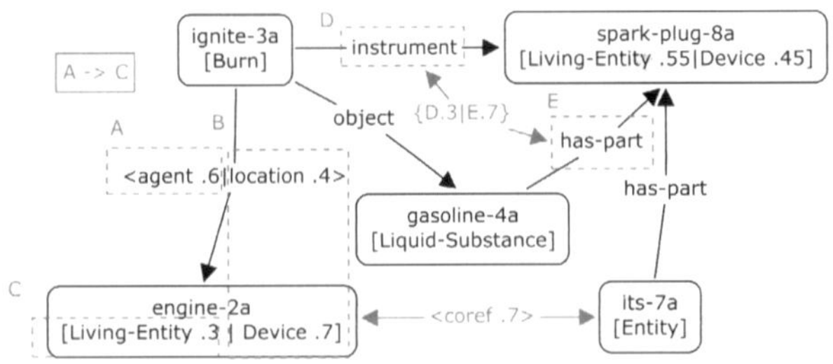

Figure 2: The PG representation for S1 (PG1)

the phrase can be attached to "ignites" (D) or "spark plug" (E). The annotation {D .3 | E .7} means either D or E (not both) is correct and the probability of each choice is respectively .3 and .7.

Co-reference ambiguity. A "co-reference" edge represents a possibility of co-reference between two nodes. For example, the edge labeled <coref .7> represents that the probability of engine-2a and its-7a being co-referent is .7.

Besides ambiguity representations above, the PG representation can also represent dependencies among different interpretations.

Simple dependency. It represents that the existence of one interpretation depends on the existence of another. For example, A $\rightarrow$ C means that if LIVING-ENTITY is found to be a wrong type for engine-2a (by subsequent evidence), the agent relation should be discarded, too.

Mutual dependency. It represents that the interpretations in a mutual dependency set depend on one another – if any interpretation in the set is found to be wrong or correct (by subsequent evidence), the others should also be rejected or confirmed. For example, the box labeled B means that if either (engine-2a type DEVICE) or (ignite-3a location engine-2a) is confirmed or rejected, the other interpretation should be confirmed or rejected.

Formally, the PG representation can be represented as a list of

- *semantic triples* – e.g., (ignite-3a type BURN), (ignite-3a instrument spark-plug-9a)
- *macros* – e.g., the symbol A refers to (ignite-3a agent engine-2a)
- *constraints* – e.g., A depends on C, D (.3) is exclusive to E (.7)

2.2 Disambiguating ambiguities in a PG representations

In this section, we briefly explain how our disambiguating algorithm resolves ambiguities in a PG representation. For details, please see (Kim et al., 2010).

The PG representation allows the system to delay commitment to an interpretation (by explicitly representing ambiguities) until enough evidence accrues to disambiguate. One source of such evidence is the other texts with redundant content. For a sentence which is hard to interpret, there may be other texts which describe the same content, but in ways that the system can better interpret. These new reliable interpretations can be used to disambiguate the original unreliable interpretations. Our algorithm is based on this approach of combining multiple PG representations to resolve their ambiguities.

The disambiguation algorithm uses graph matching. The algorithm aligns two PG representations to identify their redundant subgraphs (redundant portions of the interpretations), then increases the confidence scores of these subgraphs because the same interpretation was derived from two independent sentences (on the same topic). When the confidence scores reach a high or low threshold, the associated interpretations are confirmed or pruned. Confirming or pruning one interpretation may lead to confirming or pruning others. For example, the dependents of a pruned interpretation should also be pruned.

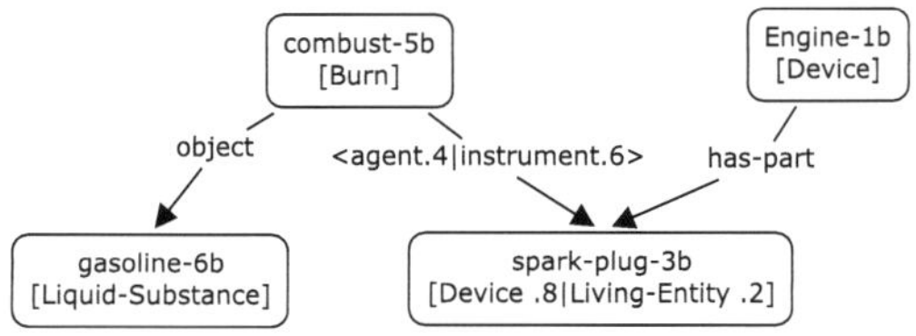

Figure 3: The PG representation for S2 (PG2), *"The engine's spark plug combusts gasoline"*

To illustrate the algorithm, we will show how PG1 (fig. 2) is merged with PG2 (fig. 3) to resolve their ambiguities.

1. engine-2 in PG1 is aligned with engine-1 in PG2. This operation chooses Device as the type of engine-2 (i.e., it discards Living-Entity) because Device is favored in both nodes

2. Deleting LIVING-ENTITY causes deletion of the *agent* edge between ignite-3a and engine-2a due to the dependency constraint A $\rightarrow$ C, (meaning *agent* (in A) depends on the existence of LIVING-ENTITY (in C)).

3. Co-reference between engine-2a and its-7a is greedily confirmed because merging the two nodes enables the alignment of (its-7a has-part spark-plug-8a) with (Engine-1b has-part spark-plug-3b).

4. The algorithm aligns (ignite-3a instrument spark-plug-8a) with (combust-5b instrument spark-plug-3b), because ignite-3a and combust-5b share the same type, [BURN]. This operation increases the score of D (the structure corresponding to PP attachment of "with its spark plug" to "ignite") over E (the structure corresponding to attachment of "with its spark plug" to "gasoline").

3 Taking advantage of the PG representation in an end-to-end system

Our experiment showed that, for ten texts with redundant content, our approach improved the interpretation accuracy by 10% (Kim et al., 2010). Encouraged by this result, we present our on-going work and future plans.

3.1 Producing PG representation

We are currently constructing a fully automated language interpretation system to produce PG representations from English sentences. The system will be able to maintain all possible interpretations generated at each step (including parsing, word sense disambiguation (WSD) and semantic relation assignment) and represent them using the PG representation. This is straightforward for WSD and semantic relation assignment because most off-the-shelf software (e.g., (Patwardhan et al., 2005) (Punyakanok et al., 2005)) outputs a list of candidate choices and confidence scores for type and relational ambiguities. (Kim et al., 2010) describes a prototype system implemented with these WSD and semantic assignment components.

However, ambiguities in parsing are more difficult because it is hard to efficiently identify structural differences among various parses. We are currently developing an algorithm (similar to (Schiehlen, 1996)) which converts a parse forest (the ambiguity-preserving chart built during PCFG parsing) (Tomita, 1986) into the syntactic-level PG representation (as shown in fig. 4). We plan to implement this algorithm in the Stanford Parser (Klein and Manning, 2003) and to evaluate it along the following dimensions.

First, we will measure the improvement in parsing accuracy that results from delaying commitment to a single best parse.

Second, even though the PG representation achieves substantial compression, its size is still bounded. The parser might generate more interpretations than will fit within the bound. We plan to handle this problem in the following way. When a PG representation grows to the bound, the system applies the components downstream of the parser to the candidate parses. Because these components use additional sources of knowledge, including knowledge derived from previous reading (Clark and Harrison, 2009), they might be able to prune some candidate interpretations. In this way, a part of a sentence may be processed early while the other parts are left unprocessed, in contrast with the traditional approach of fully processing each sentence before starting with the next.

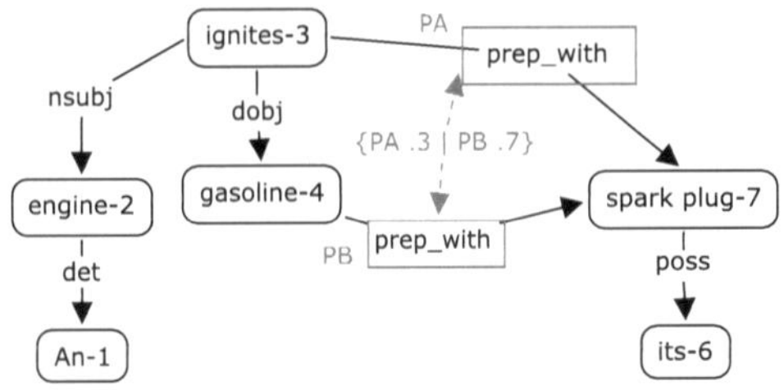

Figure 4: Syntactic-level PG representation for S1: the structural ambiguity represents an ambiguity of attaching the preposition, "with its spark plug".

3.2 System Architecture

The PG representation and its disambiguating algorithm allow an interesting property in a text understanding system: the system's interpretation capability could increase as it acquires knowledge from texts. This property can be shown in two ways. First, the ambiguities of the current text could be resolved later when the system reads subsequent texts. Second, the knowledge acquired from the prior texts could be used to resolve the ambiguities of the current text. Fig. 5 shows an architecture that exhibits this property.

Given a text, or a set of texts on the same topic, the language interpreter generates a PG representation. Then, the knowledge integration component (KI) adds the PG representation into the knowledge base. For a first text, the PG representation is simply put into the knowledge base. For subsequent texts, KI merges the subsequent PG representations with the PG representation in the knowledge base. This step may resolve ambiguities in the PG representation maintained in the knowledge base.

When the language interpreter confronts an ambiguity, it has two choices: it either (a) locally represents the ambiguity in the PG representation or (b) asks the RESOLVER to resolve the ambiguity. When the RESOLVER is called, it searches the knowledge base for information to resolve the ambiguity. If this is unsuccessful, it uses the information retrieval module (TEXT MINER) to find relevant documents from external sources which might resolve the ambiguity. The documents are added in the Text Queue to be read subsequently. In the near future, we plan to evaluate the ability of the KI and Resolver modules to resolve ambiguities as the system reads more texts.

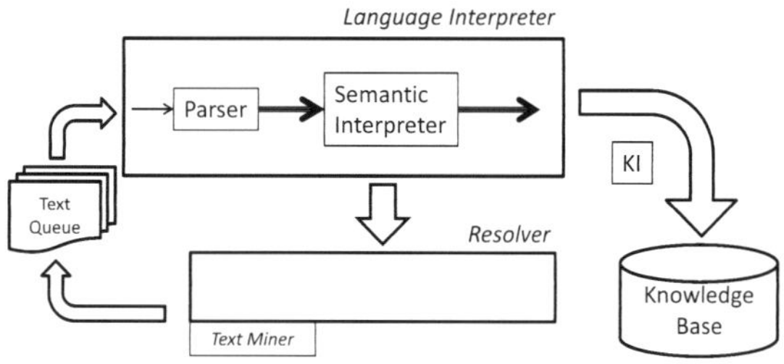

Figure 5: Architecture

4 Summary

In this paper, we discuss the development of an end-to-end text understanding system based on a packed representation. With this representation, the system can delay ambiguity resolution while avoiding combinatorial explosion, thereby effectively improving the accuracy of text interpretation.

References

Peter Clark and Philip Harrison. 2009. Large-scale extraction and use of knowledge from text. In Yolanda Gil and Natasha Fridman Noy, editors, *K-CAP*, pages 153–160. ACM.

Doo Soon Kim, Ken Barker, and Bruce Porter. 2010. Improving the quality of text understanding by delaying ambiguity resolution. Technical Report TR-10-12, University of Texas at Austin.

Dan Klein and Christopher D. Manning. 2003. Accurate unlexicalized parsing. In *Proc. of ACL*.

Siddharth Patwardhan, Satanjeev Banerjee, and Ted Pedersen. 2005. Senserelate:: Targetword-A generalized framework for word sense disambiguation. In *ACL*.

Vasin Punyakanok, Dan Roth, and Wen tau Yih. 2005. The necessity of syntactic parsing for semantic role labeling. In *IJCAI*.

Michael Schiehlen. 1996. Semantic construction from parse forests. In *COLING*, pages 907–912.

Masaru Tomita. 1986. *Efficient Parsing for Natural Language — A Fast Algorithm for Practical Systems*. Int. Series in Engineering and Computer Science. Kluwer, Hingham, MA.

Semantic Enrichment of Text with Background Knowledge

Anselmo Peñas
UNED NLP & IR Group
Juan del Rosal, 16
28040 Madrid, Spain
anselmo@lsi.uned.es

Eduard Hovy
USC Information Sciences Institute
4676 Admiralty Way
Marina del Rey, CA 90292-6695
hovy@isi.edu

Abstract

Texts are replete with gaps, information omitted since authors assume a certain amount of background knowledge. We describe the kind of information (the formalism and methods to derive the content) useful for automated filling of such gaps. We describe a stepwise procedure with a detailed example.

1 Introduction

Automated understanding of connected text remains an unsolved challenge in NLP. In contrast to systems that harvest information from large collections of text, or that extract only certain prespecified kinds of information from single texts, the task of extracting and integrating all information from a single text, and building a coherent and relatively complete representation of its full content, is still beyond current capabilities.

A significant obstacle is the fact that text always omits information that is important, but that people recover effortlessly. Authors leave out information that they assume is known to their readers, since its inclusion (under the Gricean maxim of minimality) would carry an additional, often pragmatic, import. The problem is that systems cannot perform the recovery since they lack the requisite background knowledge and inferential machinery to use it.

In this research we address the problem of automatically recovering such omitted information to 'plug the gaps' in text. To do so, we describe the background knowledge required as well as a procedure for recognizing where gaps exist and determining which kinds of background knowledge are needed.

We are looking for the synchronization between the text representation achievable by current NLP and a knowledge representation (KR) scheme that can permit further inference for text interpretation.

1.1 Vision

Clearly, producing a rich text interpretation requires both NLP and KR capabilities. The strategy we explore is the enablement of bidirectional communication between the two sides from the very beginning of the text processing. We assume that the KR system doesn't require a full representation of the text meaning, but can work with a partial interpretation, namely of the material explicitly present in the text, and can then flesh out this interpretation as required for its specific task. Although the NLP system initially provides simpler representations (even possibly ambiguous or wrong ones), the final result contains the semantics of the text according to the working domain.

In this model, the following questions arise: How much can we simplify our initial text representation and still permit the attachment of background knowledge for further inference and interpretation? How should background knowledge be represented for use by the KR system? How can the incompleteness and brittleness typical of background knowledge (its representational inflexibility, or limitation to a single viewpoint or expressive phrasing) (Barker 2007) be overcome? In what sequence can a KR system enrich an initial and/or impoverished reading, and how can the enrichment benefit subsequent text processing?

1.2 Approach

Although we are working toward it, we do not yet have such a system. The aim of our current work is to rapidly assemble some necessary pieces and explore how to (i) attach background knowledge to flesh out a simple text representation and (ii) there by make explicit the meanings attached to some of its syntactic relations. We begin with an initial simple text representation, a background knowledge base corresponding to the text, and a simple

Proceedings of the NAACL HLT 2010 First International Workshop on Formalisms and Methodology for Learning by Reading, pages 15–23,
Los Angeles, California, June 2010.

formalized procedure to attach elements from the background knowledge to the entities and implicit relations present in the initial text representation.

Surprisingly, we find that some quite simple processing can be effective if we are able to contextualize the text under interpretation.

For our exploratory experiments, we are working with a collection of 30,000 documents in the domain of US football. We parsed the collection using a standard dependency parser (Marneffe and Manning, 2008; Klein and Maning, 2003) and, after collapsing some syntactic dependencies, obtained the simple textual representations shown in Section 2. From them, we built a Background Knowledge Base by automatically harvesting propositions expressed in the collection (Section 3). Their frequency in the collection lead the enrichment process: given a new text in the same domain, we build exactly the same kind of representation, and attach the background knowledge propositions as related to the text (Section 4).

Since this is an exploratory sketch, we cannot provide a quantitative evaluation yet, but the qualitative study over some examples suggest that this simple framework is promising enough to start a long term research (Section 5). Finally, we conclude with the next steps we want to follow and the kind of evaluation we plan to do.

2 Text Representation

The starting text representation must capture the first shot of what's going on in the text, taking some excerpts into account and (unfortunately) losing others. After the first shot, in accord with the purpose of the reading, we will "contextualize" each sentence, expanding its initial representation with the relevant related background knowledge in our base.

During this process of making explicit the implicit semantic relations (which we call contextualization or interpretation) it will become apparent whether we need to recover some of the discarded elements, whether we need to expand some others, etc. So the process of interpretation is identified with the growing of the context (according to the KB) until the interpretation is possible. This is related to some well-known theories such as the Theory of Relevance (Sperber and Wilson, 1995). The particular method we envisage is related to Interpretation as Abduction (Hobbs et al. 1993).

How can the initial information be represented so as to enable the context to grow into an interpretation? We hypothesize that:

1. Behind certain syntactic dependencies there are semantic relations.
2. In the case of dependencies between nouns, this semantic relation can be made more explicit using verbs and/or prepositions. The knowledge base must help us find them.

We look for a semantic representation close enough to the syntactic representation we can obtain from the dependency graph. The main syntactic dependencies we want to represent in order to enable enrichment are:

1. Dependencies between nouns such as noun-noun compounds (nn) or possessive (poss).
2. Dependencies between nouns and verbs, such as subject and object relations.
3. Prepositions having two nouns as arguments. Then the preposition becomes the label for the relation between the two nouns, being the object of the preposition the target of the relation.

For these selected elements, we produce two very simple transformations of the syntactic dependency graph:

1. Invert the direction of the syntactic dependency for the modifiers. Since we work with the hypothesis that behind a syntactic dependency there is a semantic relation, we record the direction of the semantic relation.
2. Collapse the syntactic dependencies between verb, subject, and object into a single semantic relation. Since we are assuming that the verb is the more explicit expression of a semantic relation, we fix this in the initial representation. The subject will be the source of the relation and the object will be the target of the relation. When the verb has more arguments we consider its expansion as a new node as referred in Section 4.4.

Figure 1 shows the initial minimal representation for the sentence we will use for our discussion:

`San_Francisco's Eric_Davis intercepted a Steve_Walsh pass on the next series to set_up a seven-yard Young touchdown pass to Brent_Jones.`

Notice that some pieces of the text are lost in the initial representation of the text as for example "`on the next series`" or "`seven-yard`".

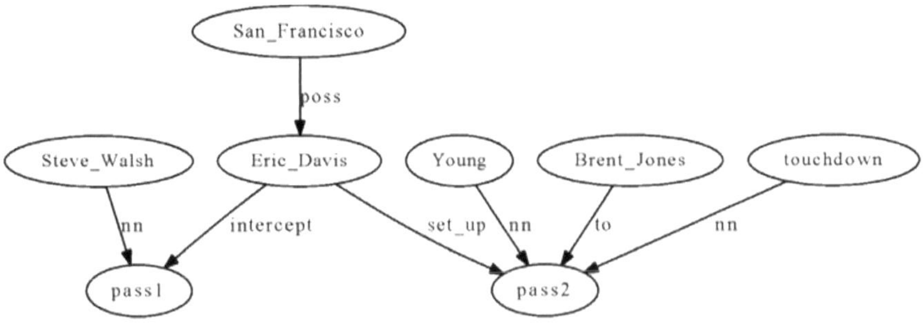

Figure 1. Representation of the sentence: `San_Francisco's Eric_Davis intercepted a Steve_Walsh pass on the next series to set_up a seven-yard Young touchdown pass to Brent_Jones.`

3 Background Knowledge Base

The Background Knowledge Base (BKB) is built from a collection in the domain of the texts we want to semanticize. The collection consists of 30,826 New York Times news about American football, similar to the kind of texts we want to interpret. The elements in the BKB (3,022,305 in total) are obtained as a result of applying general patterns over dependency trees. We take advantage of the typed dependencies (Marneffe and Manning, 2008) produced by the Stanford parser (Klein and Maning, 2003).

3.1 Types of elements in the BKB

We distinguish three elements in our Background Knowledge Base: Entities, Propositions, and Lexical relations. All of them have associated their frequency in the reference collection.

Entities

We distinguish between entity classes and entity instances:

1. Entity classes: Entity classes are denoted by the nouns that participate in a copulative relation or as noun modifier. In addition, we introduce two special classes: Person and Group. These two classes are related to the use of pronouns in text. Pronouns "I", "he" and "she" are linked to class Person. Pronouns "we" and "they" are linked to class Group. For example, the occurrence of the pronoun "he" in "He threw a pass" would produce an additional count of the proposition "person:throw:pass".
2. Entity Instances: Entity instances are indicated by proper nouns. Proper nouns are identified by the part of speech tagging. Some of these instances will participate in the "has-instance" relation (see below). When they participate in a proposition they produce proposition instances.

Propositions

Following Clark and Harrison (2009) we call *propositions* the tuples of words that have some determined pattern of syntactic relations among them. We focus on NVN, NVNPN and NPN proposition types. For example, a NVNPN proposition is a full instantiation of:

`Subject:Verb:Object:Prep:Complement`

The first three elements are the subject, the verb and the direct object. Fourth is the preposition that attaches the PP complement to the verb. For simplicity, indirect objects are considered as a Complement with the preposition "to".

The following are the most frequent NVN propositions in the BKB ordered by frequency.

NVN 2322 'NNP':'beat':'NNP'
NVN 2231 'NNP':'catch':'pass'
NVN 2093 'NNP':'throw':'pass'
NVN 1799 'NNP':'score':'touchdown'
NVN 1792 'NNP':'lead':'NNP'
NVN 1571 'NNP':'play':'NNP'
NVN 1534 'NNP':'win':'game'
NVN 1355 'NNP':'coach':'NNP'
NVN 1330 'NNP':'replace':'NNP'
NVN 1322 'NNP':'kick':'goal'
NVN 1195 'NNP':'win':'NNP'
NVN 1155 'NNP':'defeat':'NNP'
NVN 1103 'NNP':'gain':'yard'

The 'NNP' tag replaces specific proper nouns found in the proposition.

When a sentence has more than one complement, a new occurrence is counted for each complement. For example, given the sentence `"Steve_Walsh threw a pass to Brent_Jones in the first quarter"`, we would add a count to each of the following propositions:

```
Steve_Walsh:throw:pass
Steve_Walsh:throw:pass:to:Brent_Jones
Steve_Walsh:throw:pass:in:quarter
```

Notice that right now we include only the heads of the noun phrases in the propositions.

We call *proposition classes* the propositions that only involve instance classes (e.g., "`person:throw:pass`"), and *proposition instances* those that involve at least one entity instance (e.g., "`Steve_Walsh:throw:pass`").

Proposition instances are useful for the tracking of a entity instance. For example, "`'Steve_Walsh':'supplant':'John_Fourcade':'as':'quarterback'`". When a proposition instance is found, it is stored also as a proposition class replacing the proper nouns by a special word (NNP) to indicate the presence of a entity instance.

The enrichment of the text is based on the use of most frequent proposition classes.

Lexical relations

At the moment, we make use of the copulative verbs (detected by the Stanford's parser) in order to extract "is", and "has-instance" relations:

1. Is: between two entity classes. They denote a kind of identity between both entity classes, but not in any specific hierarchical relation such as hyponymy. Neither is a relation of synonymy. As a result, is somehow a kind of underspecified relation that groups those more specific. For example, if we ask the BKB what a "receiver" is, the most frequent relations are:

   290 'person':is:'receiver'
   29 'player':is:'receiver'
   16 'pick':is:'receiver'
   15 'one':is:'receiver'
   14 'receiver':is:'target'
   8 'end':is:'receiver'
   7 'back':is:'receiver'
   6 'position':is:'receiver'

   The number indicates the number of times the relation appears explicitly in the collection.

2. Has-instance: between an entity class and an entity instance. For example, if we ask for instances of team, the top 10 instances with more support in the collection are:

   192 'team':has-instance:'Jets'
   189 'team':has-instance:'Giants'
   43 'team':has-instance:'Eagles'
   40 'team':has-instance:'Bills'
   36 'team':has-instance:'Colts'
   35 'team':has-instance:'Miami'
   35 'team':has-instance:'Vikings'
   34 'team':has-instance:'Cowboys'
   32 'team':has-instance:'Patriots'
   31 'team':has-instance:'Dallas'

But we can ask also for the possible classes of an instance. For example, all the entity classes for "Eric_Davis" are:

12 'cornerback':has-instance:'Eric_Davis'
1 'hand':has-instance:'Eric_Davis'
1 'back':has-instance:'Eric_Davis'

There are other lexical relations as "part-of" and "is-value-of" in which we are still working. For example, the most frequent "is-value-of" relations are:

5178 '[0-9]-[0-9]':is-value-of:'lead'
3996 '[0-9]-[0-9]':is-value-of:'record'
2824 '[0-9]-[0-9]':is-value-of:'loss'
1225 '[0-9]-[0-9]':is-value-of:'season'

4 Enrichment procedure

The goal of the enrichment procedure is to determine what kind of events and entities are involved in the text, and what semantic relations are hidden by some syntactic dependencies such as noun-noun compound or some prepositions.

4.1 Fusion of nodes

Sometimes, the syntactic dependency ties two or more words that form a single concept. This is the case with multiword terms such as "tight end", "field goal", "running back", etc. In these cases, the meaning of the compound is beyond the syntactic dependency. Thus, we shouldn't look for its explicit meaning. Instead, we activate the fusion of the nodes into a single one.

However, there are some open issues related to the cases were fusion is not preferred. Otherwise, the process could be done with standard measures like mutual information, before the parsing step (and possibly improving its results).

The question is whether the fusion of the words into a single expression allows or not the consideration of possible paraphrases. For example, in the case of "`field:nn:goal`", we don't find other ways to express the concept in the BKB. However, in the case of "`touchdown:nn:pass`" we can find, for example, "`pass:for:touchdown`" a significant amount of times, and we want to identify them as equivalent expressions. For this reason, we find not convenient to fuse these cases.

4.2 Building context for instances

Suppose we wish to determine what kind of entity "`Steve Walsh`" is in the context of the syntactic dependency "`Steve_Walsh:nn:pass`". First, we look into the BKB for the possible entity classes of `Steve_Walsh` previously found in the collection. In this particular case, the most frequent class is "`quarterback`":

40 'quarterback':has-instance:'Steve_Walsh'
2 'junior':has-instance:'Steve_Walsh'

But, what happens if we see "`Steve_Walsh`" for the first time? Then we need to find evidence from other entities in the same syntactic context. We found that "`Marino`", "`Kelly`", "`Elway`", "`Dan_Marino`", etc. appear in the same kind of proposition ("`N:nn:pass`") where we found "`Steve_Walsh`", each of them supported by 24, 17, 15 and 10 occurrences respectively. However, some of the names can be ambiguous. For example, searching for "`Kelly`" in our BKB yields:

153 'quarterback':has-instance:'Jim_Kelly'
19 'linebacker':has-instance:'Joe_Kelly'
17 'quarterback':has-instance:'Kelly'
14 'quarterback':has-instance:'Kelly_Stouffer'
10 'quarterback':has-instance:'Kelly_Ryan'
8 'quarterback':has-instance:'Kelly_Holcomb'
7 'cornerback':has-instance:'Brian_Kelly'

Whereas others are not so ambiguous:

113 'quarterback':has-instance:'Dan_Marino'
6 'passer':has-instance:'Dan_Marino'
5 'player':has-instance:'Dan_Marino'

Taking this into account, we are able to infer that the most plausible class for an entity involved in a "`NNP:nn:pass`" proposition is a quarterback.

4.3 Building context for dependencies

Now we want to determine the meaning behind such syntactic dependencies as "`Steve_Walsh:nn:pass`", "`touchdown:nn:pass`", "`Young:nn:pass`" or "`pass:to:Brent_Jones`". We have two ways for adding more meaning to these syntactic dependencies: find the most appropriate prepositions to describe them, and find the most appropriate verbs. Whether one, the other or both is more useful has to be determined during the reasoning system development.

Finding the prepositions

There are several types of propositions in the BKB that involve prepositions. The most relevant are NPN and NVNPN. In the case of "touchdown:nn:pass", preposition "for" is clearly the best interpretation for the "nn" dependency:

NPN 712 'pass':'for':'touchdown'
NPN 24 'pass':'include':'touchdown'
NPN 3 'pass':'with':'touchdown'
NPN 2 'pass':'of':'touchdown'
NPN 1 'pass':'in':'touchdown'
NPN 1 'pass':'follow':'touchdown'
NPN 1 'pass':'to':'touchdown'

In the case of "`Steve_Walsh:nn:pass`" and "`Young:nn:pass`", assuming they are quarterbacks, we can ask for all the prepositions between "pass" and "quarterback":

NPN 23 'pass':'from':'quarterback'
NPN 14 'pass':'by':'quarterback'
NPN 2 'pass':'of':'quarterback'
NPN 1 'pass':'than':'quarterback'
NPN 1 'pass':'to':'quarterback'

Notice how lower frequencies involve more noisy options.

If we don't have any evidence on the instance class, and we know only that they are instances, the pertinent query to the BKB obtains:

NPN 1305 'pass':'to':'NNP'
NPN 1085 'pass':'from':'NNP'
NPN 147 'pass':'by':'NNP'
NPN 144 'pass':'for':'NNP'

In the case of "`Young:nn:pass`" (in "Young pass to Brent Jones"), there exists already the preposition "to" ("pass:to:Brent_Jones"), so the most promising choice become the second, "pass:from:Young", which has one order of magnitude more occurrences than the following.

In the case of "Steve_Walsh:nn:pass" (in "Eric Davis intercepted a Steve Walsh pass") we can use additional information: we know that "`Eric_Davis:intercept:pass`". So, we can try to find the appropriate preposition using NVNPN propositions in the following way:
`Eric_Davis:intercept:pass:P:Steve_Walsh"`

Asking the BKB about the propositions that involve two instances with "intercept" and "pass" we get:

NVNPN 48 'NNP':'intercept':'pass':'by':'NNP'
NVNPN 26 'NNP':'intercept':'pass':'at':'NNP'
NVNPN 12 'NNP':'intercept':'pass':'from':'NNP'

We could also query the BKB with the classes we already found for "Eric_Davis" (cornerback, player, person):

NVNPN 11 'person':'intercept':'pass':'by':'NNP'
NVNPN 4 'person':'intercept':'pass':'at':'NNP'
NVNPN 2 'person':'intercept':'pass':'in':'NNP'

NVNPN 2 'person':'intercept':'pass':'against':'NNP'
NVNPN 1 'cornerback':'intercept':'pass':'by':'NNP'

All these queries accumulate evidence over a correct preposition "by" ("pass:by:Steve_Walsh"). However, an explicit entity classification would make the procedure more robust.

Finding the verbs

Now the exercise is to find a verb able to give meaning to the syntactic dependencies such as "`Steve_Walsh:nn:pass`", "`touchdown:nn:pass`", "`Young:nn:pass`" or "`pass:to:Brent_Jones`".

We can ask the BKB what instances (NNP) do with passes. The most frequent propositions are:

NVN 2241 'NNP':'catch':'pass'
NVN 2106 'NNP':'throw':'pass'
NVN 844 'NNP':'complete':'pass'
NVN 434 'NNP':'intercept':'pass'

NVNPN 758 'NNP':'throw':'pass':'to':'NNP'
NVNPN 562 'NNP':'catch':'pass':'for':'yard'
NVNPN 338 'NNP':'complete':'pass':'to':'NNP'
NVNPN 255 'NNP':'catch':'pass':'from':'NNP'

Considering the evidence of "Brent_Jones" being instance of "end" (tight end), if we ask the BKB about the most frequent relations between "end" and "pass" we find:

NVN 28 'end':'catch':'pass'
NVN 6 'end':'drop':'pass'

So, in this case, the BKB suggests that the syntactic dependency "`pass:to:Brent_Jones`" means "Brent_Jones is an end catching a pass". Or in other words, that "Brent_Jones" has a role of "catch-ER" with respect to "pass".

If we want to accumulate more evidence on this we can consider NVNPN propositions including touchdown. We only find evidence for the most general classes (NNP and person):

NVNPN 189 'NNP':'catch':'pass':'for':'touchdown'
NVNPN 26 'NNP':'complete':'pass':'for':'touchdown'

NVNPN 84 'person':'catch':'pass':'for':'touchdown'
NVNPN 18 'person':'complete':'pass':'for':'touchdown'

This means, that when we have "touchdown", we don't have counting for the second option "Brent_Jones:drop:pass", while "catch" becomes stronger.

In the case of "Steve_Walsh:nn:pass" we hypothesize that "Steve_Walsh" is a quarterback. Asking the BKB about the most plausible relation between a quarterback and a pass we find:

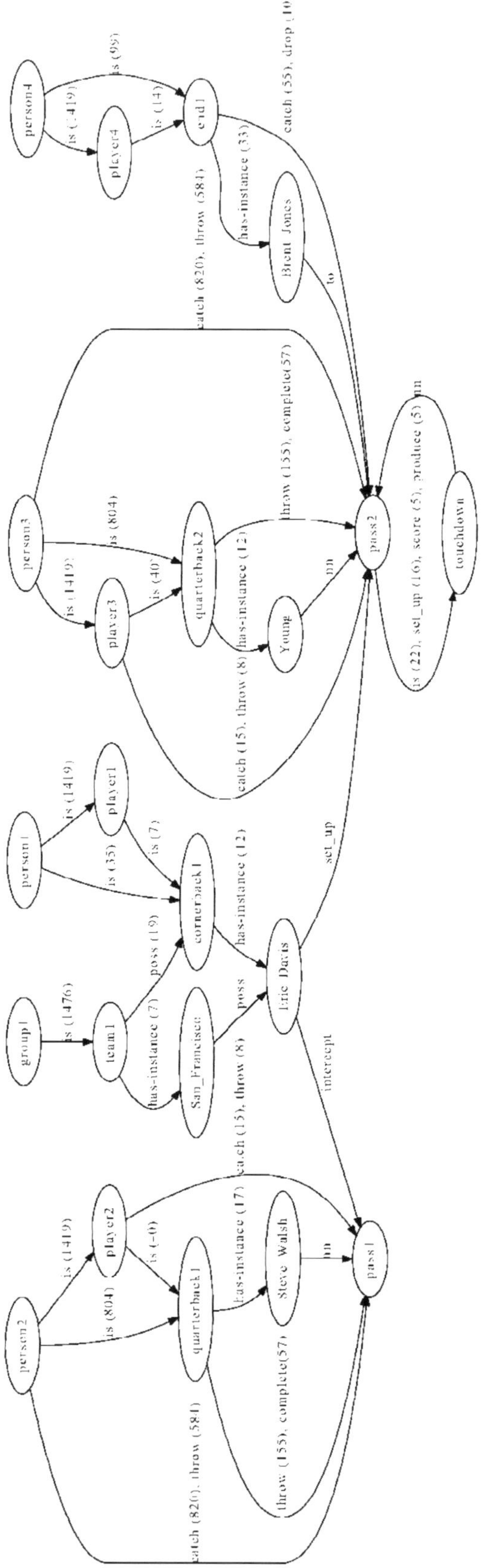

Figure 2. Graphical representation of the enriched text.

NVN 98 'quarterback':'throw':'pass'
NVN 27 'quarterback':'complete':'pass'

Again, if we take into account that it is a "`touchdown:nn:pass`", then only the second option "`Steve_Walsh:complete:pass`" is consistent with the NVNPN propositions.

So, in this case, the BKB suggests that the syntactic dependency "`Steve_Walsh:nn:pass`" means "Steve_Walsh is a quarterback completing a pass".

Finally, with respect to "`touchdown:nn:pass`", we can ask about the verbs that relate them:

NVN 14 'pass':'set_up':'touchdown'
NVN 6 'pass':'score':'touchdown'
NVN 5 'pass':'produce':'touchdown'

Figure 2 shows the graphical representation of the sentence after some enrichment.

4.4 Expansion of relations

Sometimes, the sentence shows a verb with several arguments. In our example, we have "`Eric_David:intercept:pass:on:series`". In these cases, the relation can be expanded and become a node.

In our example, the new node is the eventuality of "intercept" (let's say "intercept-ION"), "Eric_Davis" is the "intercept-ER" and "pass" is the "intercept-ED". Then, we can attach the missing information to the new node (see Figure 3).

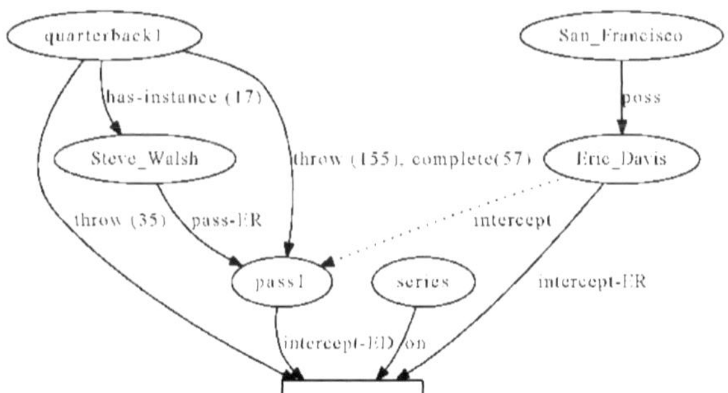

Figure 3. Expansion of the "intercept" relation.

In addition, we can proceed with the expansion of the context considering this new node. For example, we are working with the hypothesis that "Steve_Walsh" is an instance of quarterback and thus, its most plausible relations with pass are "throw" and "complete". However, now we can ask about the most frequent relation between "quarterback" and "interception". The most frequent is "`quarterback:throw:interception`" supported 35 times in the collection. From this, two actions can be done: reinforce the hypothesis of "`throw:pass`" instead of "`complete:pass`", and add the hypothesis that "`Steve_Walsh:throw:interception`".

Finally, notice that since "set_up" doesn't need to accommodate more arguments, we can maintain the collapsed edge.

4.5 Constraining the interpretations

Some of the inferences being performed are local in the sense that they involve only an entity and a relation. However, these local inferences must be coherent both with the sentence and the complete document.

To ensure this coherence we can use additional information as a way to constrain different hypotheses. In section 4.3 we showed the use of NVNPN propositions to constrain NVN ones.

Another example is the case of "`Eric_Davis:intercept:pass`". We can ask the BKB for the entity classes that participate in such kind of proposition:

NVN 75 'person':'intercept':'pass'
NVN 14 'cornerback':'intercept':'pass'
NVN 11 'defense':'intercept':'pass'
NVN 8 'safety':'intercept':'pass'
NVN 7 'group':'intercept':'pass'
NVN 5 'linebacker':'intercept':'pass'

So the local inference for the kind of entity "Eric_Davis" is (cornerback) must be coherent with the fact that it intercepted a pass. In this case "cornerback" and "person" are properly reinforced. In some sense, we are using these additional constrains as shallow selectional preferences.

5 Evaluation

The evaluation of the enrichment process is a challenge by itself. Eventually, we will use extrinsic measures such as system performance on a QA task, applied first after reading a text, and then a second time after the enrichment process. This will measure the ability of the system to absorb and use knowledge across texts to enrich the interpretation of the target text. In the near term, however, it remains unclear which intrinsic evaluation measures to apply. It is not informative simply to count the number of additional relations one can attach to representation elements, or to count the increase in degree of interlinking of the nodes in the representation of a paragraph.

6 Related Work

To build the knowledge base we take an approach closely related to DART (Clark and Harrison, 2009) which in turn is related to KNEXT (Van Durme and Schubert, 2008). It is also more distantly related to TextRunner (Banko et al. 2007).

Like DART, we make use of a dependency parser instead of partial parsing. So we capture phrase heads instead complete phrases. The main differences between the generation of our BKB and the generation of DART are:

1. We use the dependencies involving copulative verbs as a source of evidence for "is" and "has-instance" relations.
2. Instead of replacing proper nouns by "person", "place", or "organization", we consider all of them just as instances in our BKB. Furthermore, when a proposition contains a proper noun, we count it twice: one as the original proposition instance, and a second replacing the proper nouns with a generic tag indicating that there was a name.
3. We make use of the modifiers that involve an instance (proper noun) to add counting to the "has-instance" relation.
4. Instead of replacing pronouns by "person" or "thing", we replace them by "person", "group" or "thing", taking advantage of the preposition number. This is particular useful for the domain of football where players and teams are central.
5. We add a new set of propositions that relate two clauses in the same sentence (e.g., `Floyd:break:takle:add:touchdown`). We tagged these propositions NVV, NVNV, NVVN and NVNVN.
6. Instead of an unrestricted domain collection, we consider documents closely related to the domain in which we want to interpret texts.

The consideration of a specific domain collection seems a very powerful option. Ambiguity is reduced inside a domain so the counting for propositions is more robust. Also frequency distribution of propositions is different from one domain into another. For example, the list of the most frequent NVN propositions in our BKB (see Section 3.1) is, by itself, an indication of the most salient and important events in the American football domain.

7 Conclusion and Future Work

The task of inferring omitted but necessary information is a significant part of automated text interpretation. In this paper we show that even simple kinds of information, gleaned relatively straightforwardly from a parsed corpus, can be quite useful. Though they are still lexical and not even starting to be semantic, propositions consisting of verbs as relations between nouns seem to provide a surprising amount of utility. It remains a research problem to determine what kinds and levels of knowledge are most useful in the long run.

In the paper, we discuss only the propositions that are grounded in instantial statements about players and events. But for true learning by reading, a system has to be able to recognize when the input expresses general rules, and to formulate such input as axioms or inferences. In addition, augmenting that is the significant challenge of generalizing certain kinds of instantial propositions to produce inferences. At which point, for example, should the system decide that "all football players have teams", and how should it do so? How to do so remains a topic for future work.

A further topic of investigation is the time at which expansion should occur. Doing so at question time, in the manner of traditional task-oriented back-chaining inference, is the obvious choice, but some limited amount of forward chaining at reading time seems appropriate too, especially if it can significantly assist with text processing tasks, in the manner of expectation-driven understanding.

Finally, as discussed above, the evaluation of our reading augmentation procedures remains to be developed.

Acknowledgments

We are grateful to Hans Chalupsky and David Farwell for their comments and input along this work. This work has been partially supported by the Spanish Government through the "Programa Nacional de Movilidad de Recursos Humanos del Plan Nacional de I+D+i 2008-2011 (Grant PR2009-0020). We acknowledge the support of DARPA contract number: FA8750-09-C-0172.

References

1. Banko, M., Cafarella, M., Soderland, S., Broadhead, M., Etzioni, O. 2007. Open Information Extraction from the Web. IJCAI 2007.
2. Barker, K. 2007. Building Models by Reading Texts. Invited talk at the AAAI 2007 Spring Symposium on Machine Reading, Stanford University.
3. Clark, P. and Harrison, P. 2009. Large-scale extraction and use of knowledge from text. The Fifth International Conference on Knowledge Capture (K-CAP 2009). http://www.cs.utexas.edu/users/pclark/dart/
4. Hobbs, J.R., Stickel, M., Appelt, D. and Martin, P., 1993. Interpretation as Abduction. Artificial Intelligence, Vol. 63, Nos. 1-2, pp. 69-142. http://www.isi.edu/~hobbs/interp-abduct-ai.pdf
5. Klein, D. and Manning, C.D. 2003. Accurate Unlexicalized Parsing. Proceedings of the 41st Meeting of the Association for Computational Linguistics, pp. 423-430
6. Marneffe, M. and Manning, C.D. 2008. The Stanford typed dependencies representation. In COLING 2008 Workshop on Cross-framework and Cross-domain Parser Evaluation.
7. Sperber, D. and Wilson, D. 1995. Relevance: Communication and cognition (2nd ed.) Oxford, Blackwell.
8. Van Durme, B., Schubert, L. 2008. Open Knowledge Extraction through Compositional Language Processing. Symposium on Semantics in Systems for Text Processing, STEP 2008.

Large Scale Relation Detection*

Chris Welty and **James Fan** and **David Gondek** and **Andrew Schlaikjer**

IBM Watson Research Center · 19 Skyline Drive · Hawthorne, NY 10532, USA
{welty, fanj, dgondek, ahschlai}@us.ibm.com

Abstract

We present a technique for reading sentences and producing sets of hypothetical relations that the sentence may be expressing. The technique uses large amounts of instance-level background knowledge about the relations in order to gather statistics on the various ways the relation may be expressed in language, and was inspired by the observation that half of the linguistic forms used to express relations occur very infrequently and are simply not considered by systems that use too few seed examples. Some very early experiments are presented that show promising results.

1 Introduction

We are building a system that learns to read in a new domain by applying a novel combination of natural language processing, machine learning, knowledge representation and reasoning, information retrieval, data mining, etc. techniques in an integrated way. Central to our approach is the view that all parts of the system should be able to interact during any level of processing, rather than a pipeline view in which certain parts of the system only take as input the results of other parts, and thus cannot influence those results. In this paper we discuss a particular case of that idea, using large knowledge bases hand in hand with natural language processing to improve the quality of relation detection. Ultimately we define reading as representing natural language text in a way that integrates background knowledge and inference, and thus are doing the relation detection to better integrate text with pre-existing knowledge, however that should not (and does not) prevent us from using what knowledge we have to influence that integration along the way.

2 Background

The most obvious points of interaction between NLP and KR systems are named entity tagging and other forms of type instance extraction. The second major point of interaction is relation extraction, and while there are many kinds of relations that may be detected (e.g. syntactic relations such as modifiers and verb subject/object, equivalence relations like coreference or nicknames, event frame relations such as participants, etc.), the kind of relations that reading systems need to extract to support domain-specific reasoning tasks are relations that are known to be expressed in supporting knowledge-bases. We call these relations semantic relations in this paper. Compared to entity and type detection, extraction of semantic relations is significantly harder. In our work on bridging the NLP-KR gap, we have observed several aspects of what makes this task difficult, which we discuss below.

2.1 Keep reading

Humans do not read and understand text by first recognizing named entities, giving them types, and then finding a small fixed set of relations between them. Rather, humans start with the first sentence and build up a representation of what they read that expands and is refined during reading. Furthermore, humans

* Research supported in part by DARPA MRP Grant FA8750-09-C0172

Proceedings of the NAACL HLT 2010 First International Workshop on Formalisms and Methodology for Learning by Reading, pages 24–33, Los Angeles, California, June 2010.

do not "populate databases" by reading; knowledge is not only a product of reading, it is an *integral part* of it. We require knowledge during reading in order to understand what we read.

One of the central tenets of our machine reading system is the notion that reading is not performed on sentences in isolation. Often, problems in NLP can be resolved by simply waiting for the next sentence, or remembering the results from the previous, and incorporating background or domain specific knowledge. This includes parse ambiguity, coreference, typing of named entities, etc. We call this the *Keep Reading* principle.

Keep reading applies to relation extraction as well. Most relation extraction systems are implemented such that a single interpretation is forced on a sentence, based only on features of the sentence itself. In fact, this has been a shortcoming of many NLP systems in the past. However, when you apply the Keep Reading principle, multiple hypotheses from different parts of the NLP pipeline are maintained, and decisions are deferred until there is enough evidence to make a high confidence choice between competing hypotheses. Knowledge, such as those entities already known to participate in a relation and how that relation was expressed, can and should be part of that evidence. We will present many examples of the principle in subsequent sections.

2.2 Expressing relations in language

Due to the flexibility and expressive power of natural language, a specific type of semantic relation can usually be expressed in language in a myriad of ways. In addition, semantic relations are often implied by the expression of other relations. For example, all of the following sentences more or less express the same relation between an actor and a movie: (1) "Elijah wood starred in Lord of the Rings: The Fellowship of the Ring", (2) "Lord of the Rings: The Fellowship of the Ring's Elijah Wood, ...", and(3) "Elijah Wood's coming of age was clearly his portrayal of the dedicated and noble hobbit that led the eponymous fellowship from the first episode of the Lord of the Rings trilogy." No human reader would have any trouble recognizing the relation, but clearly this variability of expression presents a major problem for machine reading systems.

To get an empirical sense of the variability of natural language used to express a relation, we studied a few semantic relations and found sentences that expressed that relation, extracted simple *patterns* to account for how the relation is expressed between two arguments, mainly by removing the relation arguments (e.g. "Elijah Wood" and "Lord of the Rings: The Fellowship of the Ring" above) and replacing them with variables. We then counted the number of times each pattern was used to express the relation, producing a recognizable *very long tail* shown in Figure 1 for the top 50 patterns expressing the acted-in-movie relation in 17k sentences. More sophisticated pattern generalization (as discussed in later sections) would significantly fatten the head, bringing it closer to the traditional 50% of the area under the curve, but no amount of generalization will eliminate the tail. The patterns become increasingly esoteric, such as "The movie Death Becomes Her features a brief sequence in which Bruce Willis and Goldie Hawn's characters plan Meryl Streep's character's death by sending her car off of a cliff on Mulholland Drive," or "The best known Hawksian woman is probably Lauren Bacall, who iconically played the type opposite Humphrey Bogart in To Have and Have Not and The Big Sleep."

2.3 What relations matter

We do not consider relation extraction to be an end in and of itself, but rather as a component in larger systems that perform some task requiring interoperation between language- and knowledge-based components. Such larger tasks can include question answering, medical diagnosis, intelligence analysis, museum curation, etc. These tasks have evaluation criteria that go beyond measuring relation extraction results. The first step in applying relation detection to these larger tasks is analysis to determine what relations matter for the task and domain.

There are a number of manual and semi-automatic ways to perform such analysis. Repeating the theme of this paper, which is to use pre-existing knowledge-bases as resources, we performed this analysis using freebase and a set of 20k question-answer pairs representing our task domain. For each question, we formed tuples of each entity name in the question (QNE) with the answer, and found all

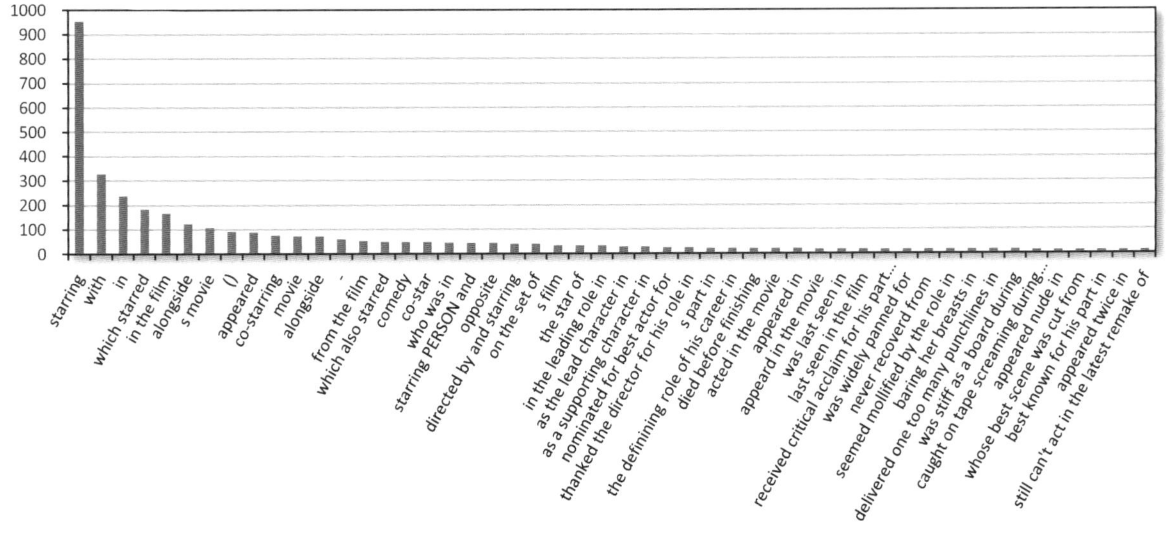

Figure 1: Pattern frequency for *acted-in-movie* relation for 17k sentences.

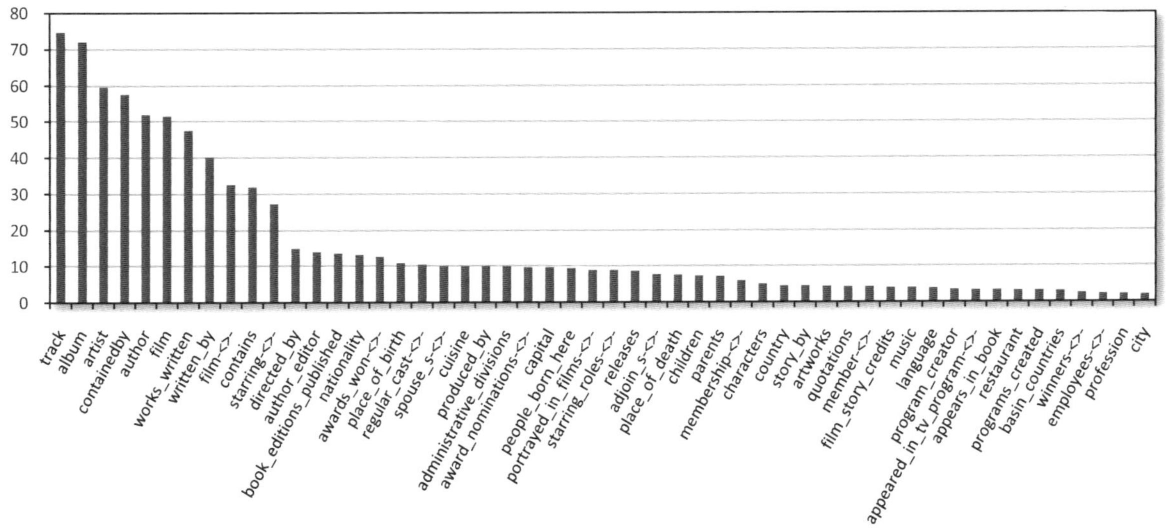

Figure 2: Relative frequency for top 50 relations in 20K question-answer pairs.

the relations in the KB connecting the entities. We kept a count for each relation of how often it connected a QNE to an answer. Of course we don't actually know for sure that the relation is the one being asked, but the intuition is that if the amount of data is big enough, you will have at least a ranked list of which relations are the most frequent.

Figure 2 shows the ranking for the top 50 relations. Note that, even when restricted to the top 50 relations, the graph has no head, it is basically all tail; The top 50 relations cover about 15% of the domain. In smaller, manual attempts to determine the most frequent relations in our domain, we had a similar result. What this means is that supporting even the top 50 relations with perfect recall covers about 15% of the questions. It is possible, of course, to narrow the domain and restrict the relations that can be queried–this is what database systems do. For reading, however, the results are the same. A reading system requires the ability to recognize hundreds of relations to have any significant impact on understanding.

2.4 Multi-relation learning on many seeds

The results shown in Figure 1 and Figure 2 confirmed much of the analysis and experiences we'd had in the past trying to apply relation extraction in the traditional way to natural language problems like question answering, building concept graphs from intelligence reports, semantic search, etc. Either by training machine learning algorithms on manually annotated data or by manually crafting finite-state transducers, relation detection is faced by this two-fold problem: the per-relation extraction hits a wall around 50% recall, and each relation itself occurs infrequently in the data.

This apparent futility of relation extraction led us to rethink our approach. First of all, the very long tail for relation patterns led us to consider how to pick up the tail. We concluded that to do so would require many more examples of the relation, but where can we get them? In the world of linked-data, huge instance-centered knowledge-bases are rapidly growing and spreading on the semantic web[1]. Resources like DBPedia, Freebase, IMDB, Geonames, the Gene Ontology, etc., are making available RDF-based data about a number of domains. These sources of structured knowledge can provide a large number of seed tuples for many different relations. This is discussed further below.

Furthermore, the all-tail nature of relation coverage led us to consider performing relation extraction on multiple relations at once. Some promising results on multi-relation learning have already been reported in (Carlson et al., 2009), and the data sources mentioned above give us many more than just the handful of seed instances used in those experiments. The idea of learning multiple relations at once also fits with our keep reading principle - multiple relation hypotheses may be annotated between the same arguments, with further evidence helping to disambiguate them.

3 Approach

One common approach to relation extraction is to start with *seed tuples* and find sentences that contain mentions of both elements of the tuple. From each such sentence a pattern is generated using at minimum universal generalization (replace the tuple elements with variables), though adding any form of generalization here can significantly improve recall. Finally, evaluate the patterns by applying them to text and evaluating the precision and recall of the tuples extracted by the patterns. Our approach, called *Large Scale Relation Detection* (LSRD), differs in three important ways:

1. We start with a knowledge-base containing a large number (thousands to millions) of tuples encoding relation instances of various types. Our hypothesis is that *only a large number of examples can possibly account for the long tail.*
2. We do not learn one relation at a time, but rather, associate a pattern with a set of relations whose tuples appear in that pattern. Thus, when a pattern is matched to a sentence during reading, each relation in its set of associated relations is posited as a hypothetical interpretation of the sentence, to be supported or refuted by further reading.
3. We use the knowledge-base as an oracle to determine negative examples of a relation. As a result the technique is semi-supervised; it requires no human intervention but does require reliable knowledge-bases as input–these knowledge-bases are readily available today.

Many relation extraction techniques depend on a prior step of named entity recognition (NER) and typing, in order to identify potential arguments. However, this limits recall to the recall of the NER step. In our approach patterns can match on any noun phrase, and typing of these NPs is simply another form of evidence.

All this means our approach is not relation extraction per se, it typically does not make conclusions about a relation in a sentence, but extracts hypotheses to be resolved by other parts of our reading system.

In the following sections, we elaborate on the technique and some details of the current implementation.

3.1 Basic pipeline

The two principle inputs are a corpus and a knowledge-base (KB). For the experiments below, we used the English Gigaword corpus[2] extended with Wikipedia and other news sources, and IMDB, DBPedia, and Freebase KBs, as shown. The intent is

[1] http://linkeddata.org/

[2] http://www.ldc.upenn.edu/Catalog/CatalogEntry.jsp?catalogId=LDC2003T05

to run against a web-scale corpus and larger linked-data sets.

Input documents are sentence delimited, tokenized and parsed. The technique can benefit dramatically from coreference resolution, however in the experiments shown, this was not present. For each pair of *proper names* in a sentence, the names are looked up in the KB, and if they are related, a *pattern* is extracted from the sentence. At minimum, pattern extraction should replace the names with variables. Depending on how patterns are extracted, one pattern may be extracted per sentence, or one pattern may be extracted per pair of proper names in the sentence. Each pattern is associated with *all the relations* known in the KB between the two proper names. If the pattern has been extracted before, the two are merged by incrementing the associated relation counts. This phase, called *pattern induction*, is repeated for the entire corpus, resulting in a large set of patterns, each pattern associated with relations. For each ¡pattern, relation¿ pair, there is a count of the number of times that pattern appeared in the corpus with names that are in the relation according to the KB.

The pattern induction phase results in *positive counts*, i.e. the number of times a pattern appeared in the corpus with named entities known to be related in the KB. However, the induction phase does not exhaustively count the number of times each pattern appears in the corpus, as a pattern may appear with entities that are not known in the KB, or are not known to be related. The second phase, called *pattern training*, goes through the entire corpus again, trying to match induced patterns to sentences, binding any noun phrase to the pattern variables. Some attempt is made to resolve the noun phrase to something (most obviously, a name) that can be looked up in the KB, and for each relation associated with the pattern, if the two names are *not* in the relation according to the KB, the *negative count* for that relation in the matched pattern is incremented. The result of the pattern training phase is an updated set of ¡pattern, relation¿ pairs with *negative counts*.

The following example illustrates the basic processing. During induction, this sentence is encountered:

> Tom Cruise and co-star Nicole Kidman appeared together at the premier.

The proper names "Tom Cruise" and "Nicole Kidman" are recognized and looked up in the KB. We find instances in the KB with those names, and the following relations: `coStar(Tom Cruise, Nicole Kidman)`; `marriedTo(Tom Cruise, Nicole Kidman)`. We extract a pattern p_1: `?`x `and co-star ?`y `appeared together at the premier` in which all the names have been replace by variables, and the associations <p_1, `costar, 1, 0`> and <p_1, `marriedTo, 1, 0`> with positive counts and zero negative counts. Over the entire corpus, we'd expect the pattern to appear a few times and end up with final positive counts like <p_1, `coStar, 14, 0`> and <p_1, `marriedTo, 2, 0`>, indicating the pattern p_1 appeared 14 times in the corpus between names known to participate in the *coStar* relation, and twice between names known to participate in the *marriedTo* relation. During training, the following sentence is encountered that matches p_1:

> Tom Hanks and co-star Daryl Hannah appeared together at the premier.

The names "Tom Hanks" and "Daryl Hannah" are looked up in the KB and in this case only the relation *coStar* is found between them, so the *marriedTo* association is updated with a negative count: <p_1, `marriedTo, 2, -1`>. Over the entire corpus, we'd expect the counts to be something like <p_1, `costar, 14, -6`> and <p_1, `marriedTo, 2, -18`>.

This is a very simple example and it is difficult to see the value of the pattern training phase, as it may appear the negative counts could be collected during the induction phase. There are several reasons why this is not so. First of all, since the first phase only induces patterns between proper names that appear and are related within the KB, a sentence in the corpus matching the pattern would be missed if it did not meet that criteria but was encountered before the pattern was induced. Secondly, for reasons that are beyond the scope of this paper, having to do with our *Keep Reading* principle, the second phase does slightly more general matching: note that it matches noun phrases instead of proper nouns.

3.2 Candidate-instance matching

An obvious part of the process in both phases is taking strings from text and matching them against names or labels in the KB. We refer to the strings in the sentences as *candidate arguments* or simply *candidates*, and refer to *instances* in the KB as entities with associated attributes. For simplicity of discussion we will assume all KBs are in RDF, and thus all KB instances are nodes in a graph with unique identifiers (URIs) and arcs connecting them to other instances or primitive values (strings, numbers, etc.). A set of specially designated arcs, called *labels*, connect instances to strings that are understood to name the instances. The reverse lookup of entity identifiers via names referred to in the previous section requires searching for the labels that match a string found in a sentence and returning the instance identifier.

This step is so obvious it belies the difficultly of the matching process and is often overlooked, however in our experiments we have found candidate-instance matching to be a significant source of error. Problems include having many instances with the same or lexically similar names, slight variations in spelling especially with non-English names, inflexibility or inefficiency in string matching in KB implementations, etc. In some of our sources, names are also encoded as URLs. In the case of movie and book titles-two of the domains we experimented with-the titles seem almost as if they were designed specifically to befuddle attempts to automatically recognize them. Just about every English word is a book or movie title, including "It", "Them", "And", etc., many years are titles, and just about every number under 1000. Longer titles are difficult as well, since simple lexical variations can prevent matching from succeeding, e.g. the Shakespeare play, *A Midsummer Night's Dream* appears often as *Midsummer Night's Dream*, *A Midsummer Night Dream*, and occasionally, in context, just *Dream*. When titles are not distinguished or delimited somehow, they can confuse parsing which may fail to recognize them as noun phrases. We eventually had to build dictionaries of multi-word titles to help parsing, but of course that was imperfect as well.

The problems go beyond the analogous ones in coreference resolution as the sources and technology themselves are different. The problems are severe enough that the candidate-instance matching problem contributes the most, of all components in this pipeline, to precision and recall failures. We have observed recall drops of as much as 15% and precision drops of 10% due to candidate-instance matching.

This problem has been studied somewhat in the literature, especially in the area of database record matching and coreference resolution (Michelson and Knoblock, 2007), but the experiments presented below use rudimentary solutions and would benefit significantly from improvements; it is important to acknowledge that the problem exists and is not as trivial as it appears at first glance.

3.3 Pattern representation

The basic approach accommodates any pattern representation, and in fact we can accommodate non pattern-based learning approaches, such as CRFs, as the primary hypothesis is principally concerned with the number of seed examples (scaling up initial set of examples is important). Thus far we have only experimented with two pattern representations: simple lexical patterns in which the known arguments are replaced in the sentence by variables (as shown in the example above), and patterns based on the spanning tree between the two arguments in a dependency parse, again with the known arguments replaced by variables. In our initial design we downplayed the importance of the pattern representation and especially generalization, with the belief that very large scale would remove the need to generalize. However, our initial experiments suggest that good pattern generalization would have a significant impact on recall, without negative impact on precision, which agrees with findings in the literature (Pantel and Pennacchiotti, 2006). Thus, these early results only employ rudimentary pattern generalization techniques, though this is an area we intend to improve. We discuss some more details of the lack of generalization below.

4 Experiment

In this section we present a set of very early proof of concept experiments performed using drastic simplifications of the LSRD design. We began, in fact, by

Relation	*Prec*	*Rec*	*F1*	*Tuples*	*Seeds*
imdb:actedIn	46.3	45.8	0.46	9M	30K
frb:authorOf	23.4	27.5	0.25	2M	2M
imdb:directorOf	22.8	22.4	0.22	700K	700K
frb:parentOf	68.2	8.6	0.16	10K	10K

Table 1: Precision and recall vs. number of tuples used for 4 freebase relations.

using single-relation experiments, despite the centrality of multiple hypotheses to our reading system, in order to facilitate evaluation and understanding of the technique. Our main focus was to gather data to support (or refute) the hypothesis that more relation examples would matter during pattern induction, and that using the KB as an oracle for training would work. Clearly, no KB is complete to begin with, and candidate-instance matching errors drop apparent coverage further, so we intended to explore the degree to which the KB's coverage of the relation impacted performance. To accomplish this, we examined four relations with different coverage characteristics in the KB.

4.1 Setup and results

The first relation we tried was the *acted-in-show* relation from IMDB; for convenience we refer to it as *imdb:actedIn*. An IMDB *show* is a movie, TV episode, or series. This relation has over 9M `<actor, show>` tuples, and its coverage was complete as far as we were able to determine. However, the version we used did not have a lot of name variations for actors. The second relation was the *author-of* relation from Freebase (*frb:authorOf*), with roughly 2M `<author, written-work>` tuples. The third relation was the *director-of-movie* relation from IMDB (*imdb:directorOf*), with 700k `<director,movie>` tuples. The fourth relation was the *parent-of* relation from Freebase (*frb:parentOf*), with roughly 10K `<parent, child>` tuples (mostly biblical and entertainment). Results are shown in Table 1.

The *imdb:actedIn* experiment was performed on the first version of the system that ran on 1 CPU and, due to resource constraints, was not able to use more than 30K seed tuples for the rule induction phase. However, the full KB (9M relation instances) was available for the training phase. With some manual effort, we selected tuples (actor-movie pairs) of popular actors and movies that we expected to appear most frequently in the corpus. In the other experiments, the full tuple set was available for both phases, but 2M tuples was the limit for the size of the KB in the implementation. With these promising preliminary results, we expect a full implementation to accommodate up to 1B tuples or more.

The evaluation was performed in decreasing degrees of rigor. The *imdb:actedIn* experiment was run against 20K sentences with roughly 1000 actor in movie relations and checked by hand. For the other three, the same sentences were used, but the ground truth was generated in a semi-automatic way by re-using the LSRD assumption that a sentence containing tuples in the relation expresses the relation, and then spot-checked manually. Thus the evaluation for these three experiments favors the LSRD approach, though spot checking revealed it is the precision and not the recall that benefits most from this, and all the recall problems in the ground truth (i.e. sentences that did express the relation but were not in the ground truth) were due to candidate-instance matching problems. An additional idiosyncrasy in the evaluation is that the sentences in the ground truth were actually questions, in which one of the arguments to the relation was the answer. Since the patterns were induced and trained on statements, there is a mismatch in style which also significantly impacts recall. Thus the precision and recall numbers should not be taken as general performance, but are useful only relative to each other.

4.2 Discussion

The results are promising, and we are continuing the work with a scalable implementation. Overall, the results seem to show a clear correlation between the number of seed tuples and relation extraction recall. However, the results do not as clearly support the many examples hypothesis as it may seem. When an actor and a film that actor starred in are mentioned in a sentence, it is very often the case that the sentence expresses that relation. However, this was less likely in the case of the parent-of relation, and as we considered other relations, we found a wide degree of variation. The borders relation between two countries, for example, is on the other extreme from actor-in-movie. Bordering nations often wage war, trade, suspend relations, deport refugees, support, oppose, etc. each other, so finding the two nations in a sentence together is not highly indicative of one relation or another. The director-of-movie relation was closer to acted-in-movie in this regard, and author-of a bit below that. The obvious next step to gather more data on the many examples hypothesis is to run the experiments with one relation, increasing the number of tuples with each experiment and observing the change in precision and recall.

The recall results do not seem particularly striking, though these experiments do not include pattern generalization (other than what a dependency parse provides) or coreference, use a small corpus, and poor candidate-instance matching. Further, as noted above there were other idiosyncrasies in the evaluation that make them only useful for relative comparison, not as general results.

Many of the patterns induced, especially for the acted-in-movie relation, were highly lexical, using e.g. parenthesis or other punctuation to signal the relation. For example, a common pattern was `actor-name (movie-name)`, or `movie-name: actor-name`, e.g. "Leonardo DiCaprio (Titanic) was considering accepting the role as Anakin Skywalker," or "Titanic: Leonardo DiCaprio and Kate Blanchett steam up the silver screen against the backdrop of the infamous disaster." Clearly patterns like this rely heavily on the context and typing to work. In general the pattern $?x$ `(`$?y$`)` is not reliable for the actor-in-movie relation unless you know $?x$ is an actor and $?y$ is a movie. However, some patterns, like $?x$ `appears in the screen epic` $?y$ is highly indicative of the relation without the types at all - in fact it is so high precision it could be used to infer the types of $?x$ and $?y$ if they were not known. This seems to fit extremely well in our larger reading system, in which the pattern itself provides one form of evidence to be combined with others, but was not a part of our evaluation.

One of the most important things to generalize in the patterns we observed was dates. If patterns like, `actor-name appears in the 1994 screen epic movie-name` could have been generalized to `actor-name appears in the date screen epic movie-name`, recall would have been boosted significantly. As it stood in these experiments, everything but the arguments had to match. Similarly, many relations often appear in lists, and our patterns were not able to generalize that away. For example the sentence, "Mark Hamill appeared in Star Wars, Star Wars: The Empire Strikes Back, and Star Wars: The Return of the Jedi," causes three patterns to be induced; in each, one of the movies is replaced by a variable in the pattern and the other two are required to be present. Then of course all this needs to be combined, so that the sentence, "Indiana Jones and the Last Crusade is a 1989 adventure film directed by Steven Spielberg and starring Harrison Ford, Sean Connery, Denholm Elliott and Julian Glover," would generate a pattern that would get the right arguments out of "Titanic is a 1997 epic film directed by James Cameron and starring Leonardo DiCaprio, Kate Winslett, Kathy Bates and Bill Paxon." At the moment the former sentence generates four patterns that require the director and dates to be exactly the same.

Some articles in the corpus were biographies which were rich with relation content but also with pervasive anaphora, name abbreviations, and other coreference manifestations that severely hampered induction and evaluation.

5 Related work

Early work in semi-supervised learning techniques such as co-training and multi-view learning (Blum and Mitchell, 1998) laid much of the ground work for subsequent experiments in bootstrapped learning for various NLP tasks, including named entity detection (Craven et al., 2000; Etzioni et al., 2005) and document classification (Nigam et al., 2006). This work's pattern induction technique also represents a semi-supervised approach, here applied to relation learning, and at face value is similar in motivation to many of the other reported experiments in large scale relation learning (Banko and Etzioni, 2008; Yates and Etzioni, 2009; Carlson et al., 2009; Carlson et al., 2010). However, previous techniques generally rely on a small set of example relation instances and/or patterns, whereas here we explicitly require a larger source of relation instances for pattern induction and training. This allows us to better evaluate the precision of all learned patterns across multiple relation types, as well as improve coverage of the pattern space for any given relation.

Another fundamental aspect of our approach lies in the fact that we attempt to learn many relations simultaneously. Previously, (Whitelaw et al., 2008) found that such a joint learning approach was useful for large-scale named entity detection, and we expect to see this result carry over to the relation extraction task. (Carlson et al., 2010) also describes relation learning in a multi-task learning framework, and attempts to optimize various constraints posited across all relation classes.

Examples of the use of negative evidence for learning the strength of associations between learned patterns and relation classes as proposed here has not been reported in prior work to our knowledge. A number of multi-class learning techniques require negative examples in order to properly learn discriminative features of positive class instances. To address this requirement, a number of approaches have been suggested in the literature for selection or generation of negative class instances. For example, sampling from the positive instances of other classes, randomly perturbing known positive instances, or breaking known semantic constraints of the positive class (e.g. positing multiple state capitols for the same state). With this work, we treat our existing RDF store as an oracle, and assume it is sufficiently comprehensive that it allows estimation of negative evidence for all target relation classes simultaneously.

The first (induction) phase of LSRD is very similar to PORE (Wang et al., 2007) (Dolby et al., 2009; Gabrilovich and Markovitch, 2007) and (Nguyen et al., 2007), in which positive examples were extracted from Wikipedia infoboxes. These also bear striking similarity to (Agichtein and Gravano, 2000), and all suffer from a significantly smaller number of seed examples. Indeed, its not using a database of specific tuples that distinguishes LSRD, but that it uses so many; the scale of the induction in LSRD is designed to capture far less frequent patterns by using significantly more seeds

In (Ramakrishnan et al., 2006) the same intuition is captured that knowledge of the structure of a database should be employed when trying to interpret text, though again the three basic hypotheses of LSRD are not supported.

In (Huang et al., 2004), a similar phenomenon to what we observed with the *acted-in-movie* relation was reported in which the chances of a protein interaction relation being expressed in a sentence are already quite high if two proteins are mentioned in that sentence.

6 Conclusion

We have presented an approach for Large Scale Relation Detection (LSRD) that is intended to be used within a machine reading system as a source of hypothetical interpretations of input sentences in natural language. The interpretations produced are semantic relations between named arguments in the sentences, and they are produced by using a large knowledge source to generate many possible patterns for expressing the relations known by that source.

We have specifically targeted the technique at the problem that the frequency of patterns occurring in text that express a particular relation has a *very long tail* (see Figure 1), and without enough seed examples the extremely infrequent expressions of the relation will never be found and learned. Further, we do not commit to any learning strategy at this stage of processing, rather we simply produce counts, for each relation, of how often a particular pattern produces tuples that are in that relation, and how often it doesn't. These counts are simply used as evidence for different possible interpretations, which can be supported or refuted by other components in the reading system, such as type detection.

We presented some very early results which while promising are not conclusive. There were many idiosyncrasies in the evaluation that made the results meaningful only with respect to other experiments that were evaluated the same way. In addition, the evaluation was done at a component level, as if the technique were a traditional relation extraction component, which ignores one of its primary differentiators–that it produces sets of hypothetical interpretations. Instead, the evaluation was done only on the top hypothesis independent of other evidence.

Despite these problems, the intuitions behind LSRD still seem to us valid, and we are investing in a truly large scale implementation that will overcome the problems discussed here and can provide more valid evidence to support or refute the hypotheses LSRD is based on:

1. A large number of examples can account for the long tail in relation expression;
2. Producing sets of hypothetical interpretations of the sentence, to be supported or refuted by further reading, works better than producing one;
3. Using existing, large, linked-data knowledge-bases as oracles can be effective in relation detection.

References

[Agichtein and Gravano2000] E. Agichtein and L. Gravano. 2000. Snowball: extracting relations from large plain-text collections. In *Proceedings of the 5th ACM Conference on Digital Libraries*, pages 85–94, San Antonio, Texas, United States, June. ACM.

[Banko and Etzioni2008] Michele Banko and Oren Etzioni. 2008. The tradeoffs between open and traditional relation extraction. In *Proceedings of the 46th Annual Meeting of the Association for Computational Linguistics*.

[Blum and Mitchell1998] A. Blum and T. Mitchell. 1998. Combining labeled and unlabeled data with co-training. In *Proceedings of the 1998 Conference on Computational Learning Theory*.

[Carlson et al.2009] A. Carlson, J. Betteridge, E. R. Hruschka Jr., and T. M. Mitchell. 2009. Coupling semi-supervised learning of categories and relations. In *Proceedings of the NAACL HLT 2009 Workshop on Semi-supervised Learning for Natural Language Processing*.

[Carlson et al.2010] A. Carlson, J. Betteridge, R. C. Wang, E. R. Hruschka Jr., and T. M. Mitchell. 2010. Coupled semi-supervised learning for information extraction. In *Proceedings of the 3rd ACM International Conference on Web Search and Data Mining*.

[Craven et al.2000] Mark Craven, Dan DiPasquo, Dayne Freitag, Andrew McCallum, Tom Mitchell, Kamal Nigam, and Sean Slattery. 2000. Learning to construct knowledge bases from the World Wide Web. *Artificial Intelligence*, 118(1–2):69–113.

[Dolby et al.2009] Julian Dolby, Achille Fokoue, Aditya Kalyanpur, Edith Schonberg, and Kavitha Srinivas. 2009. Extracting enterprise vocabularies using linked open data. In *Proceedings of the 8th International Semantic Web Conference*.

[Etzioni et al.2005] Oren Etzioni, Michael Cafarella, Doug Downey, Ana-Maria Popescu, Tal Shaked, Stephen Soderland, Daniel S. Weld, and Alexander Yates. 2005. Unsupervised named-entity extraction from the web: An experimental study. *Artificial Intelligence*, 165(1):91–134, June.

[Gabrilovich and Markovitch2007] Evgeniy Gabrilovich and Shaul Markovitch. 2007. Computing semantic relatedness using wikipedia-based explicit semantic analysis. In *IJCAI*.

[Huang et al.2004] Minlie Huang, Xiaoyan Zhu, Yu Hao, Donald G. Payan, Kunbin Qu, and Ming Li. 2004. Discovering patterns to extract protein-protein interactions from full texts. *Bioinformatics*, 20(18).

[Michelson and Knoblock2007] Matthew Michelson and Craig A. Knoblock. 2007. Mining heterogeneous transformations for record linkage. In *Proceedings of the 6th International Workshop on Information Integration on the Web*, pages 68–73.

[Nguyen et al.2007] Dat P. Nguyen, Yutaka Matsuo, , and Mitsuru Ishizuka. 2007. Exploiting syntactic and semantic information for relation extraction from wikipedia. In *IJCAI*.

[Nigam et al.2006] K. Nigam, A. McCallum, , and T. Mitchell, 2006. *Semi-Supervised Learning*, chapter Semi-Supervised Text Classification Using EM. MIT Press.

[Pantel and Pennacchiotti2006] Patrick Pantel and Marco Pennacchiotti. 2006. Espresso: Leveraging generic patterns for automatically harvesting semantic relations. In *Proceedings of the 21st international Conference on Computational Linguistics and the 44th Annual Meeting of the Association For Computational Linguistics*, Sydney, Australia, July.

[Ramakrishnan et al.2006] Cartic Ramakrishnan, Krys J. Kochut, and Amit P. Sheth. 2006. A framework for schema-driven relationship discovery from unstructured text. In *ISWC*.

[Wang et al.2007] Gang Wang, Yong Yu, and Haiping Zhu. 2007. PORE: Positive-only relation extraction from wikipedia text. In *ISWC*.

[Whitelaw et al.2008] C. Whitelaw, A. Kehlenbeck, N. Petrovic, , and L. Ungar. 2008. Web-scale named entity recognition. In *Proceeding of the 17th ACM Conference on information and Knowledge Management*, pages 123–132, Napa Valley, California, USA, October. ACM.

[Yates and Etzioni2009] Alexander Yates and Oren Etzioni. 2009. Unsupervised methods for determining object and relation synonyms on the web. *Artificial Intelligence*, 34:255–296.

Mining Script-Like Structures from the Web

Niels Kasch
Department of Computer Science
and Electrical Engineering
University of Maryland,
Baltimore County
Baltimore, MD 21250, USA
nkasch1@umbc.edu

Tim Oates
Department of Computer Science
and Electrical Engineering
University of Maryland,
Baltimore County
Baltimore, MD 21250, USA
oates@cs.umbc.edu

Abstract

This paper presents preliminary work to extract script-like structures, called events and event sets, from collections of web documents. Our approach, contrary to existing methods, is topic-driven in the sense that event sets are extracted for a specified topic. We introduce an iterative system architecture and present methods to reduce noise problems with web corpora. Preliminary results show that LSA-based event relatedness yields better event sets from web corpora than previous methods.

1 Introduction

In this paper, we present a preliminary system to extract script-like structures in a goal-directed fashion from the web. For language processing purposes, humans appear to have knowledge of many stylized situations, such as what typically happens when going to a restaurant or riding a bus. This knowledge is shared among a large part of the population and lets us predict the next step in a sequence in a familiar situation, allows us to act appropriately, and enables us to omit details when communicating with others while ensuring common ground is maintained between communication partners. It seems we have such knowledge for a vast variety of situations and scenarios, and thus natural language processing systems need access to equivalent information if they are to understand, converse, or reason about these situations.

These knowledge structures, comparable to scripts (Schank and Abelson, 1977) or narrative chains (Chambers and Jurafsky, 2008), describe typical sequences of events in a particular context. Given the number of potential scripts, their development by hand becomes a resource intensive process. In the past, some work has been devoted to automatically construct script-like structures from compiled corpora (Fujiki et al., 2003) (Chambers and Jurafsky, 2008). Such approaches, however, only produce scripts that are directly related to the topics represented in such corpora. Therefore, newspaper corpora (e.g., the Reuters Corpus) are likely to contain scripts relating to government, crime and financials, but neglect other subject areas. We present a system that extracts scripts from the web and removes the constraints of specialized corpora and domain limitations. We hope our iterative technique will produce scripts for a vast variety of topics, and has the potential to produce more complete scripts.

Another drawback of existing approaches lies with their passive extraction mechanisms. A user/system does not have the ability to obtain scripts for a specific topic, but rather is bound to obtain the most prevalent scripts for the underlying corpus. Furthermore, scripts derived in this fashion lack an absolute labeling or description of their topics. This can be problematic when a user/system is looking for specific scripts to apply to a given scenario. In contrast, our system facilitates the search for scripts given a topic. This goal oriented approach is superior in that (1) scripts are labeled by a descriptive topic and can be organized, accessed and searched by topic, (2) scripts can be constructed by topic and are not reliant on existing and potentially limiting corpora and (3) script coarseness and de-

Proceedings of the NAACL HLT 2010 First International Workshop on Formalisms and Methodology for Learning by Reading, pages 34–42,
Los Angeles, California, June 2010.

tail can be be controlled through iterative script improvement and augmentation based on additional information retrieved from the web.

2 Related Work

Lin and Pantel describe an unsupervised algorithm for discovering inference rules from text (DIRT) (Lin and Pantel, 2001a) (Lin and Pantel, 2001b). Inference rules are derived from paths in dependency trees. If two paths occur in similar contexts (i.e., the words/fillers of their slots are distributionally similar) then the meaning of the paths is similar. VerbOcean (Chklovski and Pantel, 2004) is a resource of strongly associated verb pairs and their semantic relationship. Verbs are considered strongly associated if DIRT deems dependency paths, which contain the verbs, as being similar. A form of mutual information between verb pairs and lexico-syntactic patterns indicative of semantic relationship types is used to categorize the verb pairs according to similarity, strength, antonymy, happens-before and enablement.

(Fujiki et al., 2003) describe a method to extract script knowledge from the first paragraph of Japanese newspaper articles. The first paragraph of such articles is assumed to narrate its contents in temporal order. This circumvents the need to order events as they can be extracted in presumed order. Events are defined in terms of actions, where an action consists of a tuple composed of a transitive verb and its subject and object. The method's goal is to find sequences of pairs of actions by (1) using co-occurrence of subjects and objects in neighboring sentences, (2) locating sentences where two verbs share the same subject and (3) identifying sentences where two verbs share the same object. Once pairs of events are extracted, their subject and objects are generalized into semantic entities similar to semantic roles.

(Chambers and Jurafsky, 2008) attempt to identify narrative chains in newspaper corpora. They utilize the notion of protagonist overlap or verbs sharing co-referring arguments to establish semantic coherence in a story. Co-referring arguments are taken as indicators of a common discourse structure. This assumption is used to find pairwise events in an unsupervised fashion. Point wise mutual information (PMI) is used to indicate the relatedness between event pairs. A global narrative score, aiming to maximize the PMI of a set of events is utilized to generate a ranked list of events most likely to participate in the narrative chain. Temporal order is established by labeling events with temporal attributes and using those labels, along with other linguistic features, to classify the relationship (before or other) between two events.

For the purposes of our work, finding documents related to a term and identifying similar terms is an important step in the script creation process. (Deerwester et al., 1990) describe Latent Semantic Analysis/Indexing (LSA) as a technique superior to term matching document retrieval. LSA aims to facilitate document retrieval based on the conceptual content of documents, thereby avoiding problems with synonomy and polysemy of individual search terms (or in documents). LSA employs singular-value-decomposition (SVD) of a term-by-document matrix to construct a "semantic space" in which related documents and terms are clustered together.

3 Approach

In this work we aim to extract scripts from the web. We define a script as a collection of typically related events that participate in temporal relationships amongst each other. For example, e_1 `happens-before` e_2 denotes a relationship such that event e_1 occurs prior to event e_2. An event is defined as a tuple consisting of a verb, a grammatical function and a set of arguments (i.e., words) which act out the grammatical function in relation to the verb. Figure 1 shows the structure of events.

e [verb, grammatical function, {set of arguments}]

Figure 1: The structure of an event. An event is a tuple consisting of a verb, a grammatical function and a set of arguments (i.e., instances of words filling the grammatical function).

The set of arguments represents actual instances found during the script extraction process. Figure 2 illustrates an incomplete script for the topic *eating at a restaurant*.

3.1 The Task

We define the task of goal driven script extraction as: (1) given a topic, compile a "relevant" corpus of doc-

e_1 [enter, nsubj, {customer, John})]
e_2 [enter, dobj, {restaurant}]
e_3 [order, nsubj, {customer}]
e_4 [order, dobj, {food}]
e_5 [eat, nsubj, {customer}]
e_6 [eat, dobj, {food}]
e_7 [pay, nsubj, {customer}]
e_8 [pay, dobj, {bill}]
e_9 [leave, nsubj, {customer}]
e_{10} [leave, dobj, {restaurant}]

Temporal Ordering = $e_1 < e_2 < e_3 < e_4$
$e_4 < e_5 < e_6 < e_7 < e_8 < e_9 < e_{10}$

Figure 2: An excerpt of a script for the topic *eating at a restaurant*. The script denotes the stylized actions of a customer dining at a restaurant. The $<$ relation denotes event e_i `happens_before` event e_j.

uments from a subset of documents on the web, (2) extract events relevant for the topic, (3) (optional) refine the topic and restart at 1, and (4) establish a temporal ordering for the events.

We currently impose restrictions on the form of acceptable topics. For our purposes, a topic is a short description of a script, and contains at least a verb and a noun from the script's intended domain. For example, the topic for a passenger's typical actions while using public transportation (i.e. a bus) can be described by the topic *riding on a bus*.

3.2 System Architecture

The script extraction system consists of a variety of modules where each module is responsible for a certain task. Modules are combined in a mixed fashion such that sequential processing is combined with an iterative improvement procedure. Figure 3 illustrates the system architecture and flow of information between modules. The following sections describe each module in detail.

3.2.1 Document Retrieval

Our system utilizes the web as its underlying information source to circumvent domain limitations of fixed corpora. However, using the entire web to extract a script for a specific topic is, on one hand, infeasible due to the size of the web and, on the other hand, impractical in term of document relevancy. Since only a subset of pages is potentially

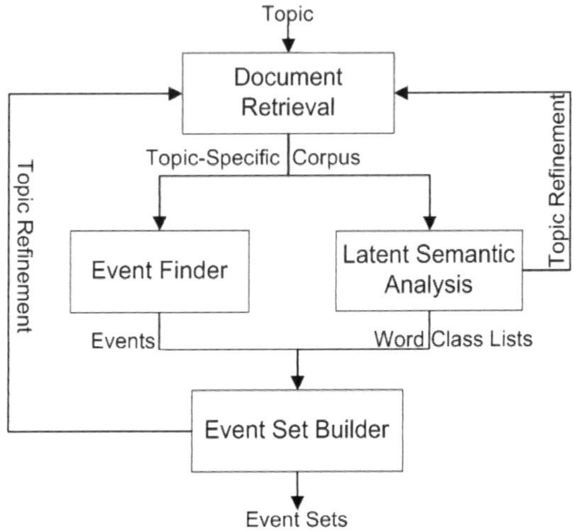

Figure 3: System Architecture and flow of information.

relevant to a given topic, the web needs to be filtered such that mostly relevant web pages are retrieved. The document retrieval module makes use of existing search engines for this purpose.[1]

The document retrieval module is presented with the topic for a script and issues this topic as a query to the search engines. The search engines produce a relevancy ranked list of documents/URLs (Brin and Page, 1998) which, in turn, are downloaded. The number of downloaded pages depends on the current iteration number of the system (i.e., how often the *retrieval-analysis* cycle has been executed for a given topic[2]).

The document retrieval module is also responsible for cleaning the documents. The cleaning process aims to remove "boilerplate" elements such as navigational menus and advertising from web pages while preserving content elements.[3] The collection of cleaned documents for a given topic is considered to be a *topic-specific corpus*.

3.2.2 Latent Semantic Analysis (LSA)

The aim of the LSA module is to identify words (verbs, nouns and adjectives) that are closely related

[1]The Google and Yahoo API's are used to establish communication with these search engines.

[2]At the first iteration, we have arbitrarily choosesn to retrieve the first 1000 unduplicated documents.

[3]The Special Interest Group of the ACL on Web as Corpus (SIGWAC) is interested in web cleaning methods for corpus construction. Our web page cleaner uses a support vector machine to classify blocks of a web page as content or non-content. The cleaner achieves $\approx 85\%$ F1 on a random set of web pages.

to the topic presented to the document retrieval module. To find such words, the topic-specific corpus is (1) part-of-speech tagged and (2) transformed into a term-document matrix. Each cell represents the log-entropy for its respective term in a document. Note that we consider a term to be a tuple consisting of a word and its POS. The advantage of using word-POS tag combinations over words only is the ability to query LSA's concept space for words by their word class. A concept space is created by applying SVD to the term-document matrix, reducing the dimensionality of the scaling matrix and reconstructing the term-document matrix using the reduced scaling matrix.

Once the concept space is constructed, the space is searched for all terms having a high correlation with the original topic. Terms from the original topic are located in the concept space (i.e., term vectors are located) and other term vectors with high cosine similarity are retrieved from the space. A list of $n = 50$ terms[4] for each word class $\in$ {verb, noun, adjective} is obtained and filtered using a stop list. The stop list currently contains the 100 most common words in the English language. The idea behind the stop list is to remove low content words from the list. The resulting set of words is deemed to have high information content with respect to the topic. This set is used for two purposes: (1) to augment the original topic and to restart the document collection process using the augmented topic and (2) identify event pairs constructed by the event finding module which contain these highly correlated terms (either as events or event arguments). The first purpose aims to use an iterative process to construct a higher quality topic-specific corpus. A new corpus created in this fashion presumably represents documents that are richer and more relevant to the augmented topic. The second purpose steers the extraction of events towards events containing those constituents judged most relevant. This fact can be incorporated into a maximization calculation based on pointwise mutual information to find highly correlated events.

[4]The number was chosen experimentally and is based on the correlation score (cosine similarity) between word vectors. After about 50 words, the correlation score begins to drop significantly indicating weaker relatedness.

3.2.3 Event Finding

The collection of documents (or topic-specific corpus) is then processed to facilitate finding event pairs. Finding event pairs involves the notion of verb argument overlap using the assumption that two events in a story are related if they share at least one semantic argument across grammatical functions. This virtue of discourse structure of coherent stories has been described in (Trabasso et al., 1984) and applied by (Fujiki et al., 2003) as subject and object overlap and by (Chambers and Jurafsky, 2008) as following a common protagonist in a story. For example, in the sentences "John ordered a drink. He enjoyed it very much." we can establish that events *order* and *enjoy* are part of a common theme because the arguments (or loosely semantic roles) of *order* and *enjoy* refer to the same entities, that is *John* = *He* and *a drink* = *it*.

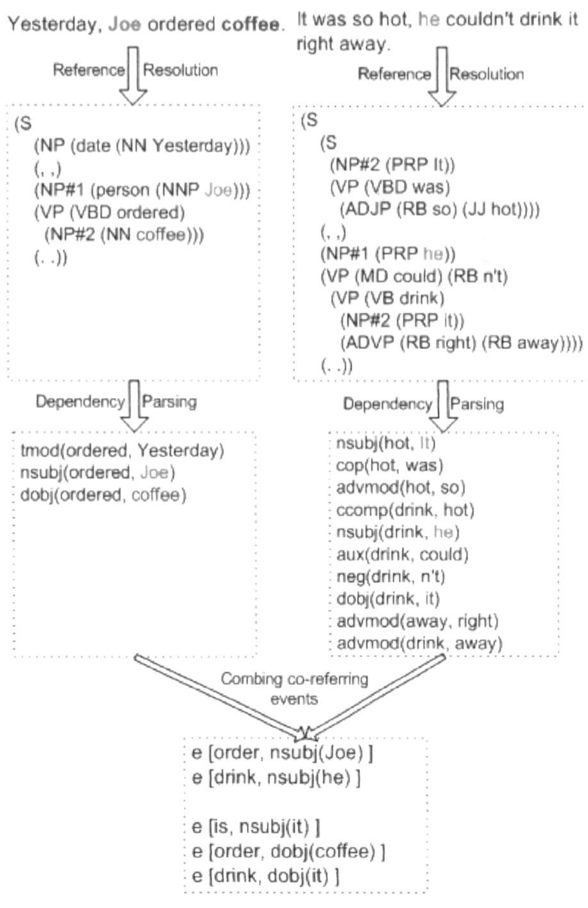

Figure 4: Example processing of the sentences "Yesterday, Joe ordered coffee. It was so hot, he couldn't drink it right away". The output after dependency parsing, reference resolution and event finding is a set of event pairs.

To identify such pairs, the topic specific corpus is (1) co-reference resolved[5] and (2) dependency parsed[6]. Sentences containing elements referring to the same mention of an element are inspected for verb argument overlap. Figure 4 illustrates this procedure for the sentences "Yesterday, Joe ordered coffee. It was so hot, he couldn't drink it right away".

Co-reference resolution tells us that mention *he* refers to *Joe* and mention(s) *it* refer to *coffee*. By our previous assumption of discourse coherence, it is possible to deduce that events *was* and *drink* are associated with event *order*. In a similar fashion, event *drink* is associated with event *was*. This is due to the fact that all events share at least one argument (in the case of events *order* and *drink* two arguments are shared). For each pair of events sharing arguments in a particular grammatic function, an event pair is generated indicating where the overlap occurred.

3.2.4 Constructing Event Sets

Sets of events representing script-like structures are constructed through the use of pointwise mutual information in combination with the lists of related words found by Latent Semantic Analysis. We utilize the definition of PMI described in (Chambers and Jurafsky, 2008). For two events e_1 and e_2

$$pmi(e1, e2) = log\frac{P(e_1, e_2)}{P(e_1)P(e_2)} \quad (1)$$

where

$$P(e_1, e_2) = \frac{C(e_1, e_2)}{\sum_{i,j} C(e_i, e_j)} \quad (2)$$

and $C(e_1, e_2)$ is the number of times events e_1 and e_2 had coreferring arguments.

We extend the definition of PMI between events to assign more weight to events whose constituents are contained in the list of words (verbs, nouns and adjectives) judged by Latent Semantic Analysis to be most relevant to the topic. For notational purposes, these lists are denoted L. Thus, we can calculate the weighted LSA PMI $LP(e_1, e_2)$ as follows:

$$LP(e_1, e_2) = P(e_1, e_2) + LSA(e_1, e_2) \quad (3)$$

where

$$LSA(e_1, e_2) = \alpha * (E(e_1) + E(e_2)) \quad (4)$$

$$\alpha = \begin{cases} 2 & \text{if } e_{1_{verb}} \in L \text{ and } e_{2_{verb}} \in L \\ 1 & \text{otherwise} \end{cases} \quad (5)$$

$$\begin{aligned} E(e) &= (||e_{verb} \cap L|| + 1) \\ &* (\frac{||e_{Args} \cap L||}{||e_{Args}||} + 1) \end{aligned} \quad (6)$$

To construct the set of n events related to the topic, the LP scores are first calculated for each event pair in the corpus. The set can then be constructed by maximizing:

$$\max_{i<k\leq n} \sum_{i=0}^{k-1} LP(e_i, e_k) \quad (7)$$

Therefore, events that share a larger number of constituents with the LSA relevancy list are preferred for inclusion in the event set. This practice distributes the relatedness weight among the frequency of events and LSA. The noisy nature of our proposed corpus generation method makes such a technique essential as we will see in section 4.3.

3.2.5 Ordering Events

At this time, we only establish a naive temporal ordering on the events. The ordering process simply assumes that an event appearing in the corpus prior to another event also occurs earlier in time. We realize that this assumption does not always hold, but delay a more sophisticated ordering process as future work.

4 Experiments

This section describes experimental results, obstacles we have encountered, various approaches to overcome these obstacles and lessons learned from our work. Unless mentioned otherwise, the results pertain to the topic *eating at a restaurant*. This topic has been chosen for our investigation since previous work (Schank and Abelson, 1977) establishes a comprehensive reference as to what a script for this domain may entail.

4.1 Domain Richness

The first step in our work was to confirm the notion that the web can be used as the underlying information source for topic-specific script extraction.

[5]OpenNLP's Co-Reference Engine is utilized `http://opennlp.sourceforge.net/`.

[6]The Stanford Parser is utilized `http://nlp.stanford.edu/software/lex-parser.shtml`

The overall goal was to investigate whether a topic-specific corpus contains sufficiently useful information which is conducive to the script extraction task.

Latent Semantic Analysis was performed on the Part-of-Speech tagged topic specific corpus. The semantic space was queried using the main constituents of the original topic. Hence, this resulted in two queries, namely *eating* and *restaurant*. For each query, we identified the most related verbs, nouns and adjectives/adverbs and placed them in respective lists. Lists are then combined according to word class, lemmatized, and pruned. Auxiliary verbs such as *be*, *do* and *have* consistently rank in the top 10 most similar words in the un-pruned lists. This result is expected due to the frequency distribution of auxiliaries in the English language. It is a natural conclusion to exclude auxiliaries from further consideration since their information content is relatively low. Furthermore, we extend this notion to exclude the 100 most frequent words in English from these lists using the same justification. By the inverse reasoning, it is desirable to include words in further processing that occur infrequently in natural language. We can hypothesize that such words are significant to a given script because their frequency appears to be elevated in the corpus. Table 1 (left) shows the resulting word class lists for both queries. Duplicates (i.e., words with identical lemma) have been removed.

The table reveals that some words also appear in the restaurant script as suggested by (Schank and Abelson, 1977). In particular, **bold** verbs resemble Schank's *scenes* and **bold** nouns resemble his *props*. We can also see that the list of adverbs/adjectives appear to not contribute any significant information. Note that any bold words have been hand selected using a human selector's subjective experience about the *eating at a restaurant* domain. Furthermore, while some script information appears to be encoded in these lists, there is a significant amount of noise, i.e., normal font words that are seemingly unimportant to the script at hand.

For our purposes, we aim to model this noise so that it can be reduced or removed to some degree. Such a model is based on the notion of overlap of noisy terms in the LSA lists derived from independent topic related corpora for the main constituents of the original topic. For example, for the topic *eating at a restaurant*, we obtain two additional corpora using the method described in Section 3.2.1, i.e., one corpus for constituent *eating* and another for the second main constituent of the original topic, *restaurant*. Both corpora are subjected to LSA analysis from which two (one for each corpus) LSA word lists are obtained. Each list was created using the respective corpus query as the LSA query. The assumption is made that words which are shared (pairwise) between all three lists (i.e., the two new LSA lists and the LSA list for topic *eating at a restaurant*) are noisy due to the fact that they occur independent of the original topic.

eating at a restaurant			**Overlap removed**		
Verbs	Nouns	A&A	Verbs	Nouns	A&A
keep	home	own	**order**	home	**fry**
need	place	still	set	hand	amaze
help	**table**	last	expect	**bowl**	green
dine	lot	open	**share**	**plate**	**grill**
love	part	full	**drink**	**cook**	chain
order	hand	off	try	**fish**	**diet**
feel	reason	long	cut	**soup**	clean
avoid	course	fat	**decide**	**service**	smart
add	side	right	watch	break	total
let	number	down	process	**drink**	relate
stay	experience	busy	save	**cheese**	worst
include	**water**	fast	**offer**	**rice**	black
tend	point	single	provide	**serve**	fit
set	**dish**	low	hear	chance	light
tell	**bowl**	free	**fill**	**portion**	exist
found	**plate**	white	forget	body	empty
bring	**bite**	wrong	write	party	live
locate	**cook**	ready	follow	rest	
eat	**fish**	true	travel	cream	
leave	**soup**	close		**taste**	

Table 1: (Left) 20 most relevant terms (after pruning) for LSA queries *eating* and *restaurant* on the *eating at a restaurant* corpus. (Right) Terms remaining after noise modeling and overlap removal. **Bold** terms in the table were manually judged by a human to be relevant.

Table 1 (right) illustrates the LSA list for topic *eating at a restaurant* after removing overlapping terms with the two other LSA lists. Bold words were judged by a human selector to be relevant to the intended script. From the table we can observe that:

1. A significant amount of words have been removed. The original table contains 50 words for each word class. The overlap reduced table contains only 19 verbs, 29 nouns, and 17 adjectives, a reduction of what we consider noise by

$\approx 57\%$

2. More words (bold) were judged to be related to the script (e.g., 6 vs. 5 relevant verbs, 12 vs. 9 nouns, and 3 vs. 0 adjectives/adverbs)
3. More relevant words appear in the top part of the list (words in the list are ordered by relevancy)
4. Some words judged to be relevant were removed (e.g., dine, bring, eat).

Using the information from the table (left and right) and personal knowledge about *eating at a restaurant*, a **human** could re-arrange the verbs and nouns into a partial script-like format of the form[7]:

e_1 [offer, nsubj, {**waiter**})]
e_2 [offer, dobj, {drink})]
Example: waiter offers a drink

e_2 [order, nsubj, {**customer**}]
e_3 [order, dobj, {fish, soup, rice}]
Example: customer orders fish

e_4 [serve/bring, nsubj, {**waiter**}]
e_5 [serve/bring, nsubj, {bowl, plate}]
Example: waiter serves/bings the bowl, plate

e_6 [eat, nsubj, {**customer**}]
e_7 [eat, dobj, {portion, cheese}]
Example: customer eats the portion, cheese
e
$_8$ [leave, nsubj, {customer}]
e_9 [leave, dobj, {table}]
Example: customer leaves the table

Note that this script-like information was not obtained by direct derivation from the information in the table. It is merely an illustration that some script information is revealed by LSA. Table 1 neither implies any ordering nor suggest semantic arguments for a verb. However, the analysis confirms that the web contains information that can be used in the script extraction process.

4.2 Processing Errors

As mentioned in section 3.2.3, events with co-referring arguments are extracted in a pairwise fashion. In the following section we describe observations about the characteristics of events extracted this way. However, we note that each step in our system architecture is imperfect, meaning that errors are introduced in each module as the result of processing. We have already seen such errors in the form of words with incorrect word class in the LSA lists as the result of incorrect POS tagging. Such errors are amplified through imprecise parsing (syntactic and dependency parsing). Other errors, such as omissions, false positives and incorrect class detection, are introduced by the named entity recognizer and the co-reference module. With this in mind, it comes as no surprise that some extracted events, as seen later, are malformed. For example, human analysis reveals that the verb slot of these events are sometimes "littered" with words from other word classes, or that the arguments of a verb were incorrectly detected. A majority of these errors can be attributed to ungrammatical sentences and phrases in the topic-specific corpus, the remainder is due to the current state of the art of the parsers and reference resolution engine.

4.3 Observations about events

To compare relations between events, we looked at three different metrics. The first metric $M1$ simply observes the frequency counts of pairwise events in the corpus. The second metric $M2$ utilizes point wise mutual information as defined in (Chambers and Jurafsky, 2008). The third metric $M3$ is our LSA based PMI calculation as defined in section 3.2.4.

$M1$ reveals that uninformative event pairs tend to have a high number of occurrences. These pairs are composed of low content, frequently occurring events. For example, event pair [e [have, nsubj,{}], e [say, nsubj, {}]] occurred 123 times in our topic-specific corpus. More sophisticated metrics, such as $M2$, consider the frequency distributions of individual events and allocate more weight to co-occurring events with lower frequency counts of their individual events.

In this fashion, $M2$ is capable of identifying strongly related events. For example, Table 2 lists the five pairwise events with highest PMI for our topic-specific corpus.

From Table 2, it is apparent that these pairs participate in mostly meaningful (in terms of human comprehensibility) relationships. For example, it does

[7]Bold terms do not appear in the LSA lists, but were added for readability.

Event Pairs	
e[sack, dobj, {the, employees}]	e[reassign, dobj, {them}]
e[identify, nsubj, {we, Willett}]	e[assert, nsubj, {Willett}]
e[pour, dobj, {a sweet sauce}]	e[slide, dobj, {the eggs}]
e[walk, nsubj, {you, his sister}]	e[fell, nsubj, {Daniel}]
e[use, nsubj, {the menu}]	e[access, dobj, {you}]

Table 2: Pairwise events with highest PMI according to Equation 1.

not require a leap of faith to connect that *sack*ing employees is related to *reassign*ing them in the context of a corporate environment.

e(eat, nsubj), e(gobble, nsubj), e(give, nsubj), e(live, nsubj), e(know, nsubj), e(go, nsubj), e(need, nsubj), e(buy, nsubj), e(have, nsubj), e(make, nsubj), e(say, nsubj), e(work, nsubj), e(try, nsubj), e(like, nsubj), e(tell, dobj), e(begin, nsubj), e(think, nsubj), e(tailor, nsubj), e(take, nsubj), **e(open, nsubj)**,e(be, nsubj)

Figure 5: An event set obtained through metric $M2$ (using the PMI between events). Temporal ordering is not implied. Event arguments are omitted. Bold events indicate subjectively judged strong relatedness to the *eating at a restaurant* topic.

Figure 5 shows a set of events for our topic. The set was created by greedily adding event e_n such that for all events $e_1, e_2, ...e_{n-1}$ already in the set $\forall_i^{n-1} pmi(e_i, e_n)$ is largest (see (Chambers and Jurafsky, 2008)). The topic constituent *eating* (i.e., *eat*) was used as the initial event in the set. If this set is intended to approximate a script for the *eating at a restaurant* domain, then it is easy to see that virtually no information from Schank's *restaurant* reference script is represented. Furthermore, by human standards, the presented set appears to be incoherent. From this observation, we can conclude that $M2$ is unsuitable for topic-specific script extraction.

Figure 6 illustrates an event set constructed using metric $M3$. Note that the sets in Figures 5 and 6 do not imply any ordering on the events. The bold events indicate events that appear in our reference script or were judged by a human evaluator to be logically coherent with the *eating at a restaurant* domain. The evaluation was conducted using the evaluators personal experience of the domain. In the future, we intend to formalize this evaluation process.

Figure 6 signifies an improvement of the results of

e(eat, nsubj), **e(wait, dobj)**, e(total, nsubj) e(write, dobj), e(place, dobj), e(complete, dobj) e(exist, nsubj), e(include, dobj), e(top, nsubj) e(found, dobj), e(keep, dobj), e(open, dobj) **e(offer, dobj)**, e(average, nsubj), **e(fill, dobj)** **e(taste, nsubj)**, **e(drink, dobj)**, **e(cook, dobj)** **e(read, dobj)**, **e(enjoy, dobj)**,e(buy, dobj)

Figure 6: An event set obtained through metric $M3$ (weighing PMI and LSA between events). Temporal ordering is not implied. Event arguments are omitted. Bold events indicate subjectively judged strong relatedness to the *eating at a restaurant* topic.

Figure 5 in terms of the number of events judged to belong to the restaurant script. This leads us to the conclusion that a metric based on scaled PMI and LSA appears more suitable for the web based topic driven script extraction task. Once a temporal order is imposed on the events in Figure 6, these events could, by themselves, serve as a partial event set for their domain.

5 Discussion and Future Work

We have presented preliminary work on extracting script-like information in a topic driven fashion from the web. Our work shows promise to identify script knowledge in a topic-specific corpus derived from an unordered collection of web pages. We have shown that while web documents contain significant amounts of noise (both boilerplate elements and topic unrelated content), a subset of content can be identified as script-like knowledge.

Latent Semantic Analysis allows for the filtering and pruning of lists of related words by word classes. LSA furthermore facilitates noise removal through overlap detection of word class list elements between independent corpora of topic constituents. Our method of weighted LSA and PMI for event relatedness produces more promising partial event sets than existing metrics.

For future work, we leave the automated evaluation of partial sets and the establishing of temporal relations between events in a set. Our system architecture features an iterative model to event set improvement. We hope that this approach will allow us to improve upon the quality of event sets by using extracted sets from one iteration to bootstrap a new iteration of event extraction.

References

Sergey Brin and Lawrence Page. 1998. The anatomy of a large-scale hypertextual web search engine. *Comput. Netw. ISDN Syst.*, 30(1-7):107–117.

Nathanael Chambers and Dan Jurafsky. 2008. Unsupervised learning of narrative event chains. In *Proceedings of ACL-08: HLT*, pages 789–797, Columbus, Ohio, June. Association for Computational Linguistics.

Timothy Chklovski and Patrick Pantel. 2004. VerbOcean: Mining the Web for Fine-Grained Semantic Verb Relations. In *Proceedings of Conference on Empirical Methods in Natural Language Processing*, pages 33–40, Barcelona, Spain, July. Association for Computational Linguistics.

Scott Deerwester, T. Susan Dumais, W. George Furnas, K. Thomas Landauer, and Richard Harshman. 1990. Indexing by Latent Semantic Analysis. *Journal of the American Society for Information Science*, 41:391–407.

Toshiaki Fujiki, Hidetsugu Nanba, and Manabu Okumura. 2003. Automatic acquisition of script knowledge from a text collection. In *EACL '03: Proceedings of the tenth conference on European chapter of the Association for Computational Linguistics*, pages 91–94, Morristown, NJ, USA. Association for Computational Linguistics.

Dekang Lin and Patrick Pantel. 2001a. DIRT - Discovery of Inference Rules from Text. In *KDD '01: Proceedings of the seventh ACM SIGKDD international conference on Knowledge discovery and data mining*, pages 323–328, New York, NY, USA. ACM.

Dekang Lin and Patrick Pantel. 2001b. Discovery of Inference Rules for Question-Answering. *Nat. Lang. Eng.*, 7(4):343–360.

Roger C. Schank and Robert P. Abelson. 1977. *Scripts, Plans, Goals and Understanding*. Lawrence Erlbaum Associates, Hillsdale, NJ.

Tom Trabasso, T. Secco, and Paul van den Broek. 1984. Causal Cohesion and Story Coherence. In *Heinz Mandl, N.L. Stein and Tom Trabasso (eds). Learning and Comprehension of Text.*, pages 83–111, Hillsdale, NJ, USA. Lawrence Erlbaum Associates.

Open-domain Commonsense Reasoning Using Discourse Relations from a Corpus of Weblog Stories

Matt Gerber
Department of Computer Science
Michigan State University
gerberm2@msu.edu

Andrew S. Gordon and **Kenji Sagae**
Institute for Creative Technologies
University of Southern California
{gordon,sagae}@ict.usc.edu

Abstract

We present a method of extracting open-domain commonsense knowledge by applying discourse parsing to a large corpus of personal stories written by Internet authors. We demonstrate the use of a linear-time, joint syntax/discourse dependency parser for this purpose, and we show how the extracted discourse relations can be used to generate open-domain textual inferences. Our evaluations of the discourse parser and inference models show some success, but also identify a number of interesting directions for future work.

1 Introduction

The acquisition of open-domain knowledge in support of commonsense reasoning has long been a bottleneck within artificial intelligence. Such reasoning supports fundamental tasks such as textual entailment (Giampiccolo et al., 2008), automated question answering (Clark et al., 2008), and narrative comprehension (Graesser et al., 1994). These tasks, when conducted in open domains, require vast amounts of commonsense knowledge pertaining to states, events, and their causal and temporal relationships. Manually created resources such as FrameNet (Baker et al., 1998), WordNet (Fellbaum, 1998), and Cyc (Lenat, 1995) encode many aspects of commonsense knowledge; however, coverage of causal and temporal relationships remains low for many domains.

Gordon and Swanson (2008) argued that the commonsense tasks of prediction, explanation, and imagination (collectively called *envisionment*) can be supported by knowledge mined from a large corpus of personal stories written by Internet weblog authors.[1] Gordon and Swanson (2008) identified three primary obstacles to such an approach. First, stories must be distinguished from other weblog content (e.g., lists, recipes, and reviews). Second, stories must be analyzed in order to extract the implicit commonsense knowledge that they contain. Third, inference mechanisms must be developed that use the extracted knowledge to perform the core envisionment tasks listed above.

In the current paper, we present an approach to open-domain commonsense inference that addresses each of the three obstacles identified by Gordon and Swanson (2008). We built on the work of Gordon and Swanson (2009), who describe a classification-based approach to the task of story identification. The authors' system produced a corpus of approximately one million personal stories, which we used as a starting point. We applied efficient discourse parsing techniques to this corpus as a means of extracting causal and temporal relationships. Furthermore, we developed methods that use the extracted knowledge to generate textual inferences for descriptions of states and events. This work resulted in an end-to-end prototype system capable of generating open-domain, commonsense inferences using a repository of knowledge extracted from unstructured weblog text. We focused on identifying

[1] We follow Gordon and Swanson (2009) in defining a story to be a "textual discourse that describes a specific series of causally related events in the past, spanning a period of time of minutes, hours, or days, where the author or a close associate is among the participants."

Proceedings of the NAACL HLT 2010 First International Workshop on Formalisms and Methodology for Learning by Reading, pages 43–51,
Los Angeles, California, June 2010.

strengths and weaknesses of the system in an effort to guide future work.

We structure our presentation as follows: in Section 2, we present previous research that has investigated the use of large web corpora for natural language processing (NLP) tasks. In Section 3, we describe an efficient method of automatically parsing weblog stories for discourse structure. In Section 4, we present a set of inference mechanisms that use the extracted discourse relations to generate open-domain textual inferences. We conclude, in Section 5, with insights into story-based envisionment that we hope will guide future work in this area.

2 Related work

Researchers have made many attempts to use the massive amount of linguistic content created by users of the World Wide Web. Progress and challenges in this area have spawned multiple workshops (e.g., those described by Gurevych and Zesch (2009) and Evert et al. (2008)) that specifically target the use of content that is collaboratively created by Internet users. Of particular relevance to the present work is the weblog corpus developed by Burton et al. (2009), which was used for the data challenge portion of the International Conference on Weblogs and Social Media (ICWSM). The ICWSM weblog corpus (referred to here as Spinn3r) is freely available and comprises tens of millions of weblog entries posted between August 1st, 2008 and October 1st, 2008.

Gordon et al. (2009) describe an approach to knowledge extraction over the Spinn3r corpus using techniques described by Schubert and Tong (2003). In this approach, logical propositions (known as *factoids*) are constructed via approximate interpretation of syntactic analyses. As an example, the system identified a factoid glossed as "doors to a room may be opened". Gordon et al. (2009) found that the extracted factoids cover roughly half of the factoids present in the corresponding Wikipedia[2] articles. We used a subset of the Spinn3r corpus in our work, but focused on discourse analyses of entire texts instead of syntactic analyses of single sentences. Our goal was to extract general causal and temporal propositions instead of the fine-grained properties expressed by many factoids extracted by Gordon et al. (2009).

Clark and Harrison (2009) pursued large-scale extraction of knowledge from text using a syntax-based approach that was also inspired by the work of Schubert and Tong (2003). The authors showed how the extracted knowledge tuples can be used to improve syntactic parsing and textual entailment recognition. Bar-Haim et al. (2009) present an efficient method of performing inference with such knowledge.

Our work is also related to the work of Persing and Ng (2009), in which the authors developed a semi-supervised method of identifying the causes of events described in aviation safety reports. Similarly, our system extracts causal (as well as temporal) knowledge; however, it does this in an open domain and does not place limitations on the types of causes to be identified. This greatly increases the complexity of the inference task, and our results exhibit a corresponding degradation; however, our evaluations provide important insights into the task.

3 Discourse parsing a corpus of stories

Gordon and Swanson (2009) developed a supervised classification-based approach for identifying personal stories within the Spinn3r corpus. Their method achieved 75% precision on the binary task of predicting *story* versus *non-story* on a held-out subset of the Spinn3r corpus. The extracted "story corpus" comprises 960,098 personal stories written by weblog users. Due to its large size and broad domain coverage, the story corpus offers unique opportunities to NLP researchers. For example, Swanson and Gordon (2008) showed how the corpus can be used to support open-domain collaborative story writing.[3]

As described by Gordon and Swanson (2008), story identification is just the first step towards commonsense reasoning using personal stories. We addressed the second step - knowledge extraction - by parsing the corpus using a Rhetorical Structure Theory (Carlson and Marcu, 2001) parser based on the one described by Sagae (2009). The parser performs joint syntactic and discourse dependency

[2]http://en.wikipedia.org

[3]The system (called SayAnything) is available at http://sayanything.ict.usc.edu

parsing using a stack-based, shift-reduce algorithm with runtime that is linear in the input length. This lightweight approach is very efficient; however, it may not be quite as accurate as more complex, chart-based approaches (e.g., the approach of Charniak and Johnson (2005) for syntactic parsing).

We trained the discourse parser over the causal and temporal relations contained in the RST corpus. Examples of these relations are shown below:

(1) $[_{cause}$ Packages often get buried in the load$]$ $[_{result}$ and are delivered late.$]$

(2) $[_{before}$ Three months after she arrived in L.A.$]$ $[_{after}$ she spent \$120 she didn't have.$]$

The RST corpus defines many fine-grained relations that capture causal and temporal properties. For example, the corpus differentiates between *result* and *reason* for causation and *temporal-after* and *temporal-before* for temporal order. In order to increase the amount of available training data, we collapsed all causal and temporal relations into two general relations *causes* and *precedes*. This step required normalization of asymmetric relations such as *temporal-before* and *temporal-after*.

To evaluate the discourse parser described above, we manually annotated 100 randomly selected weblog stories from the story corpus produced by Gordon and Swanson (2009). For increased efficiency, we limited our annotation to the generalized *causes* and *precedes* relations described above. We attempted to keep our definitions of these relations in line with those used by RST. Following previous discourse annotation efforts, we annotated relations over clause-level discourse units, permitting relations between adjacent sentences. In total, we annotated 770 instances of *causes* and 1,009 instances of *precedes*.

We experimented with two versions of the RST parser, one trained on the fine-grained RST relations and the other trained on the collapsed relations. At testing time, we automatically mapped the fine-grained relations to their corresponding *causes* or *precedes* relation. We computed the following accuracy statistics:

Discourse segmentation accuracy For each predicted discourse unit, we located the reference discourse unit with the highest overlap. Accuracy for the predicted discourse unit is equal to the percentage word overlap between the reference and predicted discourse units.

Argument identification accuracy For each discourse unit of a predicted discourse relation, we located the reference discourse unit with the highest overlap. Accuracy is equal to the percentage of times that a reference discourse relation (of any type) holds between the reference discourse units that overlap most with the predicted discourse units.

Argument classification accuracy For the subset of instances in which a reference discourse relation holds between the units that overlap most with the predicted discourse units, accuracy is equal to the percentage of times that the predicted discourse relation matches the reference discourse relation.

Complete accuracy For each predicted discourse relation, accuracy is equal to the percentage word overlap with a reference discourse relation of the same type.

Table 1 shows the accuracy results for the fine-grained and collapsed versions of the RST discourse parser. As shown in Table 1, the collapsed version of the discourse parser exhibits higher overall accuracy. Both parsers predicted the *causes* relation much more often than the *precedes* relation, so the overall scores are biased toward the scores for the *causes* relation. For comparison, Sagae (2009) evaluated a similar RST parser over the test section of the RST corpus, obtaining precision of 42.9% and recall of 46.2% ($F_1 = 44.5\%$).

In addition to the automatic evaluation described above, we also manually assessed the output of the discourse parsers. One of the authors judged the correctness of each extracted discourse relation, and we found that the fine-grained and collapsed versions of the parser performed equally well with a precision near 33%; however, throughout our experiments, we observed more desirable discourse segmentation when working with the collapsed version of the discourse parser. This fact, combined with the results of the automatic evaluation presented above,

	Fine-grained RST parser			Collapsed RST parser		
Accuracy metric	causes	precedes	overall	causes	precedes	overall
Segmentation	36.08	44.20	36.67	44.36	30.13	43.10
Argument identification	25.00	33.33	25.86	26.15	23.08	25.87
Argument classification	66.15	50.00	64.00	79.41	83.33	79.23
Complete	22.20	28.88	22.68	31.26	21.21	30.37

Table 1: RST parser evaluation. All values are percentages.

led us to use the collapsed version of the parser in all subsequent experiments.

Having developed and evaluated the discourse parser, we conducted a full discourse parse of the story corpus, which comprises more than 25 million sentences split into nearly 1 million weblog entries. The discourse parser extracted 2.2 million instances of the *causes* relation and 220,000 instances of the *precedes* relation. As a final step, we indexed the extracted discourse relations with the Lucene information retrieval engine.[4] Each discourse unit (two per discourse relation) is treated as a single document, allowing us to query the extracted relations using information retrieval techniques implemented in the Lucene toolkit.

4 Generating textual inferences

As mentioned previously, Gordon and Swanson (2008) cite three obstacles to performing commonsense reasoning using weblog stories. Gordon and Swanson (2009) addressed the first (story collection). We addressed the second (story analysis) by developing a discourse parser capable of extracting causal and temporal relations from weblog text (Section 3). In this section, we present a preliminary solution to the third problem - reasoning with the extracted knowledge.

4.1 Inference method

In general, we require an inference method that takes as input the following things:

1. A description of the state or event of interest. This is a free-text description of any length.

2. The type of inference to perform, either causal or temporal.

3. The inference direction, either forward or backward. Forward causal inference produces the effects of the given state or event. Backward causal inference produces causes of the given state or event. Similarly, forward and backward temporal inferences produce subsequent and preceding states and events, respectively.

As a simple baseline approach, we implemented the following procedure. First, given a textual input description d, we query the extracted discourse units using Lucene's modified version of the vector space model over TF-IDF term weights. This produces a ranked list R_d of discourse units matching the input description d. We then filter R_d, removing discourse units that are not linked to other discourse units by the given relation and in the given direction. Each element of the filtered R_d is thus linked to a discourse unit that could potentially satisfy the inference request.

To demonstrate, we perform forward causal inference using the following input description d:

(3) John traveled the world.

Below, we list the three top-ranked discourse units that matched d (left-hand side) and their associated consequents (right-hand side):

1. traveling the world → to murder

2. traveling from around the world to be there → even though this crowd was international

3. traveled across the world → to experience it

In a naïve way, one might simply choose the top-ranked clause in R_d and select its associated clause as the answer to the inference request; however, in the example above, this would incorrectly generate "to murder" as the effect of John's traveling (this is

[4] Available at http://lucene.apache.org

more appropriately viewed as the *purpose* of traveling). The other effect clauses also appear to be incorrect. This should not come as much of a surprise because the ranking was generated soley from the match score between the input description and the causes in R_d, which are quite relevant.

One potential problem with the naïve selection method is that it ignores information contained in the ranked list R'_d of clauses that are associated with the clauses in R_d. In our experiments, we often observed redundancies in R'_d that captured general properties of the desired inference. Intuitively, content that is shared across elements of R'_d could represent the core meaning of the desired inference result. In what follows, we describe various re-rankings of R'_d using this shared content. For each model described, the final inference prediction is the top-ranked element of R'_d.

Centroid similarity To approximate the shared content of discourse units in R'_d, we treat each discourse unit as a vector of TF scores. We then compute the average vector and re-rank all discourse units in R'_d based on their cosine similarity with the average vector. This favors inference results that "agree" with many alternative hypotheses.

Description score scaling In this approach, we incorporate the score from R_d into the centroid similarity score, multiplying the two and giving equal weight to each. This captures the intuition that the top-ranked element of R'_d should represent the general content of the list but should also be linked to an element of R_d that bears high similarity to the given state or event description d.

Log-length scaling When working with the centroid similarity score, we often observed top-ranked elements of R'_d that were only a few words in length. This was typically the case when components from sparse TF vectors in R'_d matched well with components from the centroid vector. Ideally, we would like more lengthy (but not too long) descriptions. To achieve this, we multiplied the centroid similarity score by the logarithm of the word length of the discourse unit in R'_d.

Description score/log-length scaling In this approach, we combine the description score scaling and log-length scaling, multiplying the centroid similarity by both and giving equal weight to all three factors.

4.2 Evaluating the generated textual inferences

To evaluate the inference re-ranking models described above, we automatically generated forward/backward causal and temporal inferences for five documents (265 sentences) drawn randomly from the story corpus. For simplicity, we generated an inference for each sentence in each document. Each inference re-ranking model is able to generate four textual inferences (forward/backward causal/temporal) for each sentence. In our experiments, we only kept the highest-scoring of the four inferences generated by a model. One of the authors then manually evaluated the final predictions for correctness. This was a subjective process, but it was guided by the following requirements:

1. The generated inference must increase the local coherence of the document. As described by Graesser et al. (1994), readers are typically required to make inferences about the text that lead to a coherent understanding thereof. We required the generated inferences to aid in this task.

2. The generated inferences must be globally valid. To demonstrate global validity, consider the following actual output:

   (4) I didn't even need a jacket (until I got there).

   In Example 4, the system-generated forward temporal inference is shown in parentheses. The inference makes sense given its local context; however, it is clear from the surrounding discourse (not shown) that a jacket was not needed at any point in time (it happened to be a warm day). As a result, this prediction was tagged as incorrect.

Table 2 presents the results of the evaluation. As shown in the table, the top-performing models are those that combine centroid similarity with one or both of the other re-ranking heuristics.

Re-ranking model	Inference accuracy (%)
None	10.19
Centroid similarity	12.83
Description score scaling	17.36
Log-length scaling	12.83
Description score/log-length scaling	16.60

Table 2: Inference generation evaluation results.

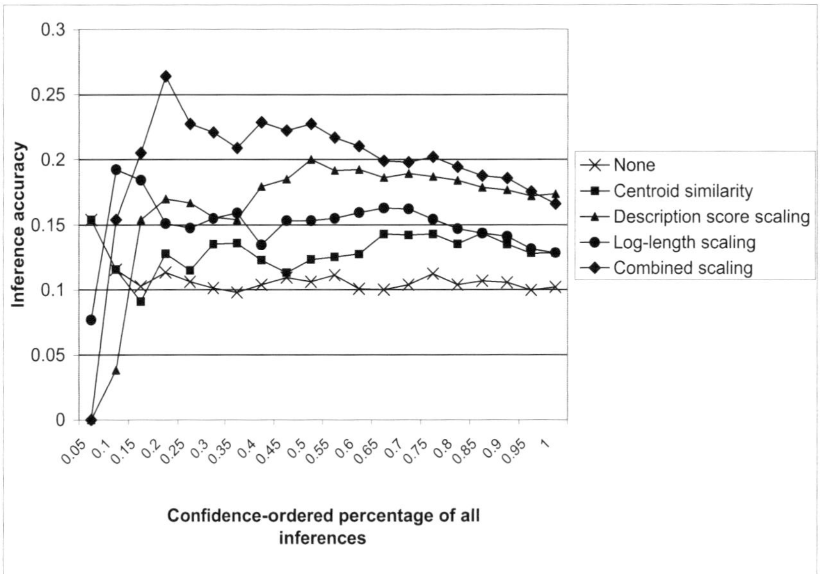

Figure 1: Inference rate versus accuracy. Values along the x-axis indicate that the top-scoring x% of all inferences were evaluated. Values along the y-axis indicate the prediction accuracy.

The analysis above demonstrates the relative performance of the models when making inferences for all sentences; however it is probably the case that many generated inferences should be rejected due to their low score. Because the output scores of a single model can be meaningfully compared across predictions, it is possible to impose a threshold on the inference generation process such that any prediction scoring at or below the threshold is withheld. We varied the prediction threshold from zero to a value sufficiently large that it excluded all predictions for a model. Doing so demonstrates the trade-off between making a large number of textual inferences and making accurate textual inferences. Figure 1 shows the effects of this variable on the re-ranking models. As shown in Figure 1, the highest inference accuracy is reached by the re-ranker that combines description score and log-length scaling with the centroid similarity measure. This accuracy is attained by keeping the top 25% most confident inferences.

5 Conclusions

We have presented an approach to commonsense reasoning that relies on (1) the availability of a large corpus of personal weblog stories and (2) the ability to analyze and perform inference with these stories. Our current results, although preliminary, suggest novel and important areas of future exploration. We group our observations according to the last two problems identified by Gordon and Swanson (2008): story analysis and envisioning with the analysis results.

5.1 Story analysis

As in other NLP tasks, we observed significant performance degradation when moving from the training genre (newswire) to the testing genre (Internet weblog stories). Because our discourse parser relies heavily on lexical and syntactic features for classification, and because the distribution of the feature values varies widely between the two genres, the performance degradation is to be expected. Recent techniques in parser adaptation for the Brown corpus (McClosky et al., 2006) might be usefully applied to the weblog genre as well.

Our supervised classification-based approach to discourse parsing could also be improved with additional training data. Causal and temporal relations are instantiated a combined 2,840 times in the RST corpus, with a large majority of these being causal. In contrast, the Penn Discourse TreeBank (Prasad et al., 2008) contains 7,448 training instances of causal relations and 2,763 training instances of temporal relations. This represents a significant increase in the amount of training data over the RST corpus. It would be informative to compare our current results with those obtained using a discourse parser trained on the Penn Discourse TreeBank.

One might also extract causal and temporal relations using traditional semantic role analysis based on FrameNet (Baker et al., 1998) or PropBank (Kingsbury and Palmer, 2003). The former defines a number of frames related to causation and temporal order, and roles within the latter could be mapped to standard thematic roles (e.g., cause) via SemLink.[5]

5.2 Envisioning with the analysis results

We believe commonsense reasoning based on weblog stories can also be improved through more sophisticated uses of the extracted discourse relations. As a first step, it would be beneficial to explore alternate input descriptions. As presented in Section 4.2, we make textual inferences at the sentence level for simplicity; however, it might be more reasonable to make inferences at the clause level, since clauses are the basis for RST and Penn Discourse TreeBank annotation. This could result in the generation of significantly more inferences due to multi-clause sentences; thus, more intelligent inference filtering will be required.

Our models use prediction scores for the tasks of rejecting inferences and selecting between multiple candidate inferences (i.e., forward/backward causal/temporal). Instead of relying on prediction scores for these tasks, it might be advantageous to first identify whether or not envisionment should be performed for a clause, and, if it should, what type and direction of envisionment would be best. For example, consider the following sentence:

(5) [$clause_1$ John went to the store] [$clause_2$ because he was hungry].

It would be better - from a local coherence perspective - to infer the cause of the second clause instead of the cause of the first. This is due to the fact that a cause for the first clause is explicitly stated, whereas a cause for the second clause is not. Inferences made about the first clause (e.g., that John went to the store because his dog was hungry), are likely to be uninformative or in conflict with explicitly stated information.

Example 5 raises the important issue of context, which we believe needs to be investigated further. Here, context refers to the discourse that surrounds the clause or sentence for which the system is attempting to generate a textual inference. The context places a number of constraints on allowable inferences. For example, in addition to content-based constraints demonstrated in Example 5, the context limits pronoun usage, entity references, and tense. Violations of these constraints will reduce local coherence.

Finally, the story corpus, with its vast size, is likely to contain a significant amount of redundancy for common events and states. Our centroid-based re-ranking heuristics are inspired by this redundancy, and we expect that aggregation techniques such as clustering might be of some use when applied to the corpus as a whole. Having identified coherent clusters of causes, it might be easier to find a consequence for a previously unseen cause.

In summary, we have presented preliminary research into the task of using a large, collaboratively constructed corpus as a commonsense knowledge repository. Rather than relying on hand-coded ontologies and event schemas, our approach relies on the implicit knowledge contained in written natural language. We have demonstrated the feasibility of obtaining the discourse structure of such a corpus via linear-time parsing models. Furthermore,

[5]Available at http://verbs.colorado.edu/semlink

we have introduced inference procedures that are capable of generating open-domain textual inferences from the extracted knowledge. Our evaluation results suggest many opportunities for future work in this area.

Acknowledgments

The authors would like to thank the anonymous reviewers for their helpful comments and suggestions. The project or effort described here has been sponsored by the U.S. Army Research, Development, and Engineering Command (RDECOM). Statements and opinions expressed do not necessarily reflect the position or the policy of the United States Government, and no official endorsement should be inferred.

References

Collin Baker, Charles Fillmore, and John Lowe. 1998. The Berkeley FrameNet project. In Christian Boitet and Pete Whitelock, editors, *Proceedings of the Thirty-Sixth Annual Meeting of the Association for Computational Linguistics and Seventeenth International Conference on Computational Linguistics*, pages 86–90, San Francisco, California. Morgan Kaufmann Publishers.

Roy Bar-Haim, Jonathan Berant, and Ido Dagan. 2009. A compact forest for scalable inference over entailment and paraphrase rules. In *Proceedings of the 2009 Conference on Empirical Methods in Natural Language Processing*, pages 1056–1065, Singapore, August. Association for Computational Linguistics.

K. Burton, A. Java, and I. Soboroff. 2009. The icwsm 2009 spinn3r dataset. In *Proceedings of the Third Annual Conference on Weblogs and Social Media.*

Lynn Carlson and Daniel Marcu. 2001. Discourse tagging manual. Technical Report ISI-TR-545, ISI, July.

Eugene Charniak and Mark Johnson. 2005. Coarse-to-fine n-best parsing and maxent discriminative reranking. In *Proceedings of the 43rd Annual Meeting on Association for Computational Linguistics.*

Peter Clark and Phil Harrison. 2009. Large-scale extraction and use of knowledge from text. In *K-CAP '09: Proceedings of the fifth international conference on Knowledge capture*, pages 153–160, New York, NY, USA. ACM.

Peter Clark, Christiane Fellbaum, Jerry R. Hobbs, Phil Harrison, William R. Murray, and John Thompson. 2008. Augmenting WordNet for Deep Understanding of Text. In Johan Bos and Rodolfo Delmonte, editors, *Semantics in Text Processing. STEP 2008 Conference Proceedings*, volume 1 of *Research in Computational Semantics*, pages 45–57. College Publications.

Stefan Evert, Adam Kilgarriff, and Serge Sharoff, editors. 2008. *4th Web as Corpus Workshop Can we beat Google?*

Christiane Fellbaum. 1998. *WordNet: An Electronic Lexical Database (Language, Speech, and Communication).* The MIT Press, May.

Danilo Giampiccolo, Hoa Trang Dang, Bernardo Magnini, Ido Dagan, and Bill Dolan. 2008. The fourth fascal recognizing textual entailment challenge. In *Proceedings of the First Text Analysis Conference.*

Andrew Gordon and Reid Swanson. 2008. Envisioning with weblogs. In *International Conference on New Media Technology.*

Andrew Gordon and Reid Swanson. 2009. Identifying personal stories in millions of weblog entries. In *Third International Conference on Weblogs and Social Media.*

Jonathan Gordon, Benjamin Van Durme, and Lenhart Schubert. 2009. Weblogs as a source for extracting general world knowledge. In *K-CAP '09: Proceedings of the fifth international conference on Knowledge capture*, pages 185–186, New York, NY, USA. ACM.

A. C. Graesser, M. Singer, and T. Trabasso. 1994. Constructing inferences during narrative text comprehension. *Psychological Review*, 101:371–395.

Iryna Gurevych and Torsten Zesch, editors. 2009. *The Peoples Web Meets NLP: Collaboratively Constructed Semantic Resources.*

Paul Kingsbury and Martha Palmer. 2003. Propbank: the next level of treebank. In *Proceedings of Treebanks and Lexical Theories.*

Douglas B. Lenat. 1995. Cyc: a large-scale investment in knowledge infrastructure. *Communications of the ACM*, 38(11):33–38.

David McClosky, Eugene Charniak, and Mark Johnson. 2006. Reranking and self-training for parser adaptation. In *ACL-44: Proceedings of the 21st International Conference on Computational Linguistics and the 44th annual meeting of the Association for Computational Linguistics*, pages 337–344, Morristown, NJ, USA. Association for Computational Linguistics.

Isaac Persing and Vincent Ng. 2009. Semi-supervised cause identification from aviation safety reports. In *Proceedings of the Joint Conference of the 47th Annual Meeting of the ACL and the 4th International Joint Conference on Natural Language Processing of the AFNLP*, pages 843–851, Suntec, Singapore, August. Association for Computational Linguistics.

Rashmi Prasad, Alan Lee, Nikhil Dinesh, Eleni Miltsakaki, Geraud Campion, Aravind Joshi, and Bonnie

Webber. 2008. Penn discourse treebank version 2.0. Linguistic Data Consortium, February.

Kenji Sagae. 2009. Analysis of discourse structure with syntactic dependencies and data-driven shift-reduce parsing. In *Proceedings of the 11th International Conference on Parsing Technologies (IWPT'09)*, pages 81–84, Paris, France, October. Association for Computational Linguistics.

Lenhart Schubert and Matthew Tong. 2003. Extracting and evaluating general world knowledge from the brown corpus. In *Proceedings of the HLT-NAACL 2003 workshop on Text meaning*, pages 7–13, Morristown, NJ, USA. Association for Computational Linguistics.

Reid Swanson and Andrew Gordon. 2008. Say anything: A massively collaborative open domain story writing companion. In *First International Conference on Interactive Digital Storytelling*.

Semantic Role Labeling for Open Information Extraction

Janara Christensen, Mausam, Stephen Soderland and Oren Etzioni
University of Washington, Seattle

Abstract

Open Information Extraction is a recent paradigm for machine reading from arbitrary text. In contrast to existing techniques, which have used only shallow syntactic features, we investigate the use of semantic features (semantic roles) for the task of Open IE. We compare TEXTRUNNER (Banko et al., 2007), a state of the art open extractor, with our novel extractor SRL-IE, which is based on UIUC's SRL system (Punyakanok et al., 2008). We find that SRL-IE is robust to noisy heterogeneous Web data and outperforms TEXTRUNNER on extraction quality. On the other hand, TEXTRUNNER performs over 2 orders of magnitude faster and achieves good precision in high locality and high redundancy extractions. These observations enable the construction of hybrid extractors that output higher quality results than TEXTRUNNER and similar quality as SRL-IE in much less time.

1 Introduction

The grand challenge of Machine Reading (Etzioni et al., 2006) requires, as a key step, a scalable system for extracting information from large, heterogeneous, unstructured text. The traditional approaches to information extraction (*e.g.*, (Soderland, 1999; Agichtein and Gravano, 2000)) do not operate at these scales, since they focus attention on a well-defined small set of relations and require large amounts of training data for each relation. The recent *Open Information Extraction* paradigm (Banko et al., 2007) attempts to overcome the knowledge acquisition bottleneck with its relation-independent nature and no manually annotated training data.

We are interested in the best possible technique for Open IE. The TEXTRUNNER Open IE system (Banko and Etzioni, 2008) employs only shallow syntactic features in the extraction process. Avoiding the expensive processing of deep syntactic analysis allowed TEXTRUNNER to process at Web scale. In this paper, we explore the benefits of semantic features and in particular, evaluate the application of semantic role labeling (SRL) to Open IE.

SRL is a popular NLP task that has seen significant progress over the last few years. The advent of hand-constructed semantic resources such as Propbank and Framenet (Martha and Palmer, 2002; Baker et al., 1998) have resulted in semantic role labelers achieving high in-domain precisions.

Our first observation is that semantically labeled arguments in a sentence almost always correspond to the arguments in Open IE extractions. Similarly, the verbs often match up with Open IE relations. These observations lead us to construct a new Open IE extractor based on SRL. We use UIUC's publicly available SRL system (Punyakanok et al., 2008) that is known to be competitive with the state of the art and construct a novel Open IE extractor based on it called SRL-IE.

We first need to evaluate SRL-IE's effectiveness in the context of large scale and heterogeneous input data as found on the Web: because SRL uses deeper analysis we expect SRL-IE to be much slower. Second, SRL is trained on news corpora using a resource like Propbank, and so may face recall loss due to out of vocabulary verbs and precision loss due to different writing styles found on the Web.

In this paper we address several empirical ques-

Proceedings of the NAACL HLT 2010 First International Workshop on Formalisms and Methodology for Learning by Reading, pages 52–60,
Los Angeles, California, June 2010.

tions. Can SRL-IE, our SRL based extractor, achieve adequate precision/recall on the heterogeneous Web text? What factors influence the relative performance of SRL-IE *vs.* that of TEXTRUNNER (*e.g.*, n-ary *vs.* binary extractions, redundancy, locality, sentence length, out of vocabulary verbs, *etc.*)? In terms of performance, what are the relative trade-offs between the two? Finally, is it possible to design a hybrid between the two systems to get the best of both the worlds? Our results show that:

1. SRL-IE is surprisingly robust to noisy heterogeneous data and achieves high precision and recall on the Open IE task on Web text.
2. SRL-IE outperforms TEXTRUNNER along dimensions such as recall and precision on complex extractions (*e.g.*, n-ary relations).
3. TEXTRUNNER is over 2 orders of magnitude faster, and achieves good precision for extractions with high system confidence or high locality or when the same fact is extracted from multiple sentences.
4. Hybrid extractors that use a combination of SRL-IE and TEXTRUNNER get the best of both worlds. Our hybrid extractors make effective use of available time and achieve a superior balance of precision-recall, better precision compared to TEXTRUNNER, and better recall compared to both TEXTRUNNER and SRL-IE.

2 Background

Open Information Extraction: The recently popular Open IE (Banko et al., 2007) is an extraction paradigm where the system makes a single data-driven pass over its corpus and extracts a large set of relational tuples without requiring any human input. These tuples attempt to capture the salient relationships expressed in each sentence. For instance, for the sentence, *"McCain fought hard against Obama, but finally lost the election"* an Open IE system would extract two tuples <McCain, fought (hard) against, Obama>, and <McCain, lost, the election>. These tuples can be binary or n-ary, where the relationship is expressed between more than 2 entities such as <Gates Foundation, invested (arg) in, 1 billion dollars, high schools>.

TEXTRUNNER is a state-of-the-art Open IE system that performs extraction in three key steps. (1) A self-supervised learner that outputs a CRF based classifier (that uses unlexicalized features) for extracting relationships. The self-supervised nature alleviates the need for hand-labeled training data and unlexicalized features help scale to the multitudes of relations found on the Web. (2) A single pass extractor that uses shallow syntactic techniques like part of speech tagging, noun phrase chunking and then applies the CRF extractor to extract relationships expressed in natural language sentences. The use of shallow features makes TEXTRUNNER highly efficient. (3) A redundancy based assessor that re-ranks these extractions based on a probabilistic model of redundancy in text (Downey et al., 2005). This exploits the redundancy of information in Web text and assigns higher confidence to extractions occurring multiple times. All these components enable TEXTRUNNER to be a high performance, general, and high quality extractor for heterogeneous Web text.

Semantic Role Labeling: SRL is a common NLP task that consists of detecting semantic arguments associated with a verb in a sentence and their classification into different roles (such as Agent, Patient, Instrument, *etc.*). Given the sentence *"The pearls I left to my son are fake"* an SRL system would conclude that for the verb 'leave', 'I' is the agent, 'pearls' is the patient and 'son' is the benefactor. Because not all roles feature in each verb the roles are commonly divided into meta-roles (A0-A7) and additional common classes such as location, time, *etc.* Each Ai can represent a different role based on the verb, though A0 and A1 most often refer to agents and patients respectively. Availability of lexical resources such as Propbank (Martha and Palmer, 2002), which annotates text with meta-roles for each argument, has enabled significant progress in SRL systems over the last few years.

Recently, there have been many advances in SRL (Toutanova et al., 2008; Johansson and Nugues, 2008; Coppola et al., 2009; Moschitti et al., 2008). We use UIUC-SRL as our base SRL system (Punyakanok et al., 2008). Our choice of the system is guided by the fact that its code is freely available and it is competitive with state of the art (it achieved the highest F1 score on the CoNLL-2005 shared task).

UIUC-SRL operates in four key steps: pruning, argument identification, argument classification and inference. Pruning involves using a full parse tree and heuristic rules to eliminate constituents that are unlikely to be arguments. Argument identification uses a classifier to identify constituents that are potential arguments. In argument classification, another classifier is used, this time to assign role labels to the candidates identified in the previous stage. Argument information is not incorporated across arguments until the inference stage, which uses an integer linear program to make global role predictions.

3 SRL-IE

Our key insight is that semantically labeled arguments in a sentence almost always correspond to the arguments in Open IE extractions. Thus, we can convert the output of UIUC-SRL into an Open IE extraction. We illustrate this conversion process via an example.

Given the sentence, *"Eli Whitney created the cotton gin in 1793,"* TextRunner extracts two tuples, one binary and one n-ary, as follows:

binary tuple:	arg0	Eli Whitney
	rel	created
	arg1	the cotton gin
n-ary tuple:	arg0	Eli Whitney
	rel	created (arg) in
	arg1	the cotton gin
	arg2	1793

UIUC-SRL labels constituents of a sentence with the role they play in regards to the verb in the sentence. UIUC-SRL will extract:

A0	Eli Whitney
verb	created
A1	the cotton gin
temporal	in 1793

To convert UIUC-SRL output to Open IE format, SRL-IE treats the verb (along with its modifiers and negation, if present) as the relation. Moreover, it assumes SRL's role-labeled arguments as the Open IE arguments related to the relation. The arguments here consist of all entities labeled Ai, as well as any entities that are marked *Direction*, *Location*, or *Temporal*. We order the arguments in the same order as they are in the sentence and with regard to the relation (except for direction, location and temporal, which cannot be arg0 of an Open IE extraction and are placed at the end of argument list). As we are interested in relations, we consider only extractions that have at least two arguments.

In doing this conversion, we naturally ignore part of the semantic information (such as distinctions between various Ai's) that UIUC-SRL provides. In this conversion process an SRL extraction that was correct in the original format will never be changed to an incorrect Open IE extraction. However, an incorrectly labeled SRL extraction could still convert to a correct Open IE extraction, if the arguments were correctly identified but incorrectly labeled.

Because of the methodology that TextRunner uses to extract relations, for n-ary extractions of the form <arg0, rel, arg1, ..., argN>, TextRunner often extracts sub-parts <arg0, rel, arg1>, <arg0, rel, arg1, arg2>, ..., <arg0, rel, arg1, ..., argN-1>. UIUC-SRL, however, extracts at most only one relation for each verb in the sentence. For a fair comparison, we create additional subpart extractions for each UIUC-SRL extraction using a similar policy.

4 Qualitative Comparison of Extractors

In order to understand SRL-IE better, we first compare with TextRunner in a variety of scenarios, such as sentences with lists, complex sentences, sentences with out of vocabulary verbs, *etc.*

Argument boundaries: SRL-IE is lenient in deciding what constitutes an argument and tends to err on the side of including too much rather than too little; TextRunner is much more conservative, sometimes to the extent of omitting crucial information, particularly post-modifying clauses and PPs. For example, TextRunner extracts <Bunsen, invented, a device> from the sentence *"Bunsen invented a device called the Spectroscope"*. SRL-IE includes the entire phrase "a device called the Spectroscope" as the second argument. Generally, the longer arguments in SRL-IE are more informative than TextRunner's succinct ones. On the other hand, TextRunner's arguments normalize better leading to an effective use of redundancy in ranking.

Lists: In sentences with a comma-separated lists of nouns, SRL-IE creates one extraction and treats the entire list as the argument, whereas TextRunner separates them into several relations, one for each item in the list.

Out of vocabulary verbs: While we expected

TEXTRUNNER to handle unknown verbs with little difficulty due to its unlexicalized nature, SRL-IE could have had severe trouble leading to a limited applicability in the context of Web text. However, contrary to our expectations, UIUC-SRL has a graceful policy to handle new verbs by attempting to identify A0 (the agent) and A1 (the patient) and leaving out the higher numbered ones. In practice, this is very effective – SRL-IE recognizes the verb and its two arguments correctly in *"Larry Page googled his name and launched a new revolution."*

Part-of-speech ambiguity: Both SRL-IE and TEXTRUNNER have difficulty when noun phrases have an identical spelling with a verb. For example, the word 'write' when used as a noun causes trouble for both systems. In the sentence, *"Be sure the file has write permission."* SRL-IE and TEXTRUNNER both extract <the file, write, permission>.

Complex sentences: Because TEXTRUNNER only uses shallow syntactic features it has a harder time on sentences with complex structure. SRL-IE, because of its deeper processing, can better handle complex syntax and long-range dependencies, although occasionally complex sentences will create parsing errors causing difficulties for SRL-IE.

N-ary relations: Both extractors suffer significant quality loss in n-ary extractions compared to binary. A key problem is prepositional phrase attachment, deciding whether the phrase associates with arg1 or with the verb.

5 Experimental Results

In our quantitative evaluation we attempt to answer two key questions: (1) what is the relative difference in performance of SRL-IE and TEXTRUNNER on precision, recall and computation time? And, (2) what factors influence the relative performance of the two systems? We explore the first question in Section 5.2 and the second in Section 5.3.

5.1 Dataset

Our goal is to explore the behavior of TEXTRUNNER and SRL-IE on a large scale dataset containing redundant information, since redundancy has been shown to immensely benefit Web-based Open IE extractors. At the same time, the test set must be a manageable size, due to SRL-IE's relatively slow processing time. We constructed a test set that approximates Web-scale distribution of extractions for five target relations – *invent, graduate, study, write,* and *develop*.

We created our test set as follows. We queried a corpus of 500M Web documents for a sample of sentences with these verbs (or their inflected forms, *e.g.*, invents, invented, *etc.*). We then ran TEXTRUNNER and SRL-IE on those sentences to find 200 distinct values of arg0 for each target relation, 100 from each system. We searched for at most 100 sentences that contain both the verb-form and arg0. This resulted in a test set of an average of 6,000 sentences per relation, for a total of 29,842 sentences. We use this test set for all experiments in this paper.

In order to compute precision and recall on this dataset, we tagged extractions by TEXTRUNNER and by SRL-IE as correct or errors. A tuple is correct if the arguments have correct boundaries and the relation accurately expresses the relationship between all of the arguments. Our definition of correct boundaries does not favor either system over the other. For instance, while TEXTRUNNER extracts <Bunsen, invented, a device> from the sentence *"Bunsen invented a device called the Spectroscope"*, and SRL-IE includes the entire phrase "a device called the Spectroscope" as the second argument, both extractions would be marked as correct.

Determining the absolute recall in these experiments is precluded by the amount of hand labeling necessary and the ambiguity of such a task. Instead, we compute pseudo-recall by taking the union of correct tuples from both methods as denominator.[1]

5.2 Relative Performance

Table 1 shows the performance of TEXTRUNNER and SRL-IE on this dataset. Since TEXTRUNNER can output different points on the precision-recall curve based on the confidence of the CRF we choose the point that maximizes F1.

SRL-IE achieved much higher recall at substantially higher precision. This was, however, at the cost of a much larger processing time. For our dataset, TEXTRUNNER took 6.3 minutes and SRL-

[1]Tuples from the two systems are considered equivalent if for the relation and each argument, the extracted phrases are equal or if one phrase is contained within the phrase extracted by the other system.

	TextRunner			SRL-IE		
	P	**R**	**F1**	**P**	**R**	**F1**
Binary	51.9	27.2	35.7	64.4	85.9	73.7
N-ary	39.3	28.2	32.9	54.4	62.7	58.3
All	47.9	27.5	34.9	62.1	79.9	69.9
Time	6.3 minutes			52.1 hours		

Table 1: SRL-IE outperforms TextRunner in both recall and precision, but has over 2.5 orders of magnitude longer run time.

IE took 52.1 hours – roughly 2.5 orders of magnitude longer. We ran our experiments on quad-core 2.8GHz processors with 4GB of memory.

It is important to note that our results for TextRunner are different from prior results (Banko, 2009). This is primarily due to a few operational criteria (such as focusing on proper nouns, filtering relatively infrequent extractions) identified in prior work that resulted in much higher precision, probably at significant cost of recall.

5.3 Comparison under Different Conditions

Although SRL-IE has higher overall precision, there are some conditions under which TextRunner has superior precision. We analyze the performance of these two systems along three key dimensions: system confidence, redundancy, and locality.

System Confidence: TextRunner's CRF-based extractor outputs a confidence score which can be varied to explore different points in the precision-recall space. Figure 1(a) and Figure 2(a) report the results from ranking extractions by this confidence value. For both binary and n-ary extractions the confidence value improves TextRunner's precision and for binary the high precision end has approximately the same precision as SRL-IE. Because of its use of an integer linear program, SRL-IE does not associate confidence values with extractions and is shown as a point in these figures.

Redundancy: In this experiment we use the redundancy of extractions as a measure of confidence. Here redundancy is the number of times a relation has been extracted from unique sentences. We compute redundancy over normalized extractions, ignoring noun modifiers, adverbs, and verb inflection.

Figure 1(b) and Figure 2(b) display the results for binary and n-ary extractions, ranked by redundancy. We use a log scale on the x-axis since high redundancy extractions account for less than 1% of the recall. For binary extractions, redundancy improved TextRunner's precision significantly, but at a dramatic loss in recall. TextRunner achieved 0.8 precision with 0.001 recall at redundancy of 10 and higher. For highly redundant information (common concepts, *etc.*) TextRunner has higher precision than SRL-IE and would be the algorithm of choice.

In n-ary relations for TextRunner and in binary relations for SRL-IE, redundancy actually hurts precision. These extractions tend to be so specific that genuine redundancy is rare, and the highest frequency extractions are often systematic errors. For example, the most frequent SRL-IE extraction was <nothing, write, home>.

Locality: Our experiments with TextRunner led us to discover a new validation scheme for the extractions – *locality*. We observed that TextRunner's shallow features can identify relations more reliably when the arguments are closer to each other in the sentence. Figure 1(c) and Figure 2(c) report the results from ranking extractions by the number of tokens that separate the first and last arguments.

We find a clear correlation between locality and precision of TextRunner, with precision 0.77 at recall 0.18 for TextRunner where the distance is 4 tokens or less for binary extractions. For n-ary relations, TextRunner can match SRL-IE's precision of 0.54 at recall 0.13. SRL-IE remains largely unaffected by locality, probably due to the parsing used in SRL.

6 A TextRunner SRL-IE Hybrid

We now present two hybrid systems that combine the strengths of TextRunner (fast processing time and high precision on a subset of sentences) with the strengths of SRL-IE (higher recall and better handling of long-range dependencies). This is set in a scenario where we have a limited budget on computational time and we need a high performance extractor that utilizes the available time efficiently.

Our approach is to run TextRunner on all sentences, and then determine the order in which to process sentences with SRL-IE. We can increase precision by filtering out TextRunner extractions that are expected to have low precision.

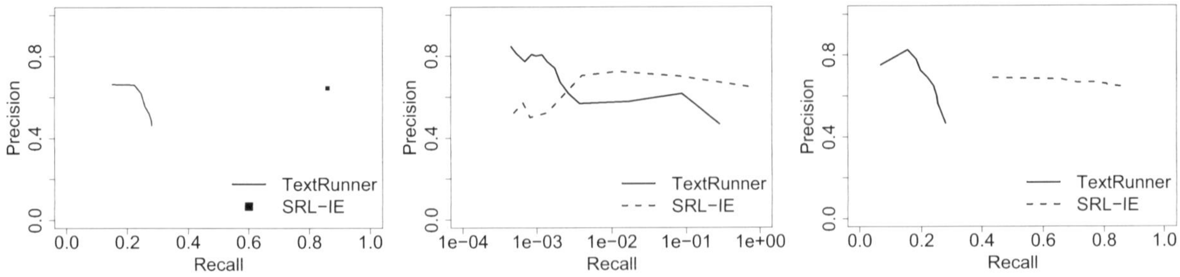

Figure 1: Ranking mechanisms for binary relations. (a) The confidence specified by the CRF improves TEXTRUNNER's precision. (b) For extractions with highest redundancy, TEXTRUNNER has higher precision than SRL-IE. Note the log scale for the x-axis. (c) Ranking by the distance between arguments gives a large boost to TEXTRUNNER's precision.

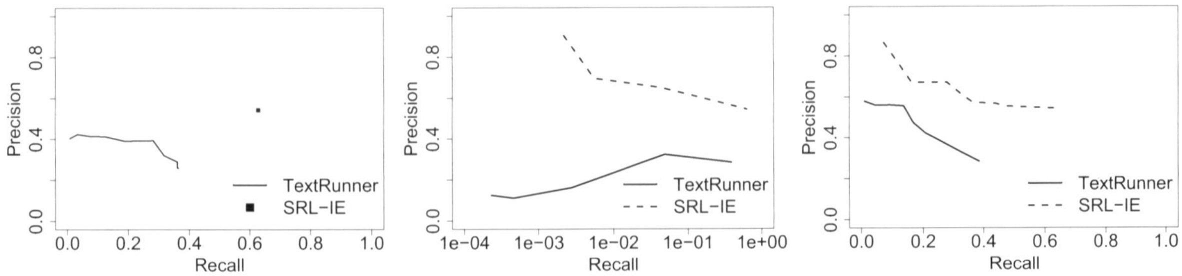

Figure 2: Ranking mechanisms for n-ary relations. (a) Ranking by confidence gives a slight boost to TEXTRUNNER's precision. (b) Redundancy helps SRL-IE, but not TEXTRUNNER. Note the log scale for the x-axis. (c) Ranking by distance between arguments raises precision for TEXTRUNNER and SRL-IE.

A naive hybrid will run TEXTRUNNER over all the sentences and use the remaining time to run SRL-IE on a random subset of the sentences and take the union of all extractions. We refer to this version as RECALLHYBRID, since this does not lose any extractions, achieving highest possible recall.

A second hybrid, which we call PRECHYBRID, focuses on increasing the precision and uses the *filter policy* and an intelligent *order of sentences for extraction* as described below.

Filter Policy for TEXTRUNNER Extractions: The results from Figure 1 and Figure 2 show that TEXTRUNNER's precision is low when the CRF confidence in the extraction is low, when the redundancy of the extraction is low, and when the arguments are far apart. Thus, system confidence, redundancy, and locality form the key factors for our filter policy: if the confidence is less than 0.5 and the redundancy is less than 2 or the distance between the arguments in the sentence is greater than 5 (if the relation is binary) or 8 (if the relation is n-ary) discard this tuple. These thresholds were determined by a parameter search over a small dataset.

Order of Sentences for Extraction: An optimal ordering policy would apply SRL-IE first to the sentences where TEXTRUNNER has low precision and leave the sentences that seem malformed (*e.g.*, incomplete sentences, two sentences spliced together) for last. As we have seen, the distance between the first and last argument is a good indicator for TEXTRUNNER precision. Moreover, a confidence value of 0.0 by TEXTRUNNER's CRF classifier is good evidence that the sentence may be malformed and is unlikely to contain a valid relation.

We rank sentences S in the following way, with SRL-IE processing sentences from highest ranking to lowest: *if* CRF.confidence = 0.0 *then* S.rank = 0, *else* S.rank = average distance between pairs of arguments for all tuples extracted by TEXTRUNNER from S.

While this ranking system orders sentences according to which sentence is likely to yield maximum new information, it misses the cost of computation. To account for computation time, we also estimate the amount of time SRL-IE will take to process each sentence using a linear model trained on the sentence length. We then choose the sentence that maximizes information gain divided by computation time.

6.1 Properties of Hybrid Extractors

The choice between the two hybrid systems is a trade-off between recall and precision: RECALLHYBRID guarantees the best recall, since it does not lose any extractions, while PRECHYBRID is designed to maximize the early boost in precision. The evaluation in the next section bears out these expectations.

6.2 Evaluation of Hybrid Extractors

Figure 3(a) and Figure 4(a) report the precision of each system for binary and n-ary extractions measured against available computation time. PRECHYBRID starts at slightly higher precision due to our filtering of potentially low quality extractions from TEXTRUNNER. For binary this precision is even better than SRL-IE's. It gradually loses precision until it reaches SRL-IE's level. RECALLHYBRID improves on TEXTRUNNER's precision, albeit at a much slower rate and remains worse than SRL-IE and PRECHYBRID throughout.

The recall for binary and n-ary extractions are shown in Figure 3(b) and Figure 4(b), again measured against available time. While PRECHYBRID significantly improves on TEXTRUNNER's recall, it does lose recall compared to RECALLHYBRID, especially for n-ary extractions. PRECHYBRID also shows a large initial drop in recall due to filtering.

Lastly, the gains in precision from PRECHYBRID are offset by loss in recall that leaves the F1 measure essentially identical to that of RECALLHYBRID (Figures 3(c),4(c)). However, for a fixed time budget both hybrid F-measures are significantly better than TEXTRUNNER and SRL-IE F-measures demonstrating the power of the hybrid extractors.

Both methods reach a much higher F1 than TEXTRUNNER: a gain of over 0.15 in half SRL-IE's processing time and over 0.3 after the full processing time. Both hybrids perform better than SRL-IE given equal processing time.

We believe that most often constructing a higher quality database of facts with a relatively lower recall is more useful than vice-versa, making PRECHYBRID to be of wider applicability than RECALLHYBRID. Still the choice of the actual hybrid extractor could change based on the task.

7 Related Work

Open information extraction is a relatively recent paradigm and hence, has been studied by only a small number of researchers. The most salient is TEXTRUNNER, which also introduced the model (Banko et al., 2007; Banko and Etzioni, 2008).

A version of KNEXT uses heuristic rules and syntactic parses to convert a sentence into an unscoped logical form (Van Durme and Schubert, 2008). This work is more suitable for extracting common sense knowledge as opposed to factual information.

Another Open IE system, Kylin (Weld et al., 2008), suggests automatically building an extractor for each relation using self-supervised training, with training data generated using Wikipedia infoboxes. This work has the limitation that it can only extract relations expressed in Wikipedia infoboxes.

A paradigm related to Open IE is Preemptive IE (Shinyama and Sekine, 2006). While one goal of Preemptive IE is to avoid relation-specificity, Preemptive IE does not emphasize Web scalability, which is essential to Open IE.

(Carlson et al., 2009) presents a semi-supervised approach to information extraction on the Web. It learns classifiers for different relations and couples the training of those classifiers with ontology defining constraints. While we attempt to learn unknown relations, it learns a pre-defined set of relations.

Another related system is WANDERLUST (Akbik and Broß, 2009). The authors of this system annotated 10,000 sentences parsed with LinkGrammar, resulting in 46 general linkpaths as patterns for relation extraction. With these patterns WANDERLUST extracts binary relations from link grammar linkages. In contrast to our approaches, this requires a large set of hand-labeled examples.

USP (Poon and Domingos, 2009) is based on Markov Logic Networks and attempts to create a full semantic parse in an unsupervised fashion. They evaluate their work on biomedical text, so its applicability to general Web text is not yet clear.

8 Discussion and Future Work

The Heavy Tail: It is well accepted that information on the Web is distributed according to Zipf's

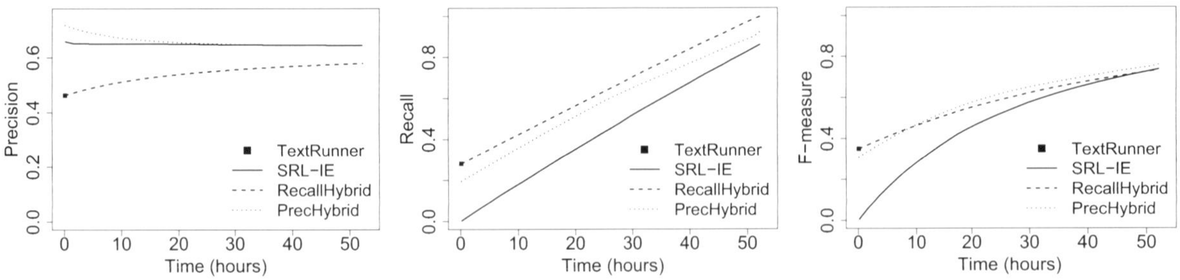

Figure 3: (a) Precision for binary extractions for PRECHYBRID starts higher than the precision of SRL-IE. (b) Recall for binary extractions rises over time for both hybrid systems, with PRECHYBRID starting lower. (c) Hybrid extractors obtain the best F-measure given a limited budget of computation time.

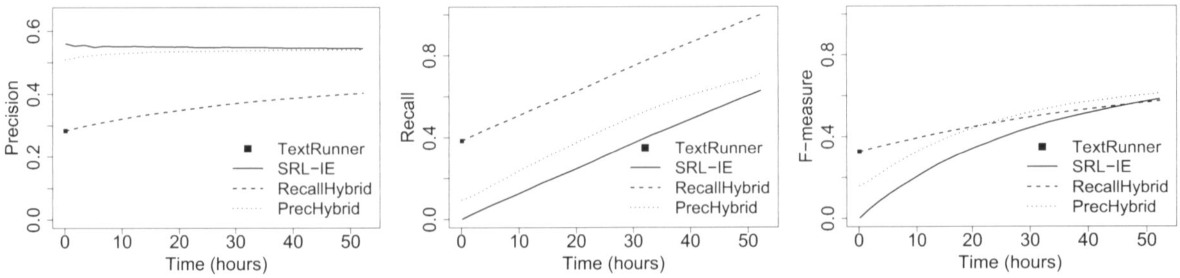

Figure 4: (a) PRECHYBRID also gives a strong boost to precision for n-ary extractions. (b) Recall for n-ary extractions for RECALLHYBRID starts substantially higher than PRECHYBRID and finally reaches much higher recall than SRL-IE alone. (c) F-measure for n-ary extractions. The hybrid extractors outperform others.

Law (Downey et al., 2005), implying that there is a heavy tail of facts that are mentioned only once or twice. The prior work on Open IE ascribes prime importance to redundancy based validation, which, as our results show (Figures 1(b), 2(b)), captures a very tiny fraction of the available information. We believe that deeper processing of text is essential to gather information from this heavy tail. Our SRL-IE extractor is a viable algorithm for this task.

Understanding SRL Components: UIUC-SRL as well as other SRL algorithms have different subcomponents – parsing, argument classification, joint inference, *etc.* We plan to study the effective contribution of each of these components. Our hope is to identify the most important subset, which yields a similar quality at a much reduced computational cost. Another alternative is to add the best performing component within TEXTRUNNER.

9 Conclusions

This paper investigates the use of semantic features, in particular, semantic role labeling for the task of open information extraction. We describe SRL-IE, the first SRL based Open IE system. We empirically compare the performance of SRL-IE with TEXTRUNNER, a state-of-the-art Open IE system and find that on average SRL-IE has much higher recall and precision, however, TEXTRUNNER outperforms in precision for the case of highly redundant or high locality extractions. Moreover, TEXTRUNNER is over 2 orders of magnitude faster.

These complimentary strengths help us design hybrid extractors that achieve better performance than either system given a limited budget of computation time. Overall, we provide evidence that, contrary to belief in the Open IE literature (Banko and Etzioni, 2008), semantic approaches have a lot to offer for the task of Open IE and the vision of machine reading.

10 Acknowledgements

This research was supported in part by NSF grant IIS-0803481, ONR grant N00014-08-1-0431, and DARPA contract FA8750-09-C-0179, and carried out at the University of Washington's Turing Center.

References

Eugene Agichtein and Luis Gravano. 2000. Snowball: Extracting relations from large plain-text collections. In *Proceedings of the Fifth ACM International Conference on Digital Libraries*.

Alan Akbik and Jügen Broß. 2009. Wanderlust: Extracting semantic relations from natural language text using dependency grammar patterns. In *Proceedings of the Workshop on Semantic Search (SemSearch 2009) at the 18th International World Wide Web Conference (WWW 2009)*.

Collin F. Baker, Charles J. Fillmore, and John B. Lowe. 1998. The berkeley framenet project. In *Proceedings of the 17th international conference on Computational linguistics*, pages 86–90.

Michele Banko and Oren Etzioni. 2008. The tradeoffs between open and traditional relation extraction. In *Proceedings of ACL-08: HLT*, pages 28–36.

Michele Banko, Michael J. Cafarella, Stephen Soderland, Matt Broadhead, and Oren Etzioni. 2007. Open information extraction from the web. In *IJCAI'07: Proceedings of the 20th international joint conference on Artifical intelligence*, pages 2670–2676.

Michele Banko. 2009. *Open Information Extraction for the Web*. Ph.D. thesis, University of Washington.

Andrew Carlson, Justin Betteridge, Estevam R. Hruschka Jr., and Tom M. Mitchell. 2009. Coupling semi-supervised learning of categories and relations. In *Proceedings of the NAACL HLT 2009 Workskop on Semi-supervised Learning for Natural Language Processing*.

Bonaventura Coppola, Alessandro Moschitti, and Giuseppe Riccardi. 2009. Shallow semantic parsing for spoken language understanding. In *NAACL '09: Proceedings of Human Language Technologies: The 2009 Annual Conference of the North American Chapter of the Association for Computational Linguistics, Companion Volume: Short Papers*, pages 85–88.

Doug Downey, Oren Etzioni, and Stephen Soderland. 2005. A probabilistic model of redundancy in information extraction. In *IJCAI '05: Proceedings of the 20th international joint conference on Artifical intelligence*, pages 1034–1041.

Oren Etzioni, Michele Banko, and Michael J. Cafarella. 2006. Machine reading. In *AAAI'06: proceedings of the 21st national conference on Artificial intelligence*, pages 1517–1519.

Richard Johansson and Pierre Nugues. 2008. The effect of syntactic representation on semantic role labeling. In *Proceedings of the 22nd International Conference on Computational Linguistics (Coling 2008)*, pages 393–400.

Paul Kingsbury Martha and Martha Palmer. 2002. From treebank to propbank. In *In Proceedings of LREC-2002*.

Alessandro Moschitti, Daniele Pighin, and Roberto Basili. 2008. Tree kernels for semantic role labeling. *Computational Linguistics*, 34(2):193–224.

Hoifung Poon and Pedro Domingos. 2009. Unsupervised semantic parsing. In *EMNLP '09: Proceedings of the 2009 Conference on Empirical Methods in Natural Language Processing*, pages 1–10.

V. Punyakanok, D. Roth, and W. Yih. 2008. The importance of syntactic parsing and inference in semantic role labeling. *Computational Linguistics*, 34(2).

Yusuke Shinyama and Satoshi Sekine. 2006. Preemptive information extraction using unrestricted relation discovery. In *Proceedings of the main conference on Human Language Technology Conference of the North American Chapter of the Association of Computational Linguistics*, pages 304–311.

Stephen Soderland. 1999. Learning information extraction rules for semi-structured and free text. *Machine Learning*, 34(1-3):233–272.

Kristina Toutanova, Aria Haghighi, and Christopher D. Manning. 2008. A global joint model for semantic role labeling. *Computational Linguistics*, 34(2):161–191.

Benjamin Van Durme and Lenhart Schubert. 2008. Open knowledge extraction through compositional language processing. In *STEP '08: Proceedings of the 2008 Conference on Semantics in Text Processing*, pages 239–254.

Daniel S. Weld, Raphael Hoffmann, and Fei Wu. 2008. Using wikipedia to bootstrap open information extraction. *SIGMOD Rec.*, 37(4):62–68.

Empirical Studies in Learning to Read

Marjorie Freedman, Edward Loper, Elizabeth Boschee, Ralph Weischedel
BBN Raytheon Technologies
10 Moulton St
Cambridge, MA 02139
{mfreedma, eloper, eboschee, weischedel}@bbn.com

Abstract

In this paper, we present empirical results on the challenge of *learning to read*. That is, given a handful of examples of the concepts and relations in an ontology and a large corpus, the system should learn to map from text to the concepts/relations of the ontology. In this paper, we report contrastive experiments on the recall, precision, and F-measure (F) of the mapping in the following conditions: (1) employing word-based patterns, employing semantic structure, and combining the two; and (2) fully automatic learning versus allowing minimal questions of a human informant.

1 Introduction

This paper reports empirical results with an algorithm that "learns to read" text and map that text into concepts and relations in an ontology specified by the user. Our approach uses unsupervised and semi-supervised algorithms to harness the *diversity* and *redundancy* of the ways concepts and relations are expressed in document collections. Diversity can be used to automatically generate patterns and paraphrases for new concepts and relations to boost recall. Redundancy can be exploited to automatically check and improve the accuracy of those patterns, allowing for system learning without human supervision.

For example, the system learns how to recognize a new relation (e.g. *invent*), starting from 5-20 instances (e.g. *Thomas Edison + the light bulb*). The system iteratively searches a collection of documents to find sentences where those instances are expressed (e.g. "*Thomas Edison's patent for the light bulb*"), induces patterns over textual features found in those instances (e.g. *patent(possessive:A, for:B)*), and repeats the cycle by applying the generated patterns to find additional instances followed by inducing more patterns from those instances. Unsupervised measures of redundancy and coverage are used to estimate the reliability of the induced patterns and learned instances; only the most reliable are added, which minimizes the amount of noise introduced at each step.

There have been two approaches to evaluation of mapping text to concepts and relations: Automatic Content Extraction (ACE)[1] and Knowledge Base Population (KBP)[2]. In ACE, complete manual annotation for a small corpus (~25k words) was possible; thus, both recall and precision could be measured across every instance in the test set. This evaluation can be termed *micro reading* in that it evaluates every concept/relation mention in the corpus. In ACE, learning algorithms had roughly 300k words of training data.

By contrast, in KBP, the corpus of documents in the test set was too large for a complete answer key. Rather than a complete answer key, relations were extracted for a list of entities; system output was pooled and judged manually. This type of reading has been termed *macro reading*[3], since finding any instance of the relation in the 1.3M document corpus is measured success, rather than finding every instance. Only 118 queries were provided, though several hundred were created and distributed by participants.

In the study in this paper, recall, precision, and F are measured for 11 relations under the following contrastive conditions

[1] http://www.nist.gov/speech/tests/ace/
[2] http://apl.jhu.edu/~paulmac/kbp.html
[3] See http://rtw.ml.cmu.edu/papers/mitchell-iswc09.pdf

Proceedings of the NAACL HLT 2010 First International Workshop on Formalisms and Methodology for Learning by Reading, pages 61–69,
Los Angeles, California, June 2010.

1. Patterns based on words vs. predicate-argument structure vs. combining both.
2. Fully automatic vs. a few periodic responses by humans to specific queries.

Though many prior studies have focused on precision, e.g., to find any text justification to answer a question, we focus equally on recall and report recall performance as well as precision. This addresses the challenge of finding information on rarely mentioned entities (no matter how challenging the expression). We believe the effect will be improved technology overall. We evaluate our system in a micro-reading context on 11 relations. In a fully automatic configuration, the system achieves an F of .48 (Recall=.37, Precision=.68). With limited human intervention, F rises to .58 (Recall=.49, Precision=.70). We see that patterns based on predicate-argument structure (text graphs) outperform patterns based on surface strings with respect to both precision and recall.

Section 2 describes our approach; section 3, some challenges; section 4, the implementation; section 5, evaluation; section 6, empirical results on extraction type; section 7, the effect of periodic, limited human feedback; section 8, related work; and section 9, lessons learned and conclusions.

2 Approach

Our approach for learning patterns that can be used to detect relations is depicted in Figure 1. Initially, a few instances of the relation tuples are provided, along with a massive corpus, e.g., the web or the gigaword corpus from the Linguistic Data Consortium (LDC). The diagram shows three inventor-invention pairs, beginning with *Thomas Edison…light bulb*. From these, we find candidate sentences in the massive corpus, e.g., *Thomas Edison invented the light bulb*. Features extracted from the sentences retrieved, for example features of the text-graph (the predicate-argument structure connecting the two arguments), provide a training instance for pattern induction. The induced patterns are added to the collection (database) of patterns. Running the extended pattern collection over the corpus finds new, previously unseen relation tuples. From these new tuples, additional sentences which express those tuples can be retrieved, and the cycle of learning can continue.

There is an analogous cycle of learning concepts from instances and the large corpus; the experiments in this paper do not report on that parallel learning cycle.

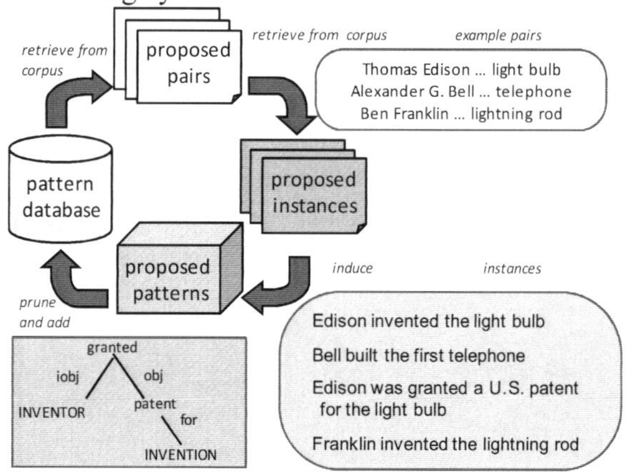

Figure 1: Approach to Learning Relations

At the ith iteration, the steps are

1. Given the set of hypothesized instances of the relation (triples HT_i), find instances of such triples in the corpus. (On the first iteration, "hypothesized" triples are manually-generated seed examples.)
2. Induce possible patterns. For each proposed pattern P:
   a. Apply pattern P to the corpus to generate a set of triples T_P
   b. Estimate precision as the confidence-weighted average of the scores of the triples in T_P. Reduce precision score by the percentage of triples in T_P that violate user-specified relation constraints (e.g. arity constraints described in 4.3)
   c. Estimate recall as the confidence-weighted percentage of triples in HT_i found by the pattern
3. Identify a set of high-confidence patterns HP_i using cutoffs automatically derived from rank-based curves for precision, recall, and F-measure (α=0.7)
4. Apply high-confidence patterns to a Web-scale corpus to hypothesize new triples. For each proposed triple T
   a. Estimate *score*(*T*) as the expected probability that T is correct, calculated by combining the respective precision and recall scores of all of the patterns that did or did not return it (using the Naïve Bayes assumption that all patterns are independent)
   b. Estimate *confidence*(*T*) as the percentage of patterns in HP_i by which T was found
5. Identify a set of high-confidence triples HT_{i+1}

using cutoffs automatically derived from rank-based curves; use these triples to begin the next iteration

3 Challenges

The iterative cycle of learning we describe above has most frequently been applied for *macro-reading* tasks. However, here we are interested in measuring performance for *micro-reading.* There are several reasons for wanting to measure performance in a micro-reading task:

- For information that is rare (e.g. relations about infrequently mentioned entities), a micro-reading paradigm may more accurately predict results.
- For some tasks or domains micro-reading may be all that we can do-- the actual corpus of interest may not be macro-scaled.
- Macro-reading frequently utilizes statistics of extraction targets from the whole corpus to improve its precision. Therefore, improving micro-reading could improve the precision of macro-reading.
- Because we are measuring performance in a micro-reading context, recall at the instance level is as important as precision. Consequently, our learning system must learn to predict patterns that incorporate nominal and pronominal mentions.
- Furthermore, while the approach we describe makes use of corpus-wide statistics during the learning process, during pattern application we limit ourselves to only information from within a single document (and in practice primarily within a single sentence). Our evaluation measures performance at the instance-level[4].

4 Implementation

4.1 Pattern Types

Boschee et al.(2008) describes two types of patterns: patterns that rely on surface strings and patterns that rely only on two types of syntactic-structure. We diverge from that early work by allowing more expressive surface-string patterns: our surface-string patterns can include wild-cards (allowing the system to make matches which require omitting words). For example for *kill(agent, victim)*, the system learns the pattern *<AGENT> <...> assassinated <VICTIM>*, which correctly matches *Booth, with hopes of a resurgent Confederacy in mind, cruelly assassinated Lincoln.*

We also diverge from the earlier work by only making use of patterns based on the normalized predicate-argument structure and not dependency parses. The normalized predicate-argument structures (text-graphs) are built by performing a set of rule-based transformations on the syntactic parse of a sentence. These transformations include finding the logical subject and object for each verb, resolving some traces, identifying temporal arguments, and attaching other verb arguments with lexicalized roles (e.g. '*of*' in Figure 2). The resulting graphs allow both noun and verb predicates.

Manually created patterns using this structure have been successfully used for event detection and template-based question answering. The text graph structures have also served as useful features in supervised, discriminative models for relation and event extraction. While the experiments described here do not include dependency tree paths, we do allow arbitrarily large text graph patterns.

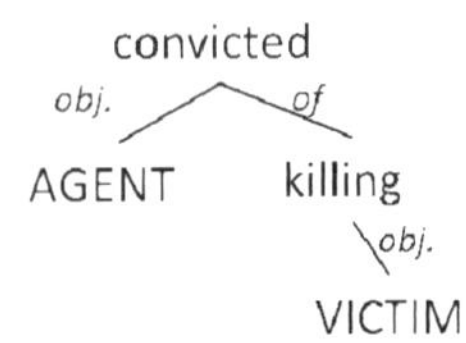

Text Graph Pattern

4.2 Co-Reference

Non-named mentions are essential for allowing high instance-level recall. In certain cases, a relation is most clearly and frequently expressed with pronouns and descriptions (e.g *her father* for the relation *child).*[5] Because non-named instances appear in different constructions than named instances, we need to learn patterns that will appear in non-named contexts. Thus, co-reference information is used during pattern induction to extract patterns from sentences where the hypothesized triples are not explicitly mentioned. In particular, any mention that is co-referent with the desired entity can be used to induce a pattern. Co-reference for 7 types of entities is produced by SERIF, a

[4] Our evaluation measures only performance in extracting the relation: that is if the text of sentence implies to an annotator that the relation is present, then the annotator has been instructed to mark the sentence as correct (regardless of whether or not outside knowledge contradicts this fact).

[5] The structure of our noun-predicates allows us to learn lexicalized patterns in cases like this. For *her father* we would induce the pattern *n:father:<ref>PARENT, <pos>CHILD.*

state of the art information extraction engine. A manually determined confidence threshold is used to discard mentions where co-reference certainty is too low.

During pattern matching, co-reference is used to find the "best string" for each element of the matched triple. In particular, pronouns and descriptors are replaced by their referents; and abbreviated names are replaced by full names. If any pronoun cannot be resolved to a description or a name, or if the co-reference threshold falls below a manually determined threshold, then the match is discarded.

Pattern scoring requires that we compare instances of triples across the whole corpus. If these instances were compared purely on the basis of strings, in many cases the same entity would appear as distinct (e.g. *US, United States).* This would interfere with the arity constraints described below. To alleviate this challenge, we use a database of name strings that have been shown to be equivalent with a combination of edit-distance and extraction statistics (Baron & Freedman, 2008). Thus, for triple(t_P) and hypothesized triples (HT_i), if $t_P \notin HT_i$, but can be mapped via the equivalent names database to some triple $t_P' \in HT_i$, then its score and confidence are adjusted towards that of t_P', weighted by the confidence of the equivalence.

4.3 Relation Set and Constraints

We ran experiments using 11 relation types. The relation types were selected as a subset of the relations that have been proposed for DARPA's machine reading program. In addition to seed examples, we provided the learning system with three types of constraints for each relation:

Symmetry: For relations where R(X,Y) = R(Y,X), the learning (and scoring process), normalizes instances of the relation so that R(X,Y) and R(Y,X) are equivalent.

Arity: For each argument of the relation, provide an expected maximum number of instances per unique instance of the other argument. These numbers are intentionally higher than the expected true value to account for co-reference mistakes. Patterns that violate the arity constraint (e.g *v:accompanied(<obj>=<X>, <sub>=<Y>* as a pattern for *spouse)* are penalized. This is one way of providing negative feedback during the unsupervised training process.

Argument Type: For each argument, specify the expected class of entities for this argument. Entity types are one of the 7 ACE types (Person, Organization, Geo-political entity, Location, Facility, Weapon, Vehicle) or Date. Currently the system only allows instance proposals when the types are correct. Potentially, the system could use pattern matches that violate type constraints as an additional type of negative example. Any implementation would need to account for the fact that in some cases, potentially too general patterns are quite effective when the type constraints are met. For example, for the relation *employed(PERSON, ORGANIZATION),* <ORG>*'s* <PER> is a fairly precise pattern, despite clearly being overly general without the type constraints.

In our relation set, only two relations (*sibling* and *spouse*) are symmetric. Table 1 below includes the other constraints. ACE types/dates are in columns labeled with the first letter of the name of the type (A is arity). We have only included those types that are an argument for some relation.

Relation	Arg1					Arg2						
	P	O	G	L	A	P	O	G	F	L	D	A
attackedOn	■	■	■	■	10						■	--
attendSchool	■				--		■					5
employed	■				--		■	■		■		5
birthDate	■				--						■	5
birthplace	■				--			■		■		5
child	■				5	■						10
kill	■				--	■						--
killedInLocation	■				--			■	■	■		5
sibling	■				10	■						10
spouse	■				5	■						5
topLeader	■				5		■	■		■		5

Table 1: Argument types of the test relations

4.4 Corpus and Seed Examples

While many other experiments using this approach have used web-scale corpora, we chose to include Wikipedia articles as well as Gigaword-3 to provide additional instances of information (e.g. *birthDate* and *sibling*) that is uncommon in news.

For each relation type, 20 seed-examples were selected randomly from the corpus by using a combination of keyword search and an ACE extraction system to identify passages that were likely to contain the relations of interest. As such, each seed example was guaranteed to occur at least once in a context that indicated the relation was present.

5 Evaluation Framework

To evaluate system performance, we ran two separate annotation-based evaluations, the first measured precision, and the second measured recall.

To measure overall precision, we ran each system's patterns over the web-scale corpora, and randomly sampled 200 of the instances it found[6]. These instances were then manually assessed as to whether they conveyed the intended relation or not. The system precision is simply the percentage of instances that were judged to be correct.

To measure recall, we began by randomly selecting 20 test-examples from the corpus, using the same process that we used to select the training seeds (but guaranteed to be distinct from the training seeds). We then searched the web-scale corpus for sentences that might possibly link these test examples together (whether directly or via coreference). We randomly sampled this set of sentences, choosing 10 sentences for each test-example, to form a collection of 200 sentences which were likely to convey the desired relation. These sentences were then manually annotated to indicate which sentences actually convey the desired relation; this set of sentences forms the *recall test set*. Once a recall set had been created for each relation, a system's recall could be evaluated by running that system's patterns over the documents in the recall set, and checking what percentage of the recall test sentences it correctly identified.

We intentionally chose to sample 10 sentences from each test example, rather than sampling from the set of all sentences found for any of the test examples, in order to prevent one or two very common instances from dominating the recall set. As a result, the recall test set is somewhat biased away from "true" recall, since it places a higher weight on the "long tail" of instances. However, we believe that this gives a more accurate indication of the system's ability to find novel instances of a relation (as opposed to novel ways of talking about known instances).

6 Effect of Pattern Type

As described in 4.1, our system is capable of learning two classes of patterns: surface-strings and text-graphs. We measured our system's performance on each of the relation types after twenty iterations. In each iteration, the system can learn multiple patterns of either type. There is currently no penalty for learning overlapping pattern types. For example, in the first iteration for the relation *killed*(), the system learns both the surface-string pattern *<AGENT> killed <VICTIM>* and the text-graph pattern: *v:killed(<sub>=<AGENT>, <obj>=<VICTIM>)*. During decoding, if multiple patterns match the same relation instance, the system accepts the relation instance, but does not make use of the additional information that there were multiple supporting patterns.

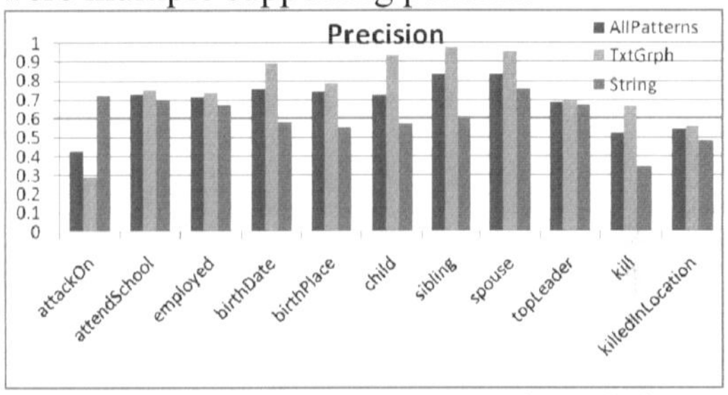

Figure 3: Precision of Pattern Types by Relation

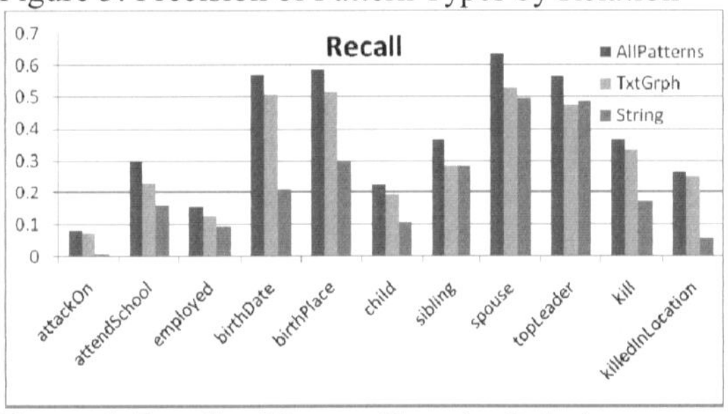

Figure 4: Recall of Pattern Type by Relation

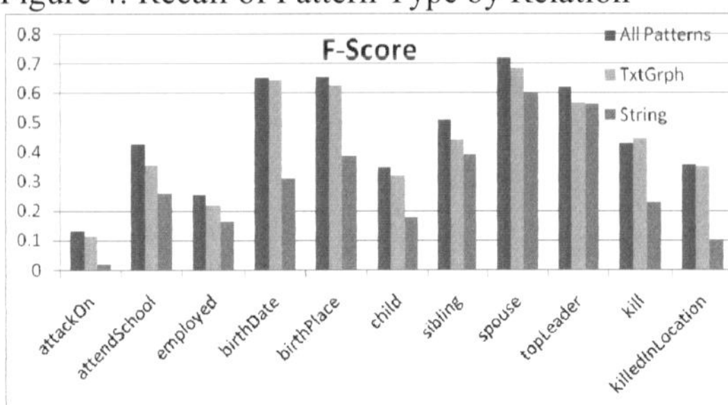

Figure 5: F-Score of Pattern Type by Relation

Figure 3, Figure 4, and Figure 5 plot precision, recall, and F-score for each of the 11 relations showing performance of all patterns vs. only text-graph patterns vs. only surface-string patterns.

- For most relations, the text-graph patterns provide both higher precision and higher recall than the surface-string patterns. The lower precision of the text-graph patterns for *attackOn* is the result of the system learning a number of overly general patterns that correlate with attacks, but do not themselves indicate the pres-

[6] While the system provides estimated precision for each pattern, we do not evaluate over the n-best matches. All patterns with estimated confidence above 50% are treated equally. We sample from the set of matches produced by these patterns.

ence of an attack. For instance, the system learns patterns with predicates *said* and *arrive*. Certainly, governments often make statements on the date of an attack and troops arrive in a location before attacking, but both patterns will produce a large number of spurious instances.

- While text-graph patterns typically have higher precision than the combined pattern set, surface-string patterns provide enough improvement in recall that typically the all-pattern F-score is higher than the text-graph F-score.

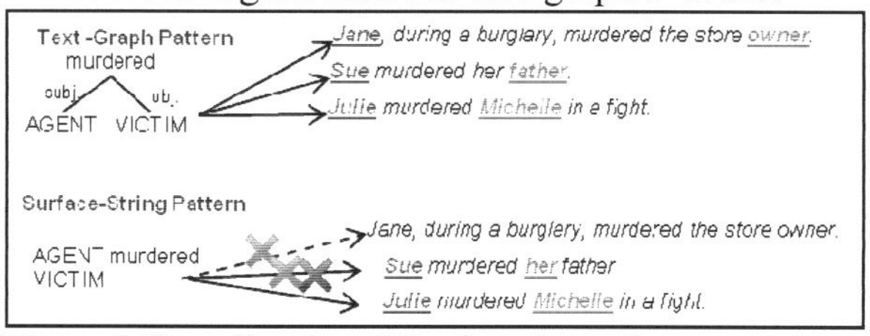

Figure 6: Text-Graph and Surface-String Patterns

A partial explanation for the higher recall and precision of the text-graph patterns is illustrated in Figure 6 which presents a simple surface-string pattern and a simple text-graph pattern that appear to represent the same information. On the right of the figure are three sentences. The text-graph pattern correctly identifies the *agent* and *victim* in each sentence. However, the surface-string pattern, misses the *killed*() relation in the first sentence and misidentifies the *victim* in the second sentence. The false-alarm in the second sentence would have been avoided by a system that restricted itself to matching named instances, but as described above in section 4.2, for the micro-reading task described here, detecting relations with pronouns is critical.

While we allowed the creation of text-graph patterns with arbitrarily long paths between the arguments, in practice, the system rarely learned such patterns. For the relation *killed(Agent, Victim)*, we learned 8 patterns that have more than one predicate (compared to 22 that only have a single predicate). For the relation *killedInLocation(Victim, Location)*, the system learned 28 patterns with more than 1 predicate (compared with 20 containing only 1 predicate). In both cases, the precision of the longer patterns was higher, but their recall was significantly lower. In the case of *killedInLocation,* none of the longer path patterns matched any of the examples in our recall set.

One strength of text-graph patterns is allowing for intelligent omission of overly specific text, for example, ignoring '*during a buglary*' in Figure 6. Surface string patterns can include wild-cards, but for surface string patterns, the omission is not syntactically defined. Approximately 30% of surface string patterns included one wild-card. An additional 17% included two. Figure 7 presents averaged precision and recall for text-graph and surface-string patterns. The final three columns break the surface-string patterns down by the number of wild-cards. It appears that with one, the patterns remain reasonably precise, but the addition of a second wild-card drops precision by more than 50%. The presence of wild-card patterns improves recall, but surface-string patterns do not reach the level of recall of text-graph patterns.

	Text Graph	Surface String			
		All	No-*	1-*	2-*
Precision	0.75	0.61	0.72	0.69	0.30
Recall	0.32	0.22	0.16	0.10	0.09

Figure 7: Performance by Number of WildCards (*)

7 Effect of Human Review

In addition to allowing the system to self-train in a completely unsupervised manner, we ran a parallel set of experiments where the system was given limited human guidance. At the end of iterations 1, 5, 10, and 20, a person provided under 10 minutes of feedback (on average 5 minutes). The person was presented with five patterns, and five sample matched instances for each pattern. The person was able to provide two types of feedback:

- The pattern is correct/incorrect (e.g. <EMPLOYEE> *said* <ORGANIZATION> is an incorrect pattern for employ(X,Y))
- The matched instances are correct/incorrect (e.g. '*Bob received a diploma from MIT*' is a correct instance, even if the pattern that produced it is debatable (e.g. *v:<received> subj:PERSON, from:ORGANIZATION*). A correct instance can also produce a new known-to-be correct seed.

Pattern judgments are stored in the database and incorporated as absolute truth. Instance judgments provide useful input into pattern scoring. Patterns were selected for annotation using a score that combines their estimated f-measure; their frequency; and their dissimilarity to patterns that were previously chosen for annotation. The matched instances for each pattern are randomly sampled, to ensure that the resulting annotation can be used to derive an unbiased precision estimate.

Figure 8, Figure 9, and Figure 10 plot precision, recall, and F-score at iterations 5 and 20 for the system running in a fully unsupervised manner and one allowing human intervention.

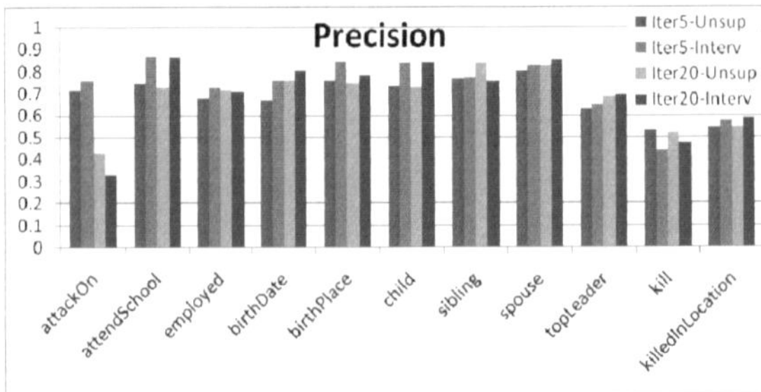

Figure 8: Precision at Iterations 5 and 20 for the Unsupervised System and the System with Intervention

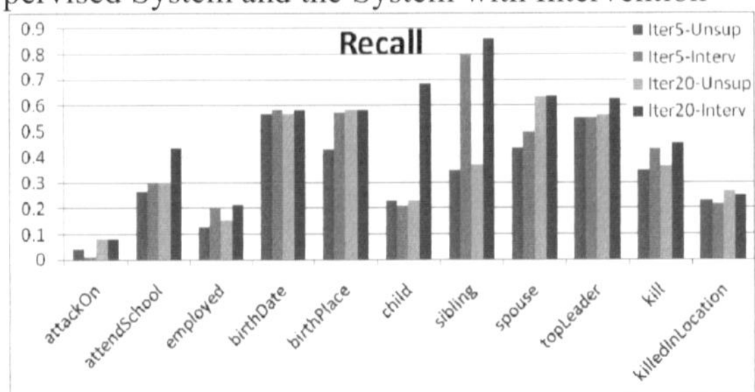

Figure 9: Recall at Iterations 5 and 20 for the Unsupervised System and the System with Intervention

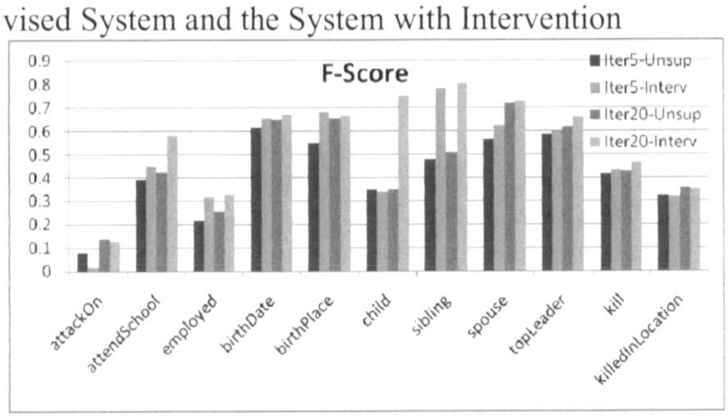

Figure 10: F-Score at Iterations 5 and 20 for the Unsupervised System and the System with Intervention

For two relations: *child* and *sibling,* recall improved dramatically with human intervention. By inspecting the patterns produced by the system, we see that in case of *sibling* without intervention, the system only learned the relation '*brother*' and not the relation '*sister.*' The limited feedback from a person was enough to allow the system to learn patterns for *sister* as well, causing the significantly improved recall. We see smaller, but frequently significant improvements in recall in a number of other relations. Interestingly, for different relations, the recall improvements are seen at different iterations. For *sibling,* the jump in recall appears within the first five iterations. Contrastingly, for *attendSchool*, there is a minor improvement in recall after iteration 5, but a much larger improvement after iteration 20. For *child,* there is actually a small decrease in recall after 5 iterations, but after 20 iterations, the system has dramatically improved.

The effect on precision is similarly varied. For 9 of the 11, human intervention improves precision; but the improvement is never as dramatic as the improvement in recall. For precision, the strongest improvements in performance appear in the early iterations. It is unclear whether this merely reflects that bootstrapping is likely to become less precise over time (as it learns more patterns), or if early feedback is truly better for improving precision.

In the case of *attackOn,* even with human intervention, after iteration 10, the system begins to learn very general patterns of the type described in the previous section (e.g. *<said in:LOCATION on:DATE>* as a pattern indicating an attack. These patterns may be correlated with experiencing an attack but are not themselves evidence of an attack. Because the overly general patterns do in fact correlate with the presence of an attack, the positive examples provided by human intervention may in fact produce more such patterns.

There is an interaction between improved precision and improved recall. If a system is very imprecise at iteration *n*, the additional instances that it proposes may not reflect the relation and be so different from each other that the system becomes unable to produce good patterns that improve recall. Conversely, if recall at iteration *n* does not produce a sufficiently diverse set of instances, it will be difficult for the system to generate instances that are used to estimate pattern precision.

8 Related Work

Much research has been done on concept and relation detection using large amounts of supervised training. This is the typical approach in programs like Automatic Content Extraction (ACE), which evaluates system performance in detecting a fixed set of concepts and relations in text. In ACE, all participating researchers are given access to a substantial amount of supervised training, e.g., 250k words of annotated data. Researchers have typically used this data to incorporate a great deal of structural syntactic information in their models (e.g. Ramshaw 2001), but the obvious weakness of these approaches is the resulting reliance on the manually annotated examples, which are expensive and time-consuming to create.

Co-training circumvents this weakness by playing off two sufficiently different views of a data set to leverage large quantities of unlabeled data (along with a few examples of labeled data), in order to improve the performance of a learning algorithm (Mitchell and Blum, 1998). Co-training will offer our approach to simultaneously learn the patterns of expressing a relation and its arguments.

Other researchers have also previously explored automatic pattern generation from unsupervised text, classically in (Riloff & Jones 1999). Ravichandran and Hovy (2002) reported experimental results for automatically generating surface patterns for relation identification; others have explored similar approaches (e.g. Agichtein & Gravano 2000 or Pantel & Pennacchiotti, 2006). More recently (Mitchell et al., 2009) has shown that for macro-reading, precision and recall can be improved by learning a large set of interconnected relations and concepts simultaneously.

We depart from this work by learning patterns that use the structural features of text-graph patterns and our particular approach to pattern and pair scoring and selection.

Most approaches to automatic pattern generation have focused on precision, e.g., Ravichandran and Hovy report results in the Text Retrieval Conference (TREC) Question Answering track, where extracting one instance of a relation can be sufficient, rather than detecting all instances. This study has also emphasized recall. Information about an entity may only be mentioned once, especially for rarely mentioned entities. A primary focus on precision allows one to ignore many instances that require co-reference or long-distance dependencies; one primary goal of our work is to measure system performance in exactly those areas.

9 Conclusion

We have shown that bootstrapping approaches can be successfully applied to micro-reading tasks. Most prior work with this approach has focused on macro-reading, and thus emphasized precision. Clearly, the task becomes much more challenging when the system must detect every instance. Despite the challenge, with very limited human intervention, we achieved F-scores of >.65 on 6 of the 11 relations (average F on the relation set was .58).

We have also replicated an earlier preliminary result (Boschee, 2008) showing that for a micro-reading task, patterns that utilize semantic/syntactic information outperform patterns that make use of only surface strings. Our result covers a larger inventory of relation types and attempts to provide a more precise measure of recall than the earlier preliminary study.

Analysis of our system's output provides insights into challenges that such a system may face.

One challenge for bootstrapping systems is that it is easy for the system to learn just a subset of relations. We observed this in both *sibling* where we learned the relation *brother* and for *employed* where we only learned patterns for leaders of an organization. For *sibling* human intervention allowed us to correct for this mistake. However for *employed* even with human intervention, our recall remains low. The difference between these two relations may be that for *sibling* there are only two sub-relations to learn, while there is a rich hierarchy of potential sub-relations under the general relation *employed.* The challenge is quite possibly exacerbated by the fact that the distribution of employment relations in the news is heavily biased towards top officials, but our recall test set intentionally does not reflect this skew.

Another challenge for this approach is continuing to learn in successive iterations. As we saw in the figures in Section 7, for many relations performance at iteration 20 is not significantly greater than performance at iteration 5. Note that seeing improvements on the long tail of ways to express a relation may require a larger recall set than the test set used here. This is exemplified by the existence of the highly precise 2-predicate patterns which in some cases never fired in our recall test set.

In future, we wish to address the subset problem and the problem of stalled improvements. Both could potentially be addressed by improved internal rescoring. For example, the system scoring could try to guarantee coverage over the whole seed-set thus promoting patterns with low recall, but high value for reflecting different information. A complementary set of improvements could explore improved uses of human intervention.

Acknowledgments

This work was supported, in part, by BBN under AFRL Contract FA8750-09-C-179.

References

E. Agichtein and L. Gravano. Snowball: extracting relations from large plain-text collections. In *Proceedings of the ACM Conference on Digital Libraries*, pp. 85-94, 2000.

A. Baron and M. Freedman, "Who is Who and What is What: Experiments in Cross Document Co-Reference". *Empirical Methods in Natural Language Processing.* 2008.

A. Blum and T. Mitchell. Combining Labeled and Unlabeled Data with Co-Training. In *Proceedings of the 1998 Conference on Computational Learning Theory*, July 1998.

E. Boschee, V. Punyakanok, R. Weischedel. An Exploratory Study Towards 'Machines that Learn to Read'. *Proceedings of AAAI BICA Fall Symposium,* November 2008.

M. Collins and Y Singer. Unsupervised Models for Named Entity Classification. EMNLP/VLC. (1999).

M Mintz, S Bills, R Snow, and D Jurafsky.. Distant supervision for relation extraction without labeled data. Proceedings of ACL-IJCNLP 200. 2009..

T. Mitchell, J. Betteridge, A. Carlson, E. Hruschka, and R. Wang. "Populating the Semantic Web by Macro-Reading Internet Text. Invited paper, *Proceedings of the 8th International Semantic Web Conference (ISWC 2009).*

P. Pantel and M. Pennacchiotti. Espresso: Leveraging Generic Patterns for Automatically Harvesting Semantic Relations. In *Proceedings of Conference on Computational Linguistics / Association for Computational Linguistics (COLING/ACL-06).* pp. 113-120. Sydney, Australia, 2006.

L. Ramshaw , E. Boschee, S. Bratus, S. Miller, R. Stone, R. Weischedel, A. Zamanian, "Experiments in multi-modal automatic content extraction", Proceedings of Human Technology Conference, March 2001.

D. Ravichandran and E. Hovy. Learning surface text patterns for a question answering system. In *Proceedings of the 40th Annual Meeting of the Association for Computational Linguistics (ACL 2002),* pages 41–47, Philadelphia, PA, 2002.

E. Riloff. Automatically generating extraction patterns from untagged text. In *Proceedings of the Thirteenth National Conference on Artificial Intelligence*, pages 1044-1049, 1996.

E. Rilof and Jones, R "Learning Dictionaries for Information Extraction by Multi-Level Bootstrapping", Proceedings of the Sixteenth National Conference on Artificial Intelligence (AAAI-99) , 1999, pp. 474-479. 1999.

R Snow, D Jurafsky, and A Y. Ng.. Learning syntactic patterns for automatic hypernym discovery . Proceedings of NIPS 17. 2005.

Towards Learning Rules from Natural Texts*

Janardhan Rao Doppa, Mohammad NasrEsfahani, Mohammad S. Sorower
Thomas G. Dietterich, Xiaoli Fern, and **Prasad Tadepalli**
School of EECS, Oregon State University
Corvallis, OR 97330, USA
{doppa,nasresfm,sorower,tgd,xfern,tadepall}@cs.orst.edu

Abstract

In this paper, we consider the problem of inductively learning rules from specific facts extracted from texts. This problem is challenging due to two reasons. First, natural texts are *radically incomplete* since there are always too many facts to mention. Second, natural texts are *systematically biased* towards novelty and surprise, which presents an unrepresentative sample to the learner. Our solutions to these two problems are based on building a generative observation model of what is mentioned and what is extracted given what is true. We first present a *Multiple-predicate Bootstrapping* approach that consists of iteratively learning if-then rules based on an implicit observation model and then imputing new facts implied by the learned rules. Second, we present an iterative *ensemble co-learning* approach, where multiple decision-trees are learned from bootstrap samples of the incomplete training data, and facts are imputed based on weighted majority.

1 Introduction

One of the principal goals of learning by reading is to make the vast amount of natural language text which is on the web accessible to automatic processing. There are at least three different ways in which this can be done. First, factual knowledge on the web can be extracted as formal relations or tuples of a data base. A number of information extraction systems, starting from the WebKb project (Craven et al., 2000), to Whirl (Cohen, 2000) to the TextRunner (Etzioni et al., 2008) project are of this kind. They typically learn patterns or rules that can be applied to text to extract instances of relations. A second possibility is to learn general knowledge, rules, or general processes and procedures by reading natural language descriptions of them, for example, extracting formal descriptions of the rules of the United States Senate or a recipe to make a dessert. A third instance of machine reading is to generalize the facts extracted from the text to learn more general knowledge. For example, one might learn by generalizing from reading the obituaries that most people live less than 90 years, or people tend to live and die in the countries they were born in. In this paper, we consider the problem of learning such general rules by reading about specific facts.

At first blush, learning rules by reading specific facts appears to be a composition of information extraction followed by rule induction. In the above example of learning from obituaries, there is reason to believe that this reductionist approach would work well. However, there are two principal reasons why this approach of learning directly from natural texts is problematic. One is that, unlike databases, the natural texts are *radically incomplete*. By this we mean that many of the facts that are relevant to predicting the target relation might be missing in the text. This

* This material is based upon work supported by the Defense Advanced Research Projects Agency (DARPA) under Contract No. FA8750-09-C-0179. Any opinions, findings and conclusions or recommendations expressed in this material are those of the author(s) and do not necessarily reflect the views of the DARPA, or the Air Force Research Laboratory (AFRL). We thank the reviewers for their insightful comments and helpful suggestions.

Proceedings of the NAACL HLT 2010 First International Workshop on Formalisms and Methodology for Learning by Reading, pages 70–77, Los Angeles, California, June 2010.

is so because in most cases the set of relevant facts is open ended.

The second problem, in some ways more worrisome, is that the natural language texts are *systematically biased* towards newsworthiness, which correlates with infrequency or novelty. This is sometimes called "the man bites a dog phenomenon."[1] Unfortunately the novelty bias violates the most common assumption of machine learning that the training data is representative of the underlying truth, or equivalently, that any missing information is missing at random. In particular, since natural langauge texts are written for people who already possess a vast amount of prior knowledge, communication efficiency demands that facts that can be easily inferred by most people are left out of the text.

To empirically validate our two hypotheses of radical incompleteness and systematic bias of natural texts, we have examined a collection of 248 documents related to the topics of people, organizations, and relationships collected by the Linguistic Data Consortium (LDC). We chose the target relationship of the birth place of a person. It turned out that the birth place of some person is only mentioned 23 times in the 248 documents, illustrating the radical incompleteness of texts mentioned earlier. Moreover, in 14 out of the 23 mentions of the birth place, the information violates some default inferences. For example, one of the sentences reads:

"Ahmed Said Khadr, an Egyptian-born Canadian, was killed last October in Pakistan."

Presumably the phrase "Egyptian-born" was considered important by the reporter because it violates our expectation that most Canadians are born in Canada. If Khadr was instead born in Canada, the reporter would mostly likely have left out "Canadian-born" because it is too obvious to mention given he is a Canadian. In all the 9 cases where the birth place does not violate the default assumptions, the story is biographical, e.g., an obituary.

In general, only a small part of the whole truth is ever mentioned in a given document. Thus, the reporter has to make some choices as to what to mention and what to leave out. The key insight of this paper is that considering how these choices are made is important in making correct statistical inferences. In the above example, wrong probabilities would be derived if one assumes that the birth place information is missing at random.

In this paper we introduce the notion of a "mention model," which models the generative process of what is mentioned in a document. We also extend this using an "extraction model," which represents the errors in the process of extracting facts from the text documents. The mention model and the extraction model together represent the probability that some facts are extracted given the true facts.

For learning, we could use an explicit mention model to score hypothesized rules by calculating the probability that a rule is satisfied by the observed evidence and then pick the rules that are most likely given the evidence. In this paper, we take the simpler approach of directly adapting the learning algorithms to an *implicit* mention model, by changing the way a rule is scored by the available evidence.

Since each text document involves multiple predicates with relationships between them, we learn rules to predict each predicate from the other predicates. Thus, the goal of the system is to learn a sufficiently large set of rules to infer all the missing information as accurately as possible. To effectively bootstrap the learning process, the learned rules are used on the incomplete training data to impute new facts, which are then used to induce more rules in subsequent iterations. This approach is most similar to the coupled semi-supervised learning of (Carlson et al., 2010) and general bootstrapping approaches in natural language processing (Yarowsky, 1995). Since this is in the context of multiple-predicate learning in inductive logic programming (ILP) (DeRaedt and Lavraøc, 1996), we call this approach "Multiple-predicate Bootstrapping."

One problem with Multiple-predicate Bootstrapping is potentially large variance. To mitigae this, we consider the bagging approach, where multiple rule sets are learned from bootstrap samples of the training data with an implicit mention model to score the rules. We then use these sets of rules as an ensemble to impute new facts, and repeat the process.

We evaluate both of these approaches on real world data processed through synthetic observation models. Our results indicate that when the assump-

[1]"When a dog bites a man, that is not news, because it happens so often. But if a man bites a dog, that is news," attributed to John Bogart of New York Sun among others.

tions of the learner suit the observation model, the learner's performance is quite good. Further, we show that the ensemble approach significantly improves the performance of Multiple-predicate Bootstrapping.

2 Probabilistic Observation Model

In this section, we will introduce a notional probabilistic observation model that captures what facts are extracted by the programs from the text given the true facts about the world and the common sense rules of the domain of discourse.

The observation model is composed of the *mention model* and the *extraction model*. The mention model $P(MentDB|TrueDB, Rules)$ models the probability distribution of mentioned facts, $MentDB$, given the set of true facts $TrueDB$ and the rules of the domain, $Rules$. For example, if a fact is always true, then the novelty bias dictates that it is *not* mentioned with a high probability. The same is true of any fact entailed by a generally valid rule that is common knowledge. For example, this model predicts that since it is common knowledge that Canadians are born in Canada, the birth place is not mentioned if a person is a Canadian and was born in Canada.

The extraction model $P(ExtrDB|MentDB)$ models the probability distribution of extracted facts, given the set of mentioned facts $MentDB$. For example, it might model that explicit facts are extracted with high probability and that the extracted facts are corrupted by coreference errors. Note that the extraction process operates only on the mentioned part of the database $MentDB$; it has no independent access to the $TrueDB$ or the $Rules$. In other words, the mentioned database $MentDB$ d-separates the extracted database $ExtrDB$ from the true database $TrueDB$ and the $Rules$, and the conditional probability decomposes.

We could also model multiple documents generated about the same set of facts $TrueDB$, and multiple databases independently extracted from the same document by different extraction systems. Given an explicit observation model, the learner can use it to consider different rule sets and evaluate their likelihood given some data. The posterior probability of a rule set given an extracted database can be obtained by marginalizing over possible true and mentioned databases. Thus, in principle, the maximum likelihood approach to rule learning could work by considering each set of rules and evaluating its posterior given the extracted database, and picking the best set. While conceptually straightforward, this approach is highly intractable due to the need to marginalize over all possible mentioned and true databases. Moreover, it seems unnecessary to force a choice between sets of rules, since different rule sets do not always conflict. In the next section, we describe a simpler approach of adapting the learning algorithms directly to score and learn rules using an *implicit* mention model.

3 Multiple-predicate Bootstrapping with an Implicit Mention Model

Our first approach, called "Multiple-predicate Bootstrapping," is inspired by several pieces of work including co-training (Blum and Mitchell, 1998), multitask learning (Caruana, 1997), coupled semi-supervised learning (Carlson et al., 2010) and self-training (Yarowsky, 1995). It is based on learning a set of rules for all the predicates in the domain given the others and using them to infer (impute) the missing facts in the training data. This is repeated for several iterations until no more facts can be inferred. The support of a rule is measured by the number of records which satisfy the body of the rule, where each record roughly corresponds to a collection of related facts that can be independently generated, e.g., information about a single football game or a single news item. The higher the support, the more statistical evidence we have for judging its predictive accuracy. To use a rule to impute facts, it needs to be "promoted," which means it should pass a certain *threshold support* level. We measure the precision of a rule as the ratio of the number of records that non-trivially satisfy the rule to the number that satisfy its body, which is a proxy for the conditional probability of the head given the body. A rule is non-trivially satisfied by a record if the rule evaluates to true on that record for all possible instantiations of its variables, and there is at least one instantiation that satisfies its body. Given multiple promoted rules which apply to a given instance, we pick the rule with the highest precision to impute its value.

3.1 Implicit Mention Models

We adapt the multiple-predicate bootstrapping approach to the case of incomplete data by adjusting the scoring function of the learning algorithm to respect the assumed mention model. Unlike in the maximum likelihood approach discussed in the previous section, there is no explicit mention model used by the learner. Instead the scoring function is optimized for a presumed *implicit* mention model. We now discuss three specific mention models and the corresponding scoring functions.

Positive Mention Model: In the "positive mention model," it is assumed that any missing fact is false. This justifies counting evidence using the negation by failure assumption of Prolog. We call this scoring method "conservative." For example, the text "Khadr, a Canadian citizen, was killed in Pakistan" is counted as not supporting the rule `citizen(X,Y)` ⇒ `bornIn(X,Y)`, as we are not told that `bornIn(Khadr,Canada)`. Positive mention model is inapplicable for most instances of learning from natural texts, except for special cases such as directory web pages.

Novelty Mention Model: In the "novelty mention model," it is assumed that facts are missing only when they are entailed by other mentioned facts and rules that are common knowledge. This suggests an "aggressive" or optimistic scoring of candidate rules, which interprets a missing fact so that it supports the candidate rule. More precisely, a rule is counted as non-trivially satisfied by a record if there is some way of imputing the missing facts in the record without causing contradiction. For example, the text "Khadr, a Canadian citizen was killed in Pakistan" is counted as non-trivially supporting the rule `citizen(X,Y)` ⇒ `bornIn(X,Y)` because, adding `bornIn(Khadr, Canada)` supports the rule without contradicting the available evidence. On the other hand, the above text does not support the rule `killedIn(X,Y)` ⇒ `citizen(X,Y)` because the rule contradicts the evidence, assuming that `citizen` is a functional relationship.

Random Mention Model: In the "random mention model," it is assumed that facts are missing at random. Since the random facts can be true or false, this mention model suggests counting the evidence fractionally in proportion to its predicted prevalence. Following the previous work on learning from missing data, we call this scoring method "distributional" (Saar-Tsechansky and Provost, 2007). In distributional scoring, we typically learn a distribution over the values of a literal given its argument and use it to assign a fractional count to the evidence. This is the approach taken to account for missing data in Quinlan's decision tree algorithm (Quinlan, 1986). We will use this as part of our Ensemble Co-Learning approach of the next section.

3.2 Experimental Results

We evaluated Multiple-predicate Bootstrapping with implicit mention models on the schema-based NFL database retrieved from `www.databasefootball.com`. We developed two different synthetic observation models. The observation models are based on the Novelty mention model and the Random mention model and assume perfect extraction in each case. The following predicates are manually provided:

- `gameWinner (Game, Team)`,
- `gameLoser(Game, Team)`,
- `homeTeam(Game, Team)`,
- `awayTeam(Game, Team)`, and
- `teamInGame(Team, Game)`,

with the natural interpretations. To simplify arithmetic reasoning we replaced the numeric team scores in the real database with two defined predicates `teamSmallerScore(Team, Game)` and `teamGreaterScore(Team, Game)` to indicate the teams with the smaller and the greater scores.

We generate two sets of synthetic data as follows. In the Random mention model, each predicate except the `teamInGame` predicate is omitted independently with probability p. The Novelty mention model, on the other hand, relies on the fact that `gameWinner`, `gameLoser`, and `teamFinalScore` are mutually correlated, as are `homeTeam` and `awayTeam`. Thus, it picks one predicate

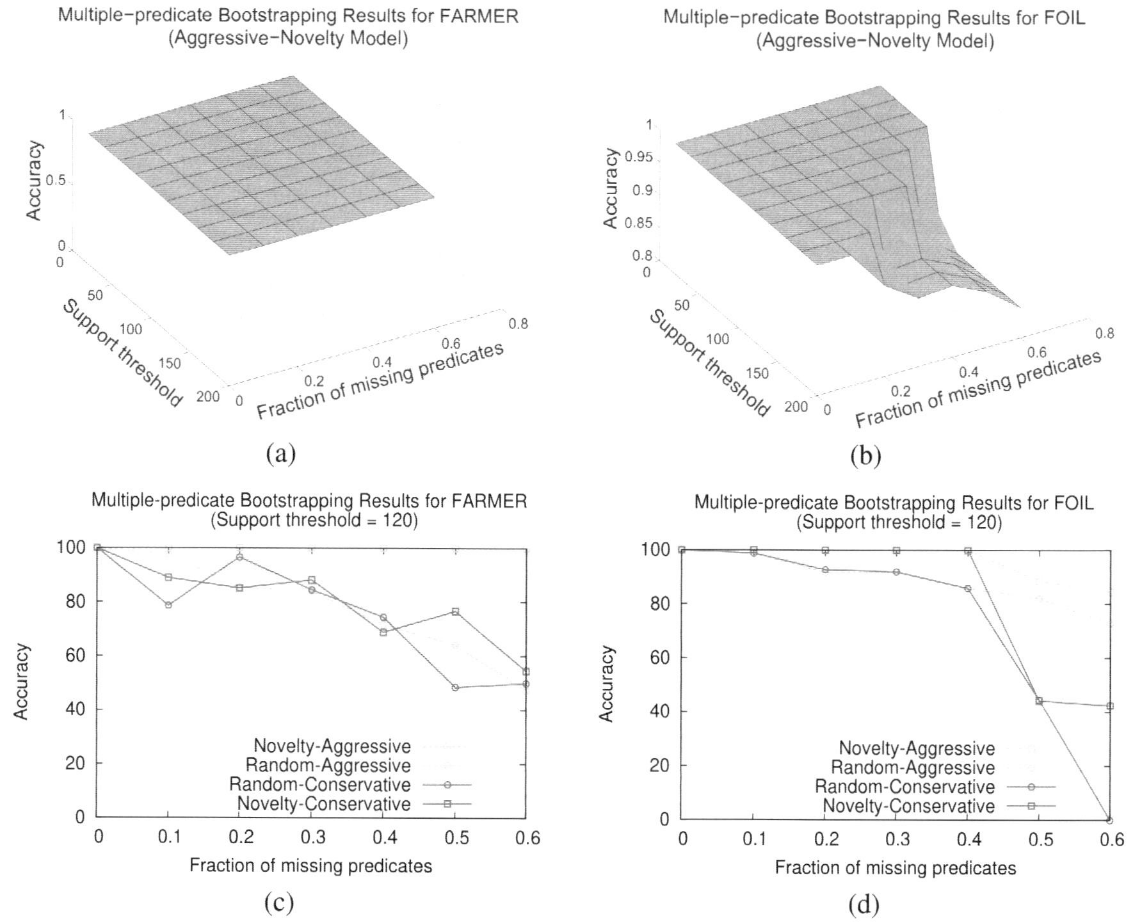

Figure 1: Multiple-predicate bootstrapping Results for (a) FARMER using aggressive-novelty model (b) FOIL using aggressive-novelty model (c) FARMER with support threshold 120 (d) FOIL with support threshold 120

from the first group to mention its values, and omitseach of the other predicates independently with some probability q. Similarly it gives a value to one of the two predicates in the second group and omits the other predicate with probability q. One consequence of this model is that it always has one of the predicates in the first group and one of the predicates in the second group, which is sufficient to infer everything if one knew the correct domain rules. We evaluate two scoring methods: the aggressive scoring and the conservative scoring.

We employed two learning systems: Quinlan's FOIL, which learns relational rules using a greedy covering algorithm (Quinlan, 1990; Cameron-Jones and Quinlan, 1994), and Nijssen and Kok's FARMER, which is a relational data mining algorithm that searches for conjunctions of literals of large support using a bottom-up depth first search (Nijssen and Kok, 2003). Both systems were applied to learn rules for all target predicates. One important difference to note here is that while FARMER seeks all rules that exceed the necessary support threshold, FOIL only learns rules that are sufficient to classify all training instances into those that satisfy the target predicate and those that do not. Secondly, FOIL tries to learn maximally deterministic rules, while FARMER is parameterized by the minimum precision of a rule. We have not modified the way they interpret missing features during learning. However, after the learning is complete, the rules learned by both approaches are scored by interpreting the missing data either aggressively or conservatively as described in the previous section.

We ran both systems on synthetic data generated using different parameters that control the fraction of missing data and the minimum support threshold needed for promotion. In Figures 1(a) and 1(b), the X and Y-axes show the fraction of missing predicates and the support threshold for the novelty mention model and aggressive scoring of rules for FOIL and FARMER. On the Z-axis is the accuracy of predictions on the missing data, which is the fraction of the total number of initially missing entries that are correctly imputed. We can see that aggressive scoring of rules with the novelty mention model performs very well even for large numbers of missing values for both FARMER and FOIL. FARMER's performance is more robust than FOIL's because FARMER learns all correct rules and uses whichever rule fires. For example, in the NFL domain, it could infer `gameWinner` from `gameLoser` or `teamSmallerScore` or `teamGreaterScore`. In contrast, FOIL's covering strategy prevents it from learning more than one rule if it finds one perfect rule. The results show that FOIL's performance degrades at larger fractions of missing data and large support thresholds.

Figures 1(c) and 1(d) show the accuracy of prediction vs. percentage of missing predicates for each of the mention models and the scoring methods for FARMER and FOIL for a support threshold of 120. They show that agressive scoring clearly outperforms conservative scoring for data generated using the novelty mention model. In FOIL, aggressive scoring also seems to outperform conservative scoring on the dataset generated by the random mention model at high levels of missing data. In FARMER, the two methods perform similarly. However, these results should be interpreted cautiously as they are derived from a single dataset which enjoys deterministic rules. We are working towards a more robust evaluation in multiple domains as well as data extracted from natural texts.

4 Ensemble Co-learning with an Implicit Mention Model

One weakness of Multiple-predicate Bootstrapping is its high variance especially when significant amounts of training data are missing. Aggressive evaluation of rules in this case would amplify the contradictory conclusions of different rules. Thus, picking only one rule among the many possible rules could lead to dangerously large variance.

One way to guard against the variance problem is to use an ensemble approach. In this section we test the hypothesis that an ensemble approach would be more robust and exhibit less variance in the context of learning from incomplete examples with an implicit mention model. For the experiments in this section, we employ a decision tree learner that uses a distributional scoring scheme to handle missing data as described in (Quinlan, 1986).

While classifying an instance, when a missing value is encountered, the instance is split into multiple pseudo-instances each with a different value for the missing feature and a weight corresponding to the estimated probability for the particular missing value (based on the frequency of values at this split in the training data). Each pseudo-instance is passed down the tree according to its assigned value. After reaching a leaf node, the frequency of the class in the training instances associated with this leaf is returned as the class-membership probability of the pseudo-instance. The overall estimated probability of class membership is calculated as the weighted average of class membership probabilities over all pseudo-instances. If there is more than one missing value, the process recurses with the weights combining multiplicatively. The process is similar at the training time, except that the information gain at the internal nodes and the class probabilities at the leaves are calculated based on the weights of the relevant pseudo-instances.

We use the *confidence level* for pruning a decision tree as a proxy for support of a rule in this case. By setting this parameter to different values, we can obtain different degrees of pruning.

Experimental Results: We use the Congressional Voting Records[2] database for our experiments. The (non-text) database includes the party affiliation and votes on 16 measures for each member of the U.S House Representatives. Although this database (just like the NFL database) is complete, we generate two different synthetic versions of it to simulate the extracted facts from typical news stories on this topic. We use all the instances including those with unknown values for training, but do not count the errors on these unknown values. We ex-

[2]http://archive.ics.uci.edu/ml/datasets/Congressional+Voting+Records

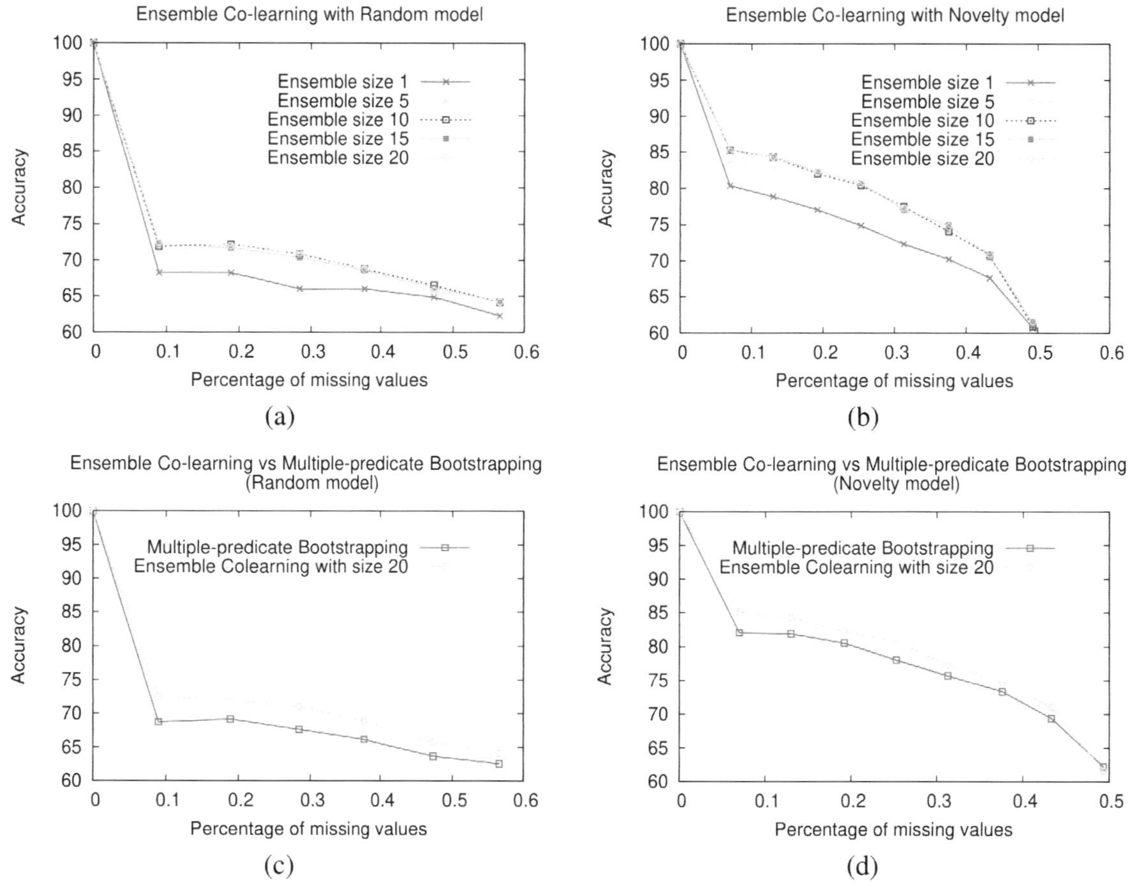

Figure 2: Results for (a) Ensemble co-learning with Random mention model (b) Ensemble co-learning with Novelty mention model (c) Ensemble co-learning vs Multiple-predicate Bootstrapping with Random mention model (d) Ensemble co-learning vs Multiple-predicate Bootstrapping with Novelty mention model

periment with two different implicit mention models: Random and Novelty. These are similar to those we defined in the previous section. In the Random mention model, each feature in the dataset is omitted independently with a probability p. Since we don't know the truely predictive rules here unlike in the football domain, we learn the novelty model from the complete dataset. Using the complete dataset which has n features, we learn a decision tree to predict each feature from all the remaining features. We use these n decision trees to define our novelty mention model in the following way. For each instance in the complete dataset, we randomly pick a feature and see if it can be predicted from all the remaining features using the predictive model. If it can be predicted, then we will omit it with probability p and mention it otherwise. We use different bootstrap samples to learn the ensemble of trees and impute the values using a majority vote. Note that, the decision tree cannot always classify an instance successfully. Therefore, we will impute the values only if the count of majority vote is greater than some minimum threshold (margin). In our experiments, we use a margin value equal to half of the ensemble size and a fixed support of 0.3 (i.e., the confidence level for pruning) while learning the decision trees. We employ J48, the WEKA version of Quinlan's C4.5 algorithm to learn our decision trees. We compute the accuracy of predictions on the missing data, which is the fraction of the total number of initially missing entries that are imputed correctly. We report the average results of 20 independent runs.

We test the hypothesis that the Ensemble Co-learning is more robust and exhibit less variance in the context of learning from incomplete examples when compared to Multiple-predicate Bootstrapping. In Figures 2(a)-(d), the X and Y-axes show the percentage of missing values and the prediction accuracy. Figures 2(a) and (b) shows the behavior with different ensemble sizes (1, 5, 10, 15 and 20) for both Random and Novelty mention model. We can see that the performance improves as the ensemble size grows for both random and novelty models. Figures 2(c) and (d) compares Multiple-predicate Bootstrapping with the best results over the different ensemble sizes. We can see that Ensemble Co-learning outperforms Multiple-predicate Bootstrapping.

5 Discussion

Learning general rules by reading natural language texts faces the challenges of radical incompleteness and systematic bias. Statistically, our notion of incompleteness corresponds to the Missing Not At Random (MNAR) case, where the probability of an entry being missed may depend on its value or the values of other observed variables (Rubin, 1976).

One of the key insights of statisticians is to build an explicit probabilistic model of missingness, which is captured by our mention model and extraction model. This missingness model might then be used in an Expectation Maximization (EM) approach (Schafer and Graham, 2002), where alternately, the missing values are imputed by their expected values according to the missingness model and the model parameters are estimated using the maximum likelihood approach. Our "Multiple-predicate Bootstrapping" is loosely analogous to this approach, except that the imputation of missing values is done implicitly while scoring the rules, and the maximum likelihood parameter learning is replaced with the learning of relational if-then rules.

In the Multiple Imputation (MI) framework of (Rubin, 1987; Schafer and Graham, 2002), the goal is to reduce the variance due to single imputation by combining the results of multiple imputations. This is analogous to Ensemble Co-learning, where we learn multiple hypotheses from different bootstrap samples of the training data and impute values using the weighted majority algorithm over the ensemble. We have shown that the ensemble approach improves performance.

References

Avrim Blum and Tom Mitchell. 1998. Combining labeled and unlabeled data with co-training. In *Proceedings of COLT*, pages 92–100. Morgan Kaufmann Publishers.

R. M. Cameron-Jones and J. R. Quinlan. 1994. Efficient top-down induction of logic programs. In *ACM SIGART Bulletin*.

Andrew Carlson, Justin Betteridge, Richard C. Wang, Estevam R. Hruschka Jr., and Tom M. Mitchell. 2010. Coupled semi-supervised learning for information extraction. In *Proceedings of the Third ACM International Conference on Web Search and Data Mining (WSDM 2010)*.

R. Caruana. 1997. Multitask learning: A knowledge-based source of inductive bias. *Machine Learning*, 28:41–75.

William W. Cohen. 2000. WHIRL: a word-based information representation language. *Artif. Intell.*, 118(1-2):163–196.

Mark Craven, Dan DiPasquo, Dayne Freitag, Andrew McCallum, Tom M. Mitchell, Kamal Nigam, and Seán Slattery. 2000. Learning to construct knowledge bases from the world wide web. *Artif. Intell.*, 118(1-2):69–113.

Luc DeRaedt and Nada Lavraøc. 1996. Multiple predicate learning in two inductive logic programming settings. *Logic Journal of the IGPL*, 4(2):227–254.

Oren Etzioni, Michele Banko, Stephen Soderland, and Daniel S. Weld. 2008. Open information extraction from the web. *Commun. ACM*, 51(12):68–74.

Siegfried Nijssen and Joost N. Kok. 2003. Efficient frequent query discovery in FARMER. In *PKDD*, pages 350–362.

Ross Quinlan. 1986. Induction of decision trees. *Machine Learning*, 1(1):81–106.

Ross Quinlan. 1990. Learning logical definitions from relations. *Machine Learning*, 5:239–266.

D. B. Rubin. 1976. Inference and missing data. *Biometrika*, 63(3):581.

D. B. Rubin. 1987. *Multiple Imputation for non-response in surveys*. Wiley New York.

Maytal Saar-Tsechansky and Foster Provost. 2007. Handling missing values when applying classification models. *Journal of Machine Learning Research*, 8:1625–1657.

J. L. Schafer and J. W. Graham. 2002. Missing data: Our view of the state of the art. *Psychological methods*, 7(2):147–177.

D. Yarowsky. 1995. Unsupervised word sense disambiguation rivaling supervised methods. In *Proceedings of ACL*.

Unsupervised techniques for discovering ontology elements from Wikipedia article links

Zareen Syed
University of Maryland, Baltimore County
1000 Hilltop Circle
Baltimore, MD 21250, USA
zarsyed1@umbc.edu

Tim Finin
University of Maryland, Baltimore County
1000 Hilltop Circle
Baltimore, MD 21250, USA
finin@umbc.edu

Abstract

We present an unsupervised and unrestricted approach to discovering an infobox like ontology by exploiting the inter-article links within Wikipedia. It discovers new slots and fillers that may not be available in the Wikipedia infoboxes. Our results demonstrate that there are certain types of properties that are evident in the link structure of resources like Wikipedia that can be predicted with high accuracy using little or no linguistic analysis. The discovered properties can be further used to discover a class hierarchy. Our experiments have focused on analyzing people in Wikipedia, but the techniques can be directly applied to other types of entities in text resources that are rich with hyperlinks.

1 Introduction

One of the biggest challenges faced by the Semantic Web vision is the availability of structured data that can be published as RDF. One approach is to develop techniques to translate information in spreadsheets, databases, XML documents and other traditional data formats into RDF (Syed et al. 2010). Another is to refine the technology needed to extract structured information from unstructured free text (McNamee and Dang, 2009).

For both approaches, there is a second problem that must be addressed: do we start with an ontology or small catalog of ontologies that will be used to encode the data or is extracting the right ontology part of the problem. We describe exploratory work on a system that can discover ontological elements as well as data from a free text with embedded hyperlinks.

Wikipedia is a remarkable and rich online encyclopedia with a wealth of general knowledge about varied concepts, entities, events and facts in the world. Its size and coverage make it a valuable resource for extracting information about different entities and concepts. Wikipedia contains both free text and structured information related to concepts in the form of infoboxes, category hierarchy and inter-article links. Infoboxes are the most structured form and are composed of a set of subject-attribute-value triples that summarize or highlight the key features of the concept or subject of the article. Resources like DBpedia (Auer et al., 2007) and Freebase (Bollacker et al., 2007) have harvested this structured data and have made it available as triples for semantic querying.

While infoboxes are a readily available source of structured data, the free text of the article contains much more information about the entity. Barker et al. (2007) unified the state of the art approaches in natural language processing and knowledge representation in their prototype system for understanding free text. Text resources which are rich in hyperlinks especially to knowledge based resources (such as encyclopedias or dictionaries) have additional information encoded in the form of links, which can be used to complement the existing systems for text understanding and knowledge discovery. Furthermore, systems such as Wikify (Mihalcea and Csomai, 2007) can be employed to link words in free text to knowledge resources like Wikipedia and thus enrich the free text with hyperlinks.

We describe an approach for unsupervised ontology discovery from links in the free text of the Wikipedia articles, without specifying a relation or set of relations in advance. We first identify candidate slots and fillers for an entity, then classify en-

Proceedings of the NAACL HLT 2010 First International Workshop on Formalisms and Methodology for Learning by Reading, pages 78–86,
Los Angeles, California, June 2010.

tities and finally derive a class hierarchy. We have evaluated our approach for the *Person* class, but it can be easily generalized to other entity types such as organizations, places, and products.

The techniques we describe are not suggested as alternatives to natural language understanding or information extraction, but as a source for additional evidence that can be used to extract ontological elements and relations from the kind of text found in Wikipedia and other heavily-linked text collections. This approach might be particularly useful in "slot fillings" tasks like the one in the Knowledge Base Population track (McNamee and Dang, 2010) at the 2009 Text Analysis Conference. We see several contributions that this work has to offer:

- Unsupervised and unrestricted ontology discovery. We describe an automatic approach that does not require a predefined list of relations or training data. The analysis uses inter-article links in the text and does not depend on existing infoboxes, enabling it to suggest slots and fillers that do not exist in any extant infoboxes.
- Meaningful slot labels. We use WordNet (Miller et al., 1990) nodes to represent and label slots enabling us to exploit WordNet's hypernym and hyponym relations as a property hierarchy.
- Entity classification and class labeling. We introduce a new feature set for entity classification, i.e. the discovered ranked slots, which performs better than other feature sets extracted from Wikipedia. We also present an approach for assigning meaningful class label vectors using WordNet nodes.
- Deriving a class hierarchy. We have developed an approach for deriving a class hierarchy based on the ranked slot similarity between classes and the label vectors.

In the remainder of the paper we describe the details of the approach, mention closely related work, present and discuss preliminary results and provide some conclusions and possible next steps.

2 Approach

Figure 1 shows our ontology discovery framework and its major steps. We describe each step in the rest of this section.

2.1 Discovering Candidate Slots and Fillers

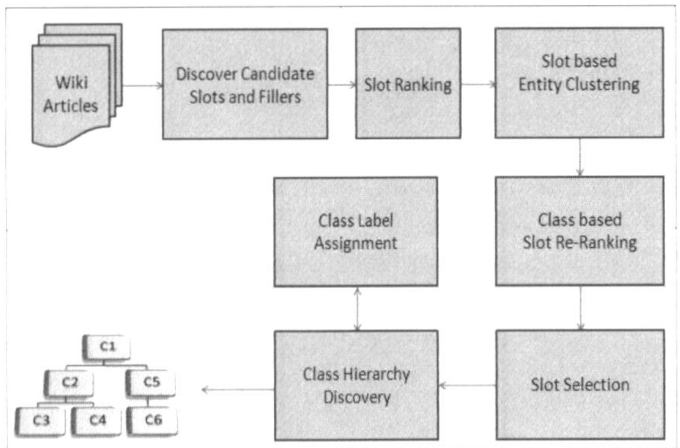

Figure 1: The ontology discovery framework comprises a number of steps, including candidate slot and filler discovery followed by slot ranking, slot selection, entity classification, slot re-ranking, class labeling, and class hierarchy discovery.

Most Wikipedia articles represent a concept, i.e., a generic class of objects (e.g., Musician), an individual object (e.g., Michael_Jackson), or a generic relation or property (e.g., age). Inter-article links within Wikipedia represent relations between concepts. In our approach we consider the linked concepts as candidate fillers for slots related to the primary article/concept. There are several cases where the filler is subsumed by the slot label for example, the infobox present in the article on "Michael_Jackson" (Figure 2) mentions *pop, rock* and *soul* as fillers for the slot *Genre* and all three of these are a type of *Genre*. The *Labels* slot contains fillers such as *Motown, Epic* and *Legacy* which are all Record Label Companies. Based on this observation, we discover and exploit "isa" relations between fillers (linked concepts) and WordNet nodes to serve as candidate slot labels.

In order to find an "isa" relation between a concept and a WordNet synset we use manually created mappings by DBpedia, which links about 467,000 articles to synsets. However, Wikipedia has more than two million articles[1], therefore, to map any remaining concepts we use the automatically generated mappings available between WordNet synsets and Wikipedia categories (Ponzetto and Navigli, 2009). A single Wikipedia article might have multiple categories associated with it and therefore multiple WordNet synsets. Wikipedia's category system serves more as a way to tag articles and facilitate navigation rather than

[1] This estimate is for the English version and does not include redirects and administrative pages such as disambiguation pages.

Figure 2. The Wikipedia infobox for the Michael_Jackson article has a number of slots from appropriate infobox templates.

to categorize them. The article on Michael Jordan, for example, has 36 categories associated with it. In order to select an individual WordNet synset as a label for the concept's type, we use two heuristics:

- **Category label extraction.** Since the first sentence in Wikipedia articles usually defines the concept, we extract a category label from the first sentence using patterns based on POS tags similar to Kazama and Torisawa (2007).
- **Assign matching WordNet synset.** We consider all the WordNet synsets associated with the categories of the article using the category to WordNet mapping (Ponzetto and Navigli, 2009) and assign the WordNet synset if any of the words in the synset matches with the extracted category label. We repeat the process with hypernyms and hyponyms of the synset up to three levels.

2.2 Slot Ranking

All slots discovered using outgoing links might not be meaningful, therefore we have developed techniques for ranking and selecting slots. Our approach is based on the observation that entities of the same type have common slots. For example, there is a set of slots common for *musical artists* whereas, a different set is common for *basketball players*. The Wikipedia infobox templates based on classes also provide a set of properties or slots to use for particular types of entities or concepts.

In case of people, it is common to note that there is a set of slots that are *generalized*, i.e., they are common across all types of persons. Examples are *name, born,* and *spouse*. There are also sets of *specialized* slots, which are generally associated with a given profession. For example, the slots for basketball players have information for basketball related activities and musical artists have slots with music related activities. The slots for "Michael_Jordan" include *Professional Team(s), NBA Draft, Position(s)* and slots for "Michael_Jackson" include *Genres, Instruments* and *Labels*.

Another observation is that people engaged in a particular profession tend to be linked to others within the same profession. Hence the maxim "A man is known by the company he keeps." For example, basketball players are linked to other basketball players and politicians are linked to other politicians. We rank the slots based on the number of linked persons having the same slots. We generated a list of person articles in Wikipedia by getting all Wikipedia articles under the *Person* type in Freebase[2]. We randomly select up to 25 linked persons (which also link back) and extract their candidate slots and vote for a slot based on the number of times it appears as a slot in a linked person normalized by the number of linked persons to assign a slot score.

2.3 Entity Classification and Slot Re-Ranking

The ranked candidate slots are used to classify entities and then further ranked based on number of times they appear among the entities in the cluster. We use complete link clustering using a simple slot similarity function:

$$sim_{slot}(p_i, p_j) = \cos(slot(p_i), slot(p_j))$$

This similarity metric for slots is computed as the cosine similarity between tf.idf weighted slot vectors, where the slot score represents the term fre-

[2] We found that the Freebase classification for Person was more extensive that DBpedia's in the datasets available to us in early 2009.

quency component and the inverse document frequency is based on the number of times the slot appears in different individuals.

We also collapsed location expressing slots (*country, county, state, district, island* etc.) into the slot labeled *location* by generating a list of location words from WordNet as these slots were causing the persons related to same type of geographical location to cluster together.

After clustering, we re-score the slots based on number of times they appear among the individuals in the cluster normalized by the cluster size. The output of clustering is a vector of scored slots associated with each cluster.

2.4 Slot Selection

The slot selection process identifies and filters out slots judged to be irrelevant. Our intuition is that *specialized* slots or attributes for a particular entity type should be somehow related to each other. For example, we would expect attributes like *league, season* and *team* for basketball players and *genre, label, song* and *album* for musical artists. If an attribute like *album* appears for basketball players it should be discarded as it is not related to other attributes.

We adopted a clustering approach for finding attributes that are related to each other. For each pair of attributes in the slot vector, we compute a similarity score based on how many times the two attribute labels appear together in Wikipedia person articles within a distance of 100 words as compared to the number of times they appear in total and weigh it using weights of the individual attributes in the slot vector. This metric is captured in the following equation, where *Df* is the document frequency and *wt* is the attribute weight.

$$sim_{attr}(a_i, a_j) = wt(a_i) \times wt(a_j) \times \frac{Df(a_i, a_j, 100)}{Df(a_i) + Df(a_j)}$$

Our initial experiments using single and complete link clustering revealed that single link was more appropriate for slot selection. We got clusters at a partition distance of 0.9 and selected the largest cluster from the set of clusters. In addition, we also added any attributes exceeding a 0.4 score into the set of selected attributes. Selected ranked slots for Michael Jackson are given in Table 1.

2.5 Class Labeling

Slot	Score	Fillers Example
Musician	1.00	ray_charles, sam_cooke ...
Album	0.99	bad_(album), ...
Location	0.97	gary, indiana, chicago, …
Music_genre	0.90	pop_music, soul_music, ...
Label	0.79	a&m_records, epic_records, ...
Phonograph_ record	0.67	give_in_to_me, this_place_hotel …
Act	0.59	singing
Movie	0.46	moonwalker …
Company	0.43	war_child_(charity), …
Actor	0.41	stan_winston, eddie_murphy,
Singer	0.40	britney_spears, …
Magazine	0.29	entertainment_weekly,…
Writing_style	0.27	hip_hop_music
Group	0.21	'n_sync, RIAA
Song	0.20	d.s._(song) …

Table 1: Fifteen slots were discovered for musician Michael Jackson along with scores and example fillers.

Assigning class labels to clusters gives additional information about the type of entities in a cluster. We generate a cluster label vector for each cluster which represents the type of entities in the cluster. We compute a list of person types by taking all hyponyms under the corresponding person sense in WordNet. That list mostly contained the professions list for persons such as basketball player, president, bishop etc. To assign a WordNet type to a person in Wikipedia we matched the entries in the list to the words in the first sentence of the person article and assigned it the set of types that matched. For example, for Michael Jordan the matching types found were *basketball_player, businessman* and *player*.

We assigned the most frequent sense to the matching word as followed by Suchanek et al. (2008) and Wu and Weld (2008), which works for majority of the cases. We then also add all the hypernyms of the matching types under the Person node. The vector for Michael Jordan has entries *basketball_player, athlete, businessperson, person, contestant, businessman* and *player*. After getting matching types and their hypernyms for all the members of the cluster, we score each type based on the number of times it occurs in its members normalized by the cluster size. For example for one of the clusters with 146 basketball players we got the following label vector: {*player*:0.97, *contestant*:0.97, *athlete*:0.96, *basketball_player*:0.96}. To select an individual label for a class we can pick the label with the highest score (the most generalized label) or the most specialized label having a score above a given threshold.

2.6 Discovering Class Hierarchy

We employ two different feature sets to discover the class hierarchy, i.e., the selected slot vectors and the class label vectors and combine both functions using their weighted sum. The similarity functions are described below.

The common slot similarity function is the cosine similarity between the common slot tf.idf vectors, where the slot score represents the tf and the idf is based on the number of times a particular slot appears in different clusters at that iteration. We re-compute the idf term in each iteration. We define the *common slot* tf.idf vector for a cluster as one where we assign a non-zero weight to only the slots that have non-zero weight for all cluster members. The label similarity function is the cosine similarity between the label vectors for clusters. The hybrid similarity function is a weighted sum of the common slot and label similarity functions. Using these similarity functions we apply complete link hierarchical clustering algorithm to discover the class hierarchy.

$$sim_{com\_slot}(c_i,c_j) = \cos(com\_slot(c_i),com\_slot(c_j))$$
$$sim_{label}(c_i,c_j) = \cos(label(c_i),label(c_j))$$
$$sim_{hyb}(c_i,c_j) = w_c \times sim_{com\_slot}(c_i,c_j) + w_l \times sim_{label}(c_i,c_j)$$
$$w_c + w_l = 1$$

3 Experiments and Evaluation

For our experiments and evaluation we used the Wikipedia dump from March 2008 and the DBpedia infobox ontology created from Wikipedia infoboxes using hand-generated mappings (Auer et al., 2007). The *Person* class is a direct subclass of the owl:Thing class and has 21 immediate subclasses and 36 subclasses at the second level. We used the persons in different classes in DBpedia ontology at level two to generate data sets for experiments.

There are several articles in Wikipedia that are very small and have very few out-links and in-links. Our approach is based on the out-links and availability of information about different related things on the article, therefore, in order to avoid data sparseness, we randomly select articles with greater than 100 in-links and out-links, at least 5KB page length and having at least five links to entities of the same type that link back (in our case persons).

We first compare our slot vector features with other features extracted from Wikipedia for entity classification task and then evaluate their accuracy. We then discover the class hierarchy and compare the different similarity functions.

3.1 Entity Classification

We did some initial experiments to compare our ranked slot features with other feature sets extracted from Wikipedia. We created a dataset composed of 25 different classes of Persons present at level 2 in the DBpedia ontology by randomly selecting 200 person articles from each class. For several classes we got less than 200 articles which fulfilled our selection criteria defined earlier. We generated twelve types of feature sets and evaluated them using ground truth from DBpedia ontology.

We compare tf.idf vectors constructed using twelve different feature sets: (1) Ranked slot features, where tf is the slot score; (2) Words in first sentence of an article; (3) Associated categories; (4) Assigned WordNet nodes (see section 2.2); (5) Associated categories tokenized into words; (6) Combined Feature Sets 1 to 5 (All); (7-11) Feature sets 7 to 11 are combinations excluding one feature set at a time; (12) Unranked slots where tf is 1 for all slots. We applied complete link clustering and evaluated the precision, recall and F-measure at different numbers of clusters ranging from one to 100. Table 2 gives the precision, recall and number of clusters where we got the maximum F-measure using different feature sets.

No.	Feature Set	k	P	R	F
1	Ranked Slots	40	0.74	0.72	0.73
2	First Sentence	89	0.07	0.53	0.12
3	Categories	1	0.05	1.00	0.10
4	WordNet Nodes	87	0.40	0.22	0.29
5	(3 tokenized)	93	0.85	0.47	0.60
6	All (1 to 5)	68	0.87	0.62	0.72
7	(All – 5)	82	0.79	0.46	0.58
8	(All – 4)	58	0.78	0.63	0.70
9	(All – 3)	53	0.76	0.65	0.70
10	(All – 2)	58	0.88	0.63	0.74
11	(All – 1)	57	0.77	0.60	0.68
12	(1 unranked)	34	0.57	0.65	0.61

Table 2: Comparison of the precision, recall and F-measure for different feature sets for entity classification. The k column shows the number of clusters that maximized the F score.

Feature set 10 (all features except feature 2) gave the best F-measure i.e. 0.74, whereas, feature set 1 (ranked slots only) gave the second best F-measure i.e. 0.73 which is very close to the best result. Feature set 12 (unranked slots) gave a lower F-measure i.e. 0.61 which shows that ranking or weighing slots based on linked entities of the same type performs better for classification.

3.2 Slot and Filler Evaluation

To evaluate our approach to finding slot fillers, we focused on DBpedia classes two levels below Person (e.g., Governor and FigureSkater). We randomly selected 200 articles from each of these classes using the criteria defined earlier to avoid data sparseness. Classes for which fewer than 20 articles were found were discarded. The resulting dataset comprised 28 classes and 3810 articles[3].

We used our ranked slots tf.idf feature set and ran a complete link clustering algorithm producing clusters at partition distance of 0.8. The slots were re-scored based on the number of times they appeared in the cluster members normalized by the cluster size. We applied slot selection over the re-scored slots for each cluster. In order to evaluate our slots and fillers we mapped each cluster to a DBpedia class based on the maximum number of members of a particular DBpedia class in our cluster. This process predicted 124 unique properties for the classes. Of these, we were able to manually align 46 to properties in either DBpedia or Freebase for the corresponding class. We initially tried to evaluate the discovered slots by comparing them with those found in the ontologies underlying DBpedia and Freebase, but were able to find an overlap in the subject and object pairs for very few properties.

We randomly selected 20 subject object pairs for each of the 46 properties from the corresponding classes and manually judged whether or not the relation was correct by consulting the correspond-

[3] For some of the classes, fewer than the full complement of 200 articles were found.

No.	Property	Accuracy
1	automobile_race	1.00
2	championship	1.00
3	expressive_style	1.00
4	fictional_character	1.00
5	label	1.00
6	racetrack	1.00
7	team_sport	1.00
8	writing_style	1.00
9	academic_degree	0.95
10	album	0.95
11	book	0.95
12	contest	0.95
13	election	0.95
14	league	0.95
15	phonograph_record	0.95
16	race	0.95
17	tournament	0.94
18	award	0.90
19	movie	0.90
20	novel	0.90
21	school	0.90
22	season	0.90
23	serial	0.90
24	song	0.90
25	car	0.85
26	church	0.85
27	game	0.85
28	musical_instrument	0.85
29	show	0.85
30	sport	0.85
31	stadium	0.85
32	broadcast	0.80
33	telecast	0.80
34	hockey_league	0.75
35	music_genre	0.70
36	trophy	0.70
37	university	0.65
38	character	0.60
39	disease	0.60
40	magazine	0.55
41	team	0.50
42	baseball_club	0.45
43	club	0.45
44	party	0.45
45	captain	0.30
46	coach	0.25
	Avg. Accuracy:	0.81

Table 3: Manual evaluation of discovered properties

Similarity Function	k (L=2)	F (L=2)	k (L=1)	F (L=1)
sim_{slot}	56	0.61	13	0.55
sim_{com_slot}	74	0.61	15	0.65
sim_{label}	50	0.63	10	0.76
sim_{hyb} w_c=w_l=0.5	59	0.63	10	0.76
sim_{hyb} w_c=0.2, w_l=0.8	61	0.63	8	0.79

Table 4: Evaluation results for class hierarchy prediction using different similarity functions.

ing Wikipedia articles (Table 3). The average accuracy for the 46 relations was 81%.

3.3 Discovering Class Hierarchy

In order to discover the class hierarchy, we took all of the clusters obtained earlier at partition distance of 0.8 and their corresponding slot vectors after slot selection. We experimented with different similarity functions and evaluated their accuracy by comparing the results with the DBpedia ontology. A complete link clustering algorithm was applied using different settings of the similarity functions and the resulting hierarchy compared to DBpedia's Person class hierarchy. Table 4 shows the highest F measure obtained for Person's immediate sub-classes (L1), "sub-sub-classes" (L2) and the number of clusters (k) for which we got the highest F-measure using a particular similarity function.

The highest F-measure both at level 2 (0.63) and level 1 (0.79) was obtained by sim_{hyb} with w_c=0.2, w_l=0.8 and also at lowest number of clusters at L1 (k=8). The sim_{hyb} (w_c=w_l=0.5) and sim_{label} functions gave almost the same F-measure at both levels. The sim_{com_slot} function gave better performance at L1 (F=0.65) than the base line sim_{slot} (F=0.55) which was originally used for entity clustering. However, both these functions gave the same F-measure at L2 (F=0.61).

4 Discussion

In case of property evaluation, properties for which the accuracy was 60% or below include *coach, captain, baseball_club, club, party, team* and *magazine*. For the *magazine* property (corresponding to *Writer* and *ComicsCreator* class) we observed that many times a magazine name was mentioned in an article because it published some news about a person rather than that person contributing any article in that magazine. For all the remaining properties we observed that these were related to some sort of competition. For example, a person played against a *team, club, coach* or *captain*. The political *party* relation is a similar case, where articles frequently mention a politician's party affiliation as well as significant opposition parties. For such properties, we need to exploit additional contextual information to judge whether the person competed "for" or "against" a particular *team, club, coach* or *party*. Even if the accuracy for fillers for such slots is low, it can still be useful to discover the kind of slots associated with an entity.

We also observed that there were some cases where the property was related to a family member of the primary person such as for *disease, school* and *university*. Certain other properties such as *spouse, predecessor, successor,* etc. require more contextual information and are not directly evident in the link structure. However, our experiments show that there are certain properties that can be predicted with high accuracy using the article links only and can be used to enrich the existing infobox ontology or for other purposes.

While our work has mostly experimented with person entities, the approach can be applied to other types as well. For example, we were able to discover *software* as a candidate slot for companies like Microsoft, Google and Yahoo!, which appeared among the top three ranked slots using our slot ranking scheme and corresponds to the *products* slot in the infoboxes of these companies.

For class hierarchy discovery, we have exploited the *specialized* slots after slot selection. One way to incorporate *generalized* slots in the hierarchy is to consider all slots for class members (without slot selection) and recursively propagate the common slots present at any level to the level above it. For example, if we find the slot *team* to be common for different types of Athletes such as basketball players, soccer players etc. we can propagate it to the Athlete class, which is one level higher in the hierarchy.

5 Related Work

Unsupervised relation discovery was initially introduced by Hasegawa et al. (2004). They developed an approach to discover relations by clustering pairs of entities based on intervening words represented as context vectors. Shinyama and Sekine (2006) generated basic patterns using parts of text syntactically connected to the entity and then generated a basic cluster composed of a set of events having the same relation.

Several approaches have used linguistic analysis to generate features for supervised or unsupervised relation extraction (Nguyen et al., 2007; Etzioni et al., 2008; Yan et al., 2009). Our approach mainly exploits the heavily linked structure of Wikipedia and demonstrates that there are several relations that can be discovered with high accuracy without the need of features generated from a linguistic analysis of the Wikipedia article text.

Suchanek et al. (2008) used Wikipedia categories and infoboxes to extract 92 relations by applying specialized heuristics for each relation and incorporated the relations in their YAGO ontology, whereas our techniques do not use specialized heuristics based on the type of relation. Kylin (Weld et al., 2008) generated infoboxes for articles by learning from existing infoboxes, whereas we can discover new fillers for several existing slots and also discover new slots for infoboxes. KOG (Wu and Weld, 2008) automatically refined the Wikipedia infobox ontology and integrated Wikipedia's infobox-class schemata with WordNet. Since we already use the WordNet nodes for representing slots, it eliminates the need for several of KOG's infobox refinement steps.

While YAGO, Kylin and KOG all rely on relations present in the infoboxes, our approach can complement these by discovering new relations evident in inter-article links in Wikipedia. For example, we could add slots like *songs* and *albums* to the infobox schema for *Musical Artists*, *movies* for the *Actors* infobox schema, and *party* for the *Politicians* schema.

6 Conclusions and Future Work

People have been learning by reading for thousands of years. The past decade, however, has seen a significant change in the way people read. The developed world now does much of its reading online and this change will soon be nearly universal. Most online content is read as hypertext via a Web browser or custom reading device. Unlike text, hypertext is semi-structured information, especially when links are drawn from global namespace, making it easy for many documents to link unambiguously to a common referent.

The structured component of hypertext augments the information in its plain text and provides an additional source of information from which both people and machines can learn. The work described in this paper is aimed at learning useful information, both about the implicit ontology and facts, from the links embedded in collection of hypertext documents.

Our approach is fully unsupervised and does not require having a pre-defined catalogue of relations. We have discovered several new slots and fillers that are not present in existing Wikipedia infoboxes and also a scheme to rank the slots based on linked entities of the same type. We compared our results with ground truth from the DBpedia infobox ontology and Freebase for the set of properties that were common and manually evaluated the accuracy of the common properties. Our results show that there are several properties that can be discovered with high accuracy from the link structure in Wikipedia and can also be used to discover a class hierarchy.

We plan to explore the discovery of slots from non-Wikipedia articles by linking them to Wikipedia concepts using existing systems like Wikify (Mihalcea and Csomai, 2007). Wikipedia articles are encyclopedic in nature with the whole article revolving around a single topic or concept. Consequently, linked articles are a good source of properties and relations. This might not be the case in other genres, such as news articles, that discuss a number of different entities and events. One way to extend this work to other genres is by first detecting the entities in the article and then only processing links in sentences that mention an entity to discover its properties.

Acknowledgements

The research described in this paper was supported in part by a Fulbright fellowship, a gift from Microsoft Research, NSF award IIS-0326460 and the Johns Hopkins University Human Language Technology Center of Excellence.

References

Sören Auer, Christian Bizer, Georgi Kobilarov, Jens Lehmann and Zachary Ives. 2007. DBpedia: A nucleus for a web of open data. In Proceedings of the 6th International Semantic Web Conference: 11–15.

Ken Barker et al. 2007. Learning by reading: A prototype system, performance baseline and lessons learned, Proceedings of the 22nd National Conference on Artificial Intelligence, AAAI Press.

K. Bollacker, R. Cook, and P. Tufts. 2007. Freebase: A Shared Database of Structured General Human Knowledge. Proceedings of the National Conference on Artificial Intelligence (Volume 2): 1962-1963.

Oren Etzioni, Michele Banko, Stephen Soderland, and Daniel S. Weld. 2008. Open information extraction from the web. Communications of the ACM 51, 12 (December): 68-74.

Takaaki Hasegawa, Satoshi Sekine, and Ralph Grishman. 2004. Discovering relations among named entities from large corpora. In Proceedings of the 42nd Annual Meeting of the Association for Computational Linguistics: 415-422.

Jun'ichi Kazama and Kentaro Torisawa. 2007. Exploiting Wikipedia as external knowledge for named entity recognition. In Proceedings of the 2007 Joint Conference on Empirical Methods in Natural Language Processing and Computational Natural Language Learning: 698–707.

Paul McNamee and Hoa Trang Dang. 2009. Overview of the TAC 2009 knowledge base population track. In Proceedings of the 2009 Text Analysis Conference. National Institute of Standards and Technology, November.

Rada Mihalcea and Andras Csomai. 2007. Wikify!: linking documents to encyclopedic knowledge. In Proceedings of the 16th ACM Conference on Information and Knowledge Management: 233–242.

George A. Miller, Richard Beckwith, Christiane Fellbaum, Derek Gross, and Katherine Miller. 1990. WordNet: An on-line lexical database. International Journal of Lexicography, 3:235–244.

Dat P. T. Nguyen, Yutaka Matsuo, and Mitsuru Ishizuka. 2007. Subtree mining for relation extraction from Wikipedia. In Proceedings of Human Language Technologies: The Annual Conference of the North American Chapter of the Association for Computational Linguistics:125–128.

Fabian M. Suchanek, Gjergji Kasneci, and Gerhard Weikum. 2008. Yago: A large ontology from Wikipedia and WordNet. Web Semantics, 6(3):203–217.

Zareen Syed, Tim Finin, Varish Mulwad and Anupam Joshi. 2010. Exploiting a Web of Semantic Data for Interpreting Tables, Proceedings of the Second Web Science Conference.

Simone P. Ponzetto and Roberto Navigli. 2009. Large-scale taxonomy mapping for restructuring and integrating Wikipedia. In Proceedings of the Twenty-First International Joint Conference on Artificial Intelligence: 2083–2088.

Yusuke Shinyama and Satoshi Sekine. 2006. Pre-emptive information extraction using unrestricted relation discovery. In Proceedings of Human Language Technologies: The Annual Conference of the North American Chapter of the Association for Computational Linguistics:.

Daniel S. Weld, Raphael Hoffmann, and Fei Wu. 2008. Using Wikipedia to bootstrap open information extrac-tion. SIGMOD Record, 37(4): 62–68.

Fei Wu and Daniel S. Weld. 2008. Automatically refining the Wikipedia infobox ontology. In Proceedings of the 17th International World Wide Web Conference, pages 635–644.

Wikipedia. 2008. Wikipedia, the free encyclopedia.

Yulan Yan, Naoaki Okazaki, Yutaka Matsuo, Zhenglu Yang, and Mitsuru Ishizuka. 2009. Unsupervised relation extraction by mining Wikipedia texts using information from the web. In Proceedings of the 47th Annual Meeting of the Association for Computational Linguistics: Volume 2: 1021–1029.

Machine Reading at the University of Washington

Hoifung Poon, Janara Christensen, Pedro Domingos, Oren Etzioni, Raphael Hoffmann, Chloe Kiddon, Thomas Lin, Xiao Ling, Mausam, Alan Ritter, Stefan Schoenmackers, Stephen Soderland, Dan Weld, Fei Wu, Congle Zhang
Department of Computer Science & Engineering
University of Washington
Seattle, WA 98195
{hoifung, janara, pedrod, etzioni, raphaelh, chloe, tlin, xiaoling, mausam, aritter, stef, soderland, weld, wufei, clzhang}@cs.washington.edu

Abstract

Machine reading is a long-standing goal of AI and NLP. In recent years, tremendous progress has been made in developing machine learning approaches for many of its subtasks such as parsing, information extraction, and question answering. However, existing end-to-end solutions typically require substantial amount of human efforts (e.g., labeled data and/or manual engineering), and are not well poised for Web-scale knowledge acquisition. In this paper, we propose a unifying approach for machine reading by bootstrapping from the easiest extractable knowledge and conquering the long tail via a self-supervised learning process. This self-supervision is powered by joint inference based on Markov logic, and is made scalable by leveraging hierarchical structures and coarse-to-fine inference. Researchers at the University of Washington have taken the first steps in this direction. Our existing work explores the wide spectrum of this vision and shows its promise.

1 Introduction

Machine reading, or learning by reading, aims to extract knowledge automatically from unstructured text and apply the extracted knowledge to end tasks such as decision making and question answering. It has been a major goal of AI and NLP since their early days. With the advent of the Web, the billions of online text documents contain virtually unlimited amount of knowledge to extract, further increasing the importance and urgency of machine reading.

In the past, there has been a lot of progress in automating many subtasks of machine reading by machine learning approaches (e.g., components in the traditional NLP pipeline such as POS tagging and syntactic parsing). However, end-to-end solutions are still rare, and existing systems typically require substantial amount of human effort in manual engineering and/or labeling examples. As a result, they often target restricted domains and only extract limited types of knowledge (e.g., a pre-specified relation). Moreover, many machine reading systems train their knowledge extractors once and do not leverage further learning opportunities such as additional text and interaction with end users.

Ideally, a machine reading system should strive to satisfy the following desiderata:

End-to-end: the system should input raw text, extract knowledge, and be able to answer questions and support other end tasks;

High quality: the system should extract knowledge with high accuracy;

Large-scale: the system should acquire knowledge at Web-scale and be open to arbitrary domains, genres, and languages;

Maximally autonomous: the system should incur minimal human effort;

Continuous learning from experience: the system should constantly integrate new information sources (e.g., new text documents) and learn from user questions and feedback (e.g., via performing end tasks) to continuously improve its performance.

These desiderata raise many intriguing and challenging research questions. Machine reading research at the University of Washington has explored

Proceedings of the NAACL HLT 2010 First International Workshop on Formalisms and Methodology for Learning by Reading, pages 87–95,
Los Angeles, California, June 2010.

a wide spectrum of solutions to these challenges and has produced a large number of initial systems that demonstrated promising performance. During this expedition, an underlying unifying vision starts to emerge. It becomes apparent that the key to solving machine reading is to:

1. Conquer the long tail of textual knowledge via a self-supervised learning process that leverages data redundancy to bootstrap from the head and propagates information down the long tail by joint inference;
2. Scale this process to billions of Web documents by identifying and leveraging ubiquitous structures that lead to sparsity.

In Section 2, we present this vision in detail, identify the major dimensions these initial systems have explored, and propose a unifying approach that satisfies all five desiderata. In Section 3, we reivew machine reading research at the University of Washington and show how they form synergistic effort towards solving the machine reading problem. We conclude in Section 4.

2 A Unifying Approach for Machine Reading

The core challenges to machine reading stem from the massive scale of the Web and *the long-tailed distribution of textual knowledge*. The heterogeneous Web contains texts that vary substantially in subject matters (e.g., finance vs. biology) and writing styles (e.g., blog posts vs. scientific papers). In addition, natural languages are famous for their myraid variations in expressing the same meaning. A fact may be stated in a straightforward way such as "kale contains calcium". More often though, it may be stated in a syntactically and/or lexically different way than as phrased in an end task (e.g., "calcium is found in kale"). Finally, many facts are not even stated explicitly, and must be inferred from other facts (e.g., "kale prevents osteoporosis" may not be stated explicitly but can be inferred by combining facts such as "kale contains calcium" and "calcium helps prevent osteoporosis"). As a result, machine reading must not rely on explicit supervision such as manual rules and labeled examples, which will incur prohibitive cost in the Web scale. Instead, it must be able to learn from indirect supervision.

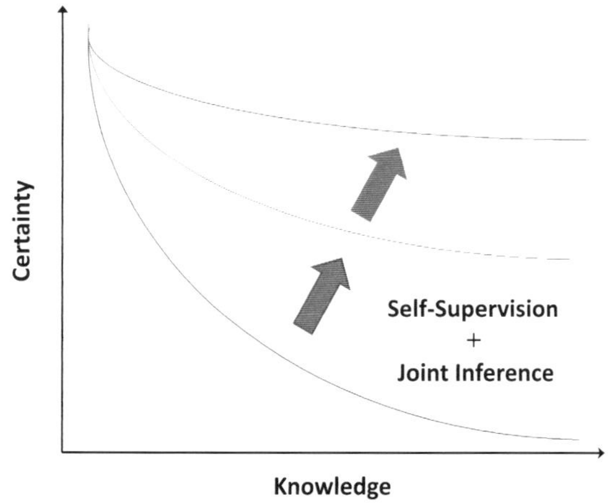

Figure 1: A unifying vision for machine reading: bootstrap from the head regime of the power-law distribution of textual knowledge, and conquer the long tail in a self-supervised learning process that raises certainty on sparse extractions by propagating information via joint inference from frequent extractions.

A key source of indirect supervision is meta knowledge about the domains. For example, the TextRunner system (Banko et al., 2007) hinges on the observation that there exist general, relation-independent patterns for information extraction. Another key source of indirect supervision is data redundancy. While a rare extracted fact or inference pattern may arise by chance of error, it is much less likely so for the ones with many repetitions (Downey et al., 2010). Such highly-redundant knowledge can be extracted easily and with high confidence, and can be leveraged for bootstrapping. For knowledge that resides in the long tail, explicit forms of redundancy (e.g., identical expressions) are rare, but this can be circumvented by joint inference. For example, expressions that are composed with or by similar expressions probably have the same meaning; the fact that kale prevents osteoporosis can be derived by combining the facts that kale contains calcium and that calcium helps prevent osteoporosis via a transitivity-through inference pattern. In general, joint inference can take various forms, ranging from simple voting to shrinkage in a probabilistic ontology to sophisticated probabilistic reasoning based on a joint model. Simple ones tend to scale better, but their capability in propagating information is limited. More sophisticated methods can uncover implicit redundancy and propagate much more information with higher quality, yet the challenge is how to make them scale as well as simple ones.

To do machine reading, a self-supervised learning process, informed by meta knowledege, stipulates what form of joint inference to use and how. Effectively, it increases certainty on sparse extractions by propagating information from more frequent ones. Figure 1 illustrates this unifying vision.

In the past, machine reading research at the University of Washington has explored a variety of solutions that span the key dimensions of this unifying vision: *knowledge representation, bootstrapping, self-supervised learning, large-scale joint inference, ontology induction, continuous learning*. See Section 3 for more details. Based on this experience, one direction seems particularly promising that we would propose here as our unifying approach for end-to-end machine reading:

Markov logic is used as the unifying framework for knowledge representation and joint inference;

Self-supervised learning is governed by a joint probabilistic model that incorporates a small amount of heuristic knowledge and large-scale relational structures to maximize the amount and quality of information to propagate;

Joint inference is made scalable to the Web by coarse-to-fine inference.

Probabilistic ontologies are induced from text to guarantee tractability in coarse-to-fine inference. This ontology induction and population are incorporated into the joint probabilistic model for self-supervision;

Continuous learning is accomplished by combining **bootstrapping** and **crowdsourced content creation** to synergistically improve the reading system from user interaction and feedback.

A distinctive feature of this approach is its emphasis on using sophisticated joint inference. Recently, joint inference has received increasing interest in AI, machine learning, and NLP, with Markov logic (Domingos and Lowd, 2009) being one of the leading unifying frameworks. Past work has shown that it can substantially improve predictive accuracy in supervised learning (e.g., (Getoor and Taskar, 2007; Bakir et al., 2007)). We propose to build on these advances, but apply joint inference beyond supervised learning, with labeled examples supplanted by indirect supervision.

Another distinctive feature is that we propose to use coarse-to-fine inference (Felzenszwalb and McAllester, 2007; Petrov, 2009) as a unifying framework to scale inference to the Web. Essentially, coarse-to-fine inference leverages the sparsity imposed by hierarchical structures that are ubiquitous in human knowledge (e.g., taxonomies/ontologies). At coarse levels (top levels in a hierarchy), ambiguities are rare (there are few objects and relations), and inference can be conducted very efficiently. The result is then used to prune unpromising refinements at the next level. This process continues down the hierarchy until decision can be made. In this way, inference can potentially be sped up exponentially, analogous to binary tree search.

Finally, we propose a novel form of continuous learning by leveraging the interaction between the system and end users to constantly improve the performance. This is straightforward to do in our approach given the self-supervision process and the availability of powerful joint inference. Essentially, when the system output is applied to an end task (e.g., answering questions), the feedback from user is collected and incorporated back into the system as a bootstrap source. The feedback can take the form of explicit supervision (e.g., via community content creation or active learning) or indirect signals (e.g., click data and query logs). In this way, we can bootstrap an online community by an initial machine reading system that provides imperfect but valuable service in end tasks, and continuously improve the quality of system output, which attracts more users with higher degree of participation, thus creating a positive feedback loop and raising the machine reading performance to a high level that is difficult to attain otherwise.

3 Summary of Progress to Date

The University of Washington has been one of the leading places for machine reading research and has produced many cutting-edge systems, e.g., WIEN (first wrapper induction system for information extraction), Mulder (first fully automatic Web-scale question answering system), KnowItAll/TextRunner (first systems to do open-domain information extraction from the Web corpus at large scale), Kylin (first self-supervised system for Wikipedia-based information extraction), UCR (first unsupervised coreference resolution system that rivals the performance of supervised systems), Holmes (first Web-scale joint inference system), USP (first unsupervised system for semantic parsing).

Figure 2 shows the evolution of the major systems; dashed lines signify influence in key ideas (e.g., Mulder inspires KnowItAll), and solid lines signify dataflow (e.g., Holmes inputs TextRunner tuples). These systems span a wide spectrum in scalability (assessed by speed and quantity in extraction) and comprehension (assessed by unit yield of knowledge at a fixed precision level). At one extreme, the TextRunner system is highly scalable, capable of extracting billions of facts, but it focuses on shallow extractions from simple sentences. At the other extreme, the USP and LOFT systems achieve much higher level of comprehension (e.g., in a task of extracting knowledge from biomedical papers and answering questions, USP obtains more than three times as many correct answers as TextRunner, and LOFT obtains more than six times as many correct answers as TextRunner), but are much less scalable than TextRunner.

In the remainder of the section, we review the progress made to date and identify key directions for future work.

3.1 Knowledge Representation and Joint Inference

Knowledge representations used in these systems vary widely in expressiveness, ranging from simple ones like relation triples (<*subject, relation, object*>; e.g., in KnowItAll and TextRunner), to clusters of relation triples or triple components (e.g., in SNE, RESOLVER), to arbitrary logical formulas and their clusters (e.g., in USP, LOFT). Similarly, a variety forms of joint inference have been used, ranging from simple voting to heuristic rules to sophisticated probabilistic models. All these can be compactly encoded in Markov logic (Domingos and Lowd, 2009), which provides a unifying framework for knowledge representation and joint inference.

Past work at Washington has shown that in supervised learning, joint inference can substantially improve predictive performance on tasks related to machine reading (e.g., citation information extraction (Poon and Domingos, 2007), ontology induction (Wu and Weld, 2008), temporal information extraction (Ling and Weld, 2010)). In addition, it has demonstrated that sophisticated joint inference can enable effective learning without any labeled information (UCR, USP, LOFT), and that joint inference can scale to millions of Web documents by leveraging sparsity in naturally occurring relations (Holmes, Sherlock), showing the promise of our unifying approach.

Simpler representations limit the expressiveness in representing knowledge and the degree of sophistication in joint inference, but they currently scale much better than more expressive ones. A key direction for future work is to evaluate this tradeoff more thoroughly, e.g., for each class of end tasks, to what degree do simple representations limit the effectiveness in performing the end tasks? Can we automate the choice of representations to strike the best tradeoff for a specific end task? Can we advance joint inference algorithms to such a degree that sophisticated inference scales as well as simple ones?

3.2 Bootstrapping

Past work at Washington has identified and leveraged a wide range of sources for bootstrapping. Examples include Wikipedia (Kylin, KOG, IIA, WOE, WPE), Web lists (KnowItAll, WPE), Web tables (WebTables), Hearst patterns (KnowItAll), heuristic rules (TextRunner), semantic role labels (SRL-IE), etc.

In general, potential bootstrap sources can be broadly divided into domain knowledge (e.g., patterns and rules) and crowdsourced contents (e.g., linguistic resources, Wikipedia, Amazon Mechanical Turk, the ESP game).

A key direction for future work is to combine bootstrapping with crowdsourced content creation for continuous learning. (Also see Subsection 3.6.)

3.3 Self-Supervised Learning

Although the ways past systems conduct self-supervision vary widely in detail, they can be divided into two broad categories. One uses heuristic rules that exploit existing semi-structured resources to generate noisy training examples for use by supervised learning methods and with cotraining (e.g.,

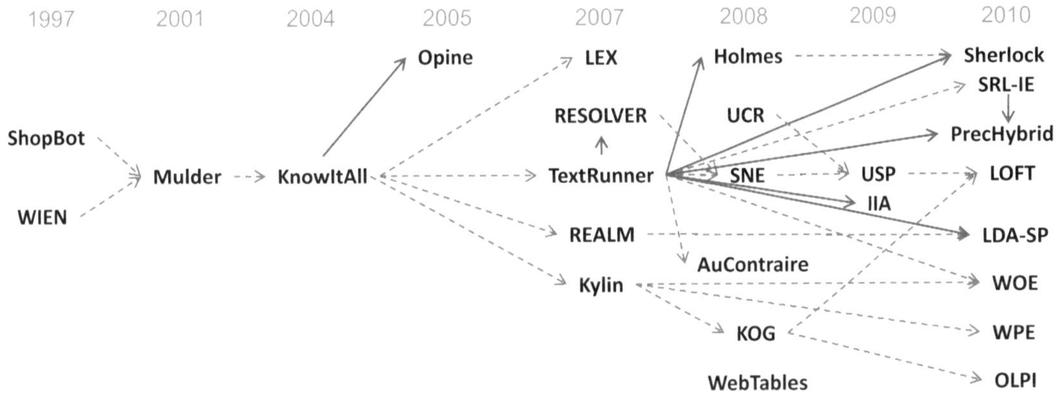

Figure 2: The evolution of major machine reading systems at the University of Washington. Dashed lines signify influence and solid lines signify dataflow. At the top are the years of publications. **ShopBot** learns comparison-shopping agents via self-supervision using heuristic knowledge (Doorenbos et al., 1997); **WIEN** induces wrappers for information extraction via self-supervision using joint inference to combine simple atomic extractors (Kushmerick et al., 1997); **Mulder** answers factoid questions by leveraging redundancy to rank candidate answers extracted from multiple search query results (Kwok et al., 2001); **KnowItAll** conducts open-domain information extraction via self-supervision bootstrapping from Hearst patterns (Etzioni et al., 2005); **Opine** builds on KnowItAll and mines product reviews via self-supervision using joint inference over neighborhood features (Popescu and Etzioni, 2005); **Kylin** populates Wikipedia infoboxes via self-supervision bootstrapping from existing infoboxes (Wu and Weld, 2007); **LEX** conducts Web-scale name entity recognition by leveraging collocation statistics (Downey et al., 2007a); **REALM** improves sparse open-domain information extraction via relational clustering and language modeling (Downey et al., 2007b); **RESOLVER** performs entity and relation resolution via relational clustering (Yates and Etzioni, 2007); **TextRunner** conducts open-domain information extraction via self-supervision bootstrapping from heuristic rules (Banko et al., 2007); **AuContraire** automatically identifies contradictory statements in a large web corpus using functional relations (Ritter et al., 2008); **HOLMES** infers new facts from TextRunner output using Markov logic (Schoenmackers et al., 2008); **KOG** learns a rich ontology by combining Wikipedia infoboxes with WordNet via joint inference using Markov Logic Networks (Wu and Weld, 2008), shrinkage over this ontology vastly improves the recall of Kylin's extractors; **UCR** performs state-of-the-art unsupervised coreference resolution by incorporating a small amount of domain knowledge and conducting joint inference among entity mentions with Markov logic (Poon and Domingos, 2008b); **SNE** constructs a semantic network over TextRunner output via relational clustering with Markov logic (Kok and Domingos, 2008); **WebTables** conducts Web-scale information extraction by leveraging HTML table structures (Cafarella et al., 2008); **IIA** learns from infoboxes to filter open-domain information extraction toward assertions that are interesting to people (Lin et al., 2009); **USP** jointly learns a semantic parser and extracts knowledge via recursive relational clustering with Markov logic (Poon and Domingos, 2009); **LDA-SP** automatically infers a compact representation describing the plausible arguments for a relation using an LDA-Style model and Bayesian Inference (Ritter et al., 2010); **LOFT** builds on USP and jointly performs ontology induction, population, and knowledge extraction via joint recursive relational clustering and shrinkage with Markov logic (Poon and Domingos, 2010); **OLPI** improves the efficiency of lifted probabilistic inference and learning via coarse-to-fine inference based on type hierarchies (Kiddon and Domingos, 2010). **SHERLOCK** induces new inference rules via relational learning (Schoenmackers et al., 2010); **SRL-IE** conducts open-domain information extraction by bootstrapping from semantic role labels, **PrecHybrid** is a hybrid version between SRL-IE and TextRunner, which given a budget of computation time does better than either system (Christensen et al., 2010); **WOE** builds on Kylin and conducts open-domain information extraction (Wu and Weld, 2010); **WPE** learns 5000 relational extractors by bootstrapping from Wikipedia and using Web lists to generate dynamic, relation-specific lexicon features (Hoffmann et al., 2010).

TextRunner, Kylin, KOG, WOE, WPE). Another uses unsupervised learning and often takes a particular form of relational clustering (e.g., objects associated with similar relations tend to be the same and vice versa, as in REALM, RESOLVER, SNE, UCR, USP, LDA-SP, LOFT, etc.).

Some distinctive types of self-supervision include shrinkage based on an ontology (KOG, LOFT, OLPI), probabilistic inference via handcrafted or learned inference patterns (Holmes, Sherlock), and cotraining using relation-specific and relation-independent (open) extraction to reinforce semantic coherence (Wu et al., 2008).

A key direction for future work is to develop a unifying framework for self-supervised learning by combining the strengths of existing methods and overcoming their limitations. This will likely take the form of a new learning paradigm that combines existing paradigms such as supervised learning, relational clustering, semi-supervised learning, and active learning into a unifying learning framework that synergistically leverages diverse forms of supervision and information sources.

3.4 Large-Scale Joint Inference

To apply sophisticated joint inference in machine reading, the major challenge is to make it scalable to billions of text documents. A general solution is to identify and leverage ubiquitous problem structures that lead to sparsity. For example, order of magnitude reduction in both memory and inference time can be achieved for relational inference by leveraging the fact that most relational atoms are false, which trivially satisfy most relational formulas (Singla and Domingos, 2006; Poon and Domingos, 2008a); joint inference with naturally occurring textual relations can scale to millions of Web pages by leveraging the fact that such relations are approximately functional (Schoenmackers et al., 2008).

More generally, sparsity arises from hierarchical structures (e.g., ontologies) that are naturally exhibited in human knowledge, and can be leveraged to do coarse-to-fine inference (OLPI).

The success of coarse-to-fine inference hinges on the availability and quality of hierarchical structures. Therefore, a key direction for future work is to automatically induce such hierarchies. (Also see next subsection.) Moreover, given the desideratum of continuous learning from experience, and the speedy evolution of the Web (new contents, formats, etc.), it is important that we develop *online methods* for self-supervision and joint inference. For example, when a new text document arrives, the reading system should not relearn from scratch, but should identify only the relevant pieces of knowledge and conduct limited-scoped inference and learning accordingly.

3.5 Ontology Induction

As mentioned in previous subsections, ontologies play an important role in both self-supervision (shrinkage) and large-scale inference (coarse-to-fine inference). A distinctive feature in our unifying approach is to induce probabilistic ontologies, which can be learned from noisy text and support joint inference. Past systems have explored two different approaches to probabilistic ontology induction. One approach is to bootstrap from existing ontological structures and apply self-supervision to correct the erroneous nodes and fill in the missing ones (KOG). Another approach is to integrate ontology induction with hierarchical smoothing, and jointly pursue unsupervised ontology induction, population and knowledge extraction (LOFT).

A key direction for future work is to combine these two paradigms. As case studies in ontology integration, prior research has devised probabilistic schema mappings and corpus-based matching algorithms (Doan, 2002; Madhavan, 2005; Dong et al., 2007), and has automatically constructed mappings between the Wikipedia infobox "ontology" and the Freebase ontology. This latter endeavor illustrated the complexity of the necessary mappings: a simple attribute in one ontology may correspond to a complex relational view in the other, comprising three join operations; searching for such matches yields a search space with billions of possible correspondences for just a single attribute.

Another key direction is to develop general methods for inducing multi-facet, multi-inheritance ontologies. Although single-inheritance, tree-like hierarchies are easier to induce and reason with, naturally occurring ontologies generally take the form of a lattice rather than a tree.

3.6 Continuous Learning

Early work at Washington proposed to construct knowledge bases by mass collaboration (Richardson and Domingos, 2003). A key challenge is to combine inconsistent knowledge sources of varying quality, which motivated the subsequent development of Markov logic. While this work did not do machine reading, its emphasis on lifelong learning from user feedback resonates with our approach on continuous learning.

Past work at Washington has demonstrated the promise of our approach. For example, (Banko and Etzioni, 2007) automated theory formation based on TextRunner extractions via a lifelong-learning process; (Hoffmann et al., 2009) show that the pairing of Kylin and community content creation benefits both by sharing Wikipedia edits; (Soderland et al., 2010) successfully adapted the TextRunner open-domain information extraction system to specific domains via active learning.

Our approach also resonates with the never-ending learning paradigm for "Reading the Web" (Carlson et al., 2010). In future work, we intend to combine our approach with related ones to enable more effective continuous learning from experience.

4 Conclusion

This paper proposes a unifying approach to machine reading that is end-to-end, large-scale, maximally autonomous, and capable of continuous learning from experience. At the core of this approach is a self-supervised learning process that conquers the long tail of textual knowledge by propagating information via joint inference. Markov logic is used as the unifying framework for knowledge representation and joint inference. Sophisticated joint inference is made scalable by coarse-to-fine inference based on induced probabilistic ontologies. This unifying approach builds on the prolific experience in cutting-edge machine reading research at the University of Washington. Past results demonstrate its promise and reveal key directions for future work.

5 Acknowledgement

This research was partly funded by ARO grant W911NF-08-1-0242, AFRL contract FA8750-09-C-0181, DARPA contracts FA8750-05-2-0283, FA8750-07-D-0185, HR0011-06-C-0025, HR0011-07-C-0060, NBCH-D030010 and FA8750-09-C-0179, NSF grants IIS-0803481 and IIS-0534881, and ONR grant N00014-08-1-0670 and N00014-08-1-0431, the WRF / TJ Cable Professorship, a gift from Google, and carried out at the University of Washington's Turing Center. The views and conclusions contained in this document are those of the authors and should not be interpreted as necessarily representing the official policies, either expressed or implied, of ARO, DARPA, NSF, ONR, or the United States Government.

References

G. Bakir, T. Hofmann, B. B. Schölkopf, A. Smola, B. Taskar, S. Vishwanathan, and (eds.). 2007. *Predicting Structured Data*. MIT Press, Cambridge, MA.

M. Banko and O. Etzioni. 2007. Strategies for lifelong knowledge extraction from the web. In *Proceedings of the Sixteenth International Conference on Knowledge Capture*, British Columbia, Canada.

Michele Banko, Michael J. Cafarella, Stephen Soderland, Matt Broadhead, and Oren Etzioni. 2007. Open information extraction from the web. In *Proceedings of the Twentieth International Joint Conference on Artificial Intelligence*, pages 2670–2676, Hyderabad, India. AAAI Press.

Michael J. Cafarella, Jayant Madhavan, and Alon Halevy. 2008. Web-scale extraction of structured data. *SIGMOD Record*, 37(4):55–61.

Andrew Carlson, Justin Betteridge, Richard C. Wang, Estevam R. Hruschka Jr., and Tom M. Mitchell. 2010. Coupled semi-supervised learning for information extraction. In *Proceedings of the Third ACM International Conference on Web Search and Data Mining*.

Janara Christensen, Mausam, Stephen Soderland, and Oren Etzioni. 2010. Semantic role labeling for open information extraction. In *Proceedings of the First International Workshop on Formalisms and Methodology for Learning by Reading*.

Anhai Doan. 2002. *Learning to Map between Structured Representations of Data*. Ph.D. thesis, University of Washington.

Pedro Domingos and Daniel Lowd. 2009. *Markov Logic: An Interface Layer for Artificial Intelligence*. Morgan & Claypool, San Rafael, CA.

Xin Dong, Alon Halevy, and Cong Yu. 2007. Data integration with uncertainty. *VLDB Journal*.

Robert B. Doorenbos, Oren Etzioni, and Daniel S. Weld. 1997. A scalable comparison-shopping agent for the world-wide web. In *Proceedings of AGENTS-97*.

Doug Downey, Matthew Broadhead, and Oren Etzioni. 2007a. Locating complex named entities in web text. In *Proceedings of the Twentieth International Joint Conference on Artificial Intelligence*.

Doug Downey, Stefan Schoenmackers, and Oren Etzioni. 2007b. Sparse information extraction: Unsupervised language models to the rescue. In *Proceedings of the Forty Fifth Annual Meeting of the Association for Computational Linguistics*.

Doug Downey, Oren Etzioni, and Stephen Soderland. 2010. Analysis of a probabilistic model of redundancy in unsupervised information extraction. In *Artificial Intelligence*.

Oren Etzioni, Michael Cafarella, Doug Downey, Ana-Maria Popescu, Tal Shaked, Stephen Soderland, Daniel S. Weld, and Alexander Yates. 2005. Unsupervised named-entity extraction from the web: An experimental study. *Artificial Intelligence*, 165(1):91–134.

Pedro F. Felzenszwalb and David McAllester. 2007. The generalized A* architecture. *Journal of Artificial Intelligence Research*, 29.

Lise Getoor and Ben Taskar, editors. 2007. *Introduction to Statistical Relational Learning*. MIT Press, Cambridge, MA.

Raphael Hoffmann, Saleema Amershi, Kayur Patel, Fei Wu, James Fogarty, and Daniel S. Weld. 2009. Amplifying community content creation using mixed-initiative information extraction. In *Proceedings of CHI-09*.

Raphael Hoffmann, Congle Zhang, and Daniel S. Weld. 2010. Learning 5000 relational extractors. In *submission*.

Chloe Kiddon and Pedro Domingos. 2010. Ontological lifted probabilistic inference. In *submission*.

Stanley Kok and Pedro Domingos. 2008. Extracting semantic networks from text via relational clustering. In *Proceedings of the Nineteenth European Conference on Machine Learning*, pages 624–639, Antwerp, Belgium. Springer.

Nicholas Kushmerick, Daniel S. Weld, and Robert Doorenbos. 1997. Wrapper induction for information extraction. In *Proceedings of the Fifteenth International Joint Conference on Artificial Intelligence*.

Cody Kwok, Oren Etzioni, and Daniel S. Weld. 2001. Scaling question answering to the web. In *Proceedings of the Tenth International Conference on World Wide Web*.

Thomas Lin, Oren Etzioni, and James Fogarty. 2009. Identifying interesting assertions from the web. In *Proceedings of the Eighteenth Conference on Information and Knowledge Management*.

Xiao Ling and Daniel S. Weld. 2010. Temporal information extraction. In *Proceedings of the Twenty Fifth National Conference on Artificial Intelligence*.

Jayant Madhavan. 2005. *Using known schemas and mappings to construct new semantic mappings*. Ph.D. thesis, University of Washington.

Slav Petrov. 2009. *Coarse-to-Fine Natural Language Processing*. Ph.D. thesis, Department of Computer Science, University of Berkeley.

Hoifung Poon and Pedro Domingos. 2007. Joint inference in information extraction. In *Proceedings of the Twenty Second National Conference on Artificial Intelligence*, pages 913–918, Vancouver, Canada. AAAI Press.

Hoifung Poon and Pedro Domingos. 2008a. A general method for reducing the complexity of relational inference and its application to mcmc. In *Proceedings of the Twenty Third National Conference on Artificial Intelligence*, pages 1075–1080, Chicago, IL. AAAI Press.

Hoifung Poon and Pedro Domingos. 2008b. Joint unsupervised coreference resolution with Markov logic. In *Proceedings of the 2008 Conference on Empirical Methods in Natural Language Processing*, pages 649–658, Honolulu, HI. ACL.

Hoifung Poon and Pedro Domingos. 2009. Unsupervised semantic parsing. In *Proceedings of the 2009 Conference on Empirical Methods in Natural Language Processing*, pages 1–10, Singapore. ACL.

Hoifung Poon and Pedro Domingos. 2010. Unsupervised ontological induction from text. In *submission*.

Ana-Maria Popescu and Oren Etzioni. 2005. Extracting product features and opinions from reviews. In *Proceedings of the Joint Conference on Human Language Technology and Empirical Methods in Natural Language Processing*.

Matt Richardson and Pedro Domingos. 2003. Building large knowledge bases by mass collaboration. In *Proceedings of the Second International Conference on Knowledge Capture*, pages 129–137, Sanibel Island, FL. ACM Press.

Alan Ritter, Doug Downey, Stephen Soderland, and Oren Etzioni. 2008. It's a contradiction – no, it's not: A case study using functional relations. In *Proceedings of the 2008 Conference on Empirical Methods in Natural Language Processing*.

Alan Ritter, Mausam, and Oren Etzioni. 2010. A latent dirichlet allocation method for selectional preferences. In *submission*.

Stefan Schoenmackers, Oren Etzioni, and Daniel S. Weld. 2008. Scaling textual inference to the web. In *Proceedings of the 2008 Conference on Empirical Methods in Natural Language Processing*.

Stefan Schoenmackers, Jesse Davis, Oren Etzioni, and Daniel S. Weld. 2010. Learning first-order horn clauses from web text. In *submission*.

Parag Singla and Pedro Domingos. 2006. Memory-efficient inference in relational domains. In *Proceedings of the Twenty First National Conference on Artificial Intelligence*.

Stephen Soderland, Brendan Roof, Bo Qin, Mausam, and Oren Etzioni. 2010. Adapting open information extraction to domain-specific relations. In *submission*.

Fei Wu and Daniel S. Weld. 2007. Automatically semantifying wikipedia. In *Proceedings of the Sixteenth Conference on Information and Knowledge Management*, Lisbon, Portugal.

Fei Wu and Daniel S. Weld. 2008. Automatically refining the wikipedia infobox ontology. In *Proceedings of the Seventeenth International Conference on World Wide Web*, Beijing, China.

Fei Wu and Daniel S. Weld. 2010. Open information extraction using wikipedia. In *submission*.

Fei Wu, Raphael Hoffmann, and Daniel S. Weld. 2008. Information extraction from Wikipedia: Moving down the long tail. In *Proceedings of the Fourteenth ACM SIGKDD International Conference on Knowledge Discovery and Data Mining*, Las Vegas, NV.

Alexander Yates and Oren Etzioni. 2007. Unsupervised resolution of objects and relations on the web. In *Proceedings of Human Language Technology (NAACL)*.

Analogical Dialogue Acts: Supporting Learning by Reading Analogies

David Barbella
Qualitative Reasoning Group
Northwestern University
2133 Sheridan Road, Evanston, IL, USA
barbella@u.northwestern.edu

Kenneth D. Forbus
Qualitative Reasoning Group
Northwestern University
2133 Sheridan Road, Evanston, IL, 60201, USA
forbus@northwestern.edu

Abstract

Analogy is heavily used in written explanations, particularly in instructional texts. We introduce the concept of *analogical dialogue acts* (ADAs) which represent the roles utterances play in instructional analogies. We describe a catalog of such acts, based on ideas from structure-mapping theory. We focus on the operations that these acts lead to while understanding instructional texts, using the Structure-Mapping Engine (SME) and dynamic case construction in a computational model. We test this model on a small corpus of instructional analogies, expressed in simplified English, which were understood via a semi-automatic natural language system using analogical dialogue acts. The model enabled a system to answer questions after understanding the analogies that it was not able to answer without them.

1 Introduction

People use analogy heavily in written explanations. Instructional texts, for example, use analogy to convey new concepts and systems of related ideas to learners. Any learning by reading system must ultimately include the capability of understanding such analogies. Here we combine Gentner's (1983) structure-mapping theory with ideas from dialogue act theory (Traum, 2000) to describe a catalog of analogical dialogue acts (ADAs) which capture the functional roles that discourse elements play in instructional analogies. We outline criteria for identifying ADAs in text and describe what operations they suggest for discourse processing. We provide evidence that this model captures important aspects of understanding instructional analogies via a simulation that uses knowledge gleaned from reading instructional analogies to answer questions.

We start by reviewing the relevant aspects of structure-mapping theory and dialogue act theory. Then we describe our catalog of analogical dialogue acts, based on a theoretical analysis of the roles structure-mapping operations can play in language understanding. A prototype implementation of these ideas is described next, followed by an experiment illustrating that these ideas can be used to understand analogies in text, based on answering questions. We close with a discussion of related and future work.

2 Background

Dialogue act theories (also called speech acts (Allen & Perrault, 1980)) are concerned with the roles utterances play in discourse and the effects they have on the world or on understanding. An utterance identified as a Requesting Information, for example, might take the syntactic form of a question that makes the information requested explicit, e.g. "What time is it?" The surface manifestation might instead be a statement, or an indirect question, e.g. "Do you have the time?" In other words, its classification is based on its function in the dialogue and the set of operations it suggests for the recipient to undertake. We claim that there exists a set of analogical dialogue acts that are used in communicating analogies. Like other dialogue acts, they have criteria by which they can be rec-

Proceedings of the NAACL HLT 2010 First International Workshop on Formalisms and Methodology for Learning by Reading, pages 96–104, Los Angeles, California, June 2010.

ognized, and a set of implied commitments and obligations for the dialogue participants. This paper focuses on instructional analogies in texts, both because they are an important phenomenon and because it allows us to factor out follow-up questions, making it a useful starting point.

There are a wide variety of dialogue act models, but all of them include some variation of acts like Inform (Traum, 2000), which indicate the intent to describe the state of the world. The analogical dialogue acts we discuss here can be viewed as specializations of Inform.

The organization of analogical dialogue acts follows directly from the concepts of structure-mapping theory. In structure-mapping, analogical matching takes as input two structured, relational representations, the *base* and *target*, and produces as output one or more *mappings*. Each mapping consists of a set of *correspondences*, identifying how entities and statements in the base align with entities and statements in the target. Mappings include a *structural evaluation score* providing an estimate of their overall quality. This estimate is based on *systematicity*, i.e., the amount of nested relational structure in the mapping, especially higher-order relations that serve as inferential connections between other statements. Causal, logical, and mathematical statements are all examples of higher-order relations. Systematicity thus serves as a local heuristic measure of the explanatory promise of a mapping.

Mappings can also contain *candidate inferences*, statements in the base that are projected onto the target, using the correspondences of the mapping. The candidate inferences represent conjectures about the target, and constitute a source of analogy's generative power. Whether or not the candidate inferences are in fact correct is evaluated outside of the matching process. In discourse, candidate inferences are often used to convey new information about the target to the learner. Candidate inferences can be forward, from base to target, or reverse, from target to base. Candidate inferences also represent differences between two representations, when they cannot be consistently projected from one description to the other.

The Structure-Mapping Engine (SME, Falkenhainer et al 1989) provides a simulation of analogical matching. SME typically produces only one mapping, but can produce a second or third mapping if they are sufficiently close to the best mapping. SME can accept input about the base and target incrementally, updating its mappings as new information becomes available (Forbus et al 1994), which can be important for modeling the incremental nature of discourse. One cost of SME's greedy match algorithm and incremental operation is that matches can go awry. Consequently, SME also supports a small set of constraints, optionally specified as part of the matcher's input, which guide it based on task constraints. Here the relevant constraints are those concerning correspondences. That is, given a base item b_i and target item t_j, either entities or statements, the following constraints are defined: *required*$(b_i\ t_j)$ means that b_i must correspond to t_j in every mapping, and *excluded*$(b_i\ t_j)$ means that b_i cannot correspond to t_j in any mapping. The following open constraints are also defined: *requiredBase*(b_i), means that something in every mapping must correspond to b_i, with *requiredTarget*(t_j) defined similarly. *excludedBase*(b_i) means that b_i cannot participate in any correspondence, with *excludedTarget*(t_j) defined similarly.

An important problem in understanding analogy in discourse concerns how the representations provided to SME are constructed. As described below, the representations that constitute an understanding of the text are produced in our model via a semi-automatic natural language understanding system, which reduces tailorability. In understanding instructional analogies, a learner is expected to draw upon their existing world knowledge. In some situations, whole cases representing a prior experience are retrieved from memory. In other situations, cases seem to be constructed dynamically from one's general knowledge of the world. We use *dynamic case construction* methods (Mostek et al 2000) to model this process. In dynamic case construction, a seed entity or concept is provided as a starting point, and facts which mention it are gathered, perhaps filtering by some criterion. For example, "The economy of India" might have India as its seed, and facts filtered based on their judged relevance to economic matters. When a reader is processing an instructional analogy, we believe that something like this process is used to create representations to be used in their understanding of the analogy.

Heat flows from one place to another because the temperature of the two places is different. A hot brick loses heat to a cool room. The temperature difference - the brick's temperature minus the room's temperature – drives the heat from the brick. Heat leaks from the brick until the temperature difference is gone. No more heat flows from the brick when it becomes as cool as the room it is in.
Similarly, a full can of water will leak volume from a hole in the side of the can. The depth of the water is higher than the depth of the hole, so the depth difference drives volume out through the hole.
Eventually, all the volume that can leak out does so. When this happens, the water depth has fallen so that it is the same as that of the hole. There is no more depth difference, so no more volume flows out through the hole. Just as a difference in temperature causes heat to flow, so a difference in depth causes volume to flow. When there is no temperature difference, heat flow ceases; when there is no depth difference, volume flow ceases.

Extend Target
Extend Base
Introduce Comparison
Candidate Inference

Figure 1: An analogy from our test corpus, hand-annotated with analogical dialogue acts.

3 Analogical Dialogue Acts

Our model of analogical dialog acts is based on an analysis of how the functional constraints on performing analogical mapping and case construction interact with the properties of discourse. To carry out an analogy, a reader must be able to infer that an analogy is required. They must understand what goes into the base and what goes into the target, which can be complex because what is stated in the text typically needs to be combined with the reader's own knowledge. Since readers often know quite a lot to begin with, figuring out which subset of what they know is relevant to the analogy can be complicated. Finally, they have to understand how the author intends the mapping to go, since there can be multiple mappings between the same domains. Analogical dialogue acts, we argue, provide readers with information that they need to perform these tasks.

Let us examine this process in more detail. To carry out an analogy, the contents of the base and target representations must be identified. A fundamental problem is that the reader must figure out an appropriate construal of the base and target, i.e., what subset of their knowledge should be brought to bear in the current comparison? A reader's starting knowledge may or may not be sufficient to guide the mapping process correctly, in order to reconstruct the mapping that the author intended. This is especially true in instructional analogies, of course. We believe that this is why one commonly finds explicit information about intended correspondences provided as part of instructional analogies. Such information provides a source of constraints that can be used to guide case construction and mapping. Similarly, and we believe for similar reasons, the desired inferences to be drawn from the analogy are often highlighted. Since there can be multiple construals (i.e., specific sets of facts retrieved) for the given base and target, mentioning candidate inferences explicitly provides clues to the reader about how to construe the base and target (i.e., the given candidate inference should be derivable) as well as information about its validity.

Next we describe our proposed analogy dialogue acts. For each act, we give an example, some criteria for identifying them, and describe what operations a reader might do when they detect such an act has occurred. At this point our focus has been on developing the basic set and the operations they entail, rather than on developing a comprehensive set of identification criteria. The first three acts are concerned with introducing the representations to be compared, and the rest are concerned with correspondences and candidate inferences. We use a greenhouse/atmosphere analogy as a source of examples.

Introduce Comparison: Introduces a comparison by providing both base and target. For example, in "We can understand the greenhouse effect by comparing it to what goes on in an actual greenhouse." the base is a greenhouse, and the target is the Earth's atmosphere. Recognizing an Introduce Comparison can require combining information across multiple sentences. In Figure 1, for example, the target is described in the paragraph above the point where the comparison is introduced. Sometimes this intent must be inferred from parallel sentence structure in subsequent sentences and other sophisticated rhetorical devices, while in other cases, like this example, the comparison is introduced explicitly.

What is the base and what is the target requires a non-local assessment about what the containing text is about. (This particular example is drawn from a book on solar energy, and the rest of the chapter makes clear that heat is the domain being taught.) Since we assume that candidate inferences can be constructed bidirectionally, an incorrect assessment is not catastrophic.

Processing an Introduce Comparison act requires finding appropriate construals of the base and target. The target, as in this case, is constrained by what has already been introduced in the text. The base, unless it has been used before in the same text and is being used in a consistent manner, must be constructed from the reader's knowledge. Whether this is done aggressively or lazily is, we suspect, a strategy that is subject to individual variation. Ambiguity in linguistic cues can lead to the need to explore multiple construals, to find combinations with significant overlap.

Extend Base, Extend Target: These acts add information to the base or target of a comparison, respectively. Such acts are identified by relationships and/or entities being mentioned in the same statement as an entity in the base or target, but which is not a statement about correspondences or candidate inferences. For example, "The glass of a greenhouse lets the short solar rays through." is extending the base, and "The earth's atmosphere admits most of the solar radiation." is an example of extending the target. Entities that are mentioned in these acts are added to the construal of the case, if not there already, by retrieving additional knowledge about them, focusing on statements involving other entities in the current construal. If the specific facts mentioned are not already known to the reader, they are provisionally accepted as being true about the base or target, as appropriate.

Introduce Correspondence: These acts provide clues as to the author's intended mapping. For example, "The Earth's atmosphere is like the glass in the greenhouse." indicates that "Earth's atmosphere" corresponds to "glass in greenhouse". Distinguishing these acts from introducing a comparison can be tricky, since "is like" is a syntactic pattern common to both. The first occurrence of "is like" in such cases is typically the introduction of the base and target, with subsequent statements introducing correspondences. Sometimes Introduce Correspondence acts are expressed as identity statements, e.g. "The glass is the atmosphere." Sometimes these acts are signaled by pairs of sentences, one expressing a fact about the base followed immediately by one about the target, with identical syntax.

When an Introduce Correspondence act is detected, the base and target are checked to see if they already contain the entities or relationships mentioned. If they do not, then the descriptions are extended to include them. The final step is introducing a *required* constraint between them as part of the input to SME. If mappings have already been generated that are not consistent with this constraint, they are discarded and new mappings are generated.

Block Correspondence: These acts are provided by the author to block a correspondence that a reader might otherwise find tempting. An example is "The greenhouse door is not like the hole in the ozone layer." We believe that these acts are relatively rare, and especially in written text compared with spoken dialogue, where there are opportunities for feedback, a matter discussed later.

When both a base and target item are mentioned, an *exclude* constraint is introduced between them. When only one of them is mentioned, the minimal operation is to add an open exclusion constraint (e.g. *excludedBase* or *excludedTarget*). The reader may decide to simply remove the excluded item from the construal, along with all of the facts that mention it. This would prevent it from being mapped, but it would also prevent it from appearing in any candidate inferences, and hence is more extreme.

Introduce Candidate Inference: These acts alert the reader to information that the author intended to convey via the analogy. An example is "Just as heat is trapped by the greenhouse roof, heat is trapped by the Earth's atmosphere." Phrases such as "just as" and "just like", or even "Like *<base statement to be projected>*, *<resulting candidate inference>*." are clues for identifying such acts. If the candidate inference can be found in the mapping that the reader has built up so far, then that surmise should be given additional weight as being true. (If it is already known by the reader, it may already be part of a mapping. This does not indicate failure, only that it is uninformative for that reader.) If the candidate inference cannot be

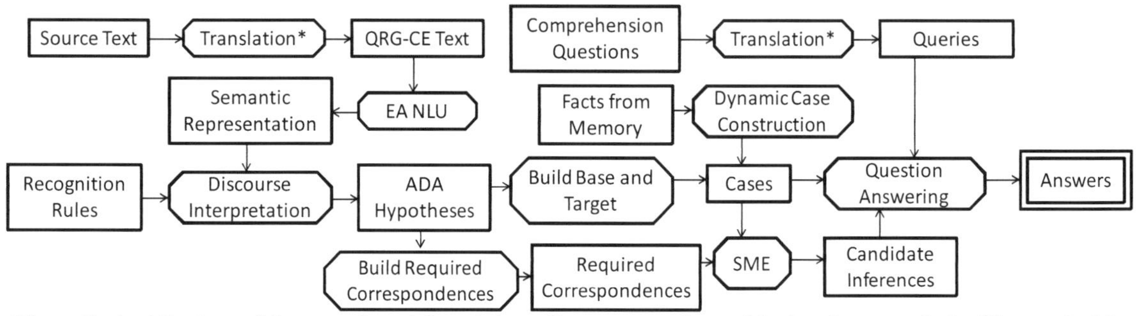

Figure 2: Architecture of the experimental prototype. Processes performed by hand are marked with an asterisk.

found, then there are several possibilities that a reader should explore: Their construal of the base and/or target might be too different from what the author expects, or they should generate a different mapping.

It is important to note that whether a statement combining information from the base and target is considered an intended correspondence versus an intended candidate inference depends to some degree on the reader's state of knowledge. If the target information is unknown, then for that reader, a candidate inference is being introduced. A very active reader may ponder whether it would be a correspondence for a more informed reader, and conversely, whether something an active and well-informed reader views as a correspondence might have been intended as a candidate inference. In both cases, considering the alternate classification would affect the reader's judgment of informativeness, so the distinction between these two types of acts is useful to make. Candidate inferences represent the point of the analogy, what it was set up to convey, and hence distinguishing them seems important.

Block Candidate Inference: These acts alert the reader that an inference that they are likely to make is not in fact correct. For example, "Unlike solar radiation, radiation heat flow reacts in the same way to different colors." If the candidate inference is part of the reader's mapping, then these acts indicate that the reader should mark them as incorrect. A reader with an aggressive processing style who did not generate this inference might explore modifications of their base and/or target to see if they can generate that inference, thereby ensuring they are more in sync with the author's intentions and thus better able to process subsequent statements. These acts are sometimes identifiable by terms such as "unlike," "however," or "you might expect… but" which include one clause expressing information about the base and one clause expressing information about the target. We believe that, like Block Correspondence, these occur relatively infrequently.

4 A prototype implementation

To explore the utility of our analogical dialogue acts theory, we implemented a simple computational model which uses ADAs to learn from instructional texts and answer questions based on what it has learned, synthesized with what it already knows (Figure 1). Our model uses the FIRE reasoning engine, which incorporates SME. The knowledge base contents are extracted from ResearchCyc[1] and extended with other knowledge, including an analogy ontology that lets analogy operations and other forms of reasoning be freely mixed (Forbus et al 2002). In addition to the natural language lexical information built into ResearchCyc, we also use the COMLEX lexicon (Macleod et al 1998) for part of speech and subcat information. For natural language understanding, we use EA NLU (Tomai & Forbus, 2009), which also uses FIRE and the same knowledge base. EA NLU uses Allen's (1994) parser for syntactic processing and construction of initial semantic representations. It uses Discourse Representation Theory (Kamp & Reyle, 1993) for dealing with tense, quotation, logical and numerical quantification, and counterfactuals.

EA NLU is useful for this type of learning by reading experiment because it focuses on generating rich semantic representations. It does so at the expense of syntactic coverage: We restrict inputs syntactically, using QRG-CE (Kuehne & Forbus, 2004), a form of simplified English much like CPL (Clark et al 2005). For example, complex sen-

[1] http://research.cyc.com

tences are broken up into a number of shorter, simpler sentences. Explicit object references (e.g. "the greenhouse greenhouse12" every time the same greenhouse is mentioned) are used to factor out the difficulty of anaphora resolution. EA NLU provides facilities for semi-automatic processing; In this mode, the ambiguities it cannot resolve on its own are presented as choices to the experimenter. This keeps tailorability low, while allowing the system to process more complex texts.

As noted above, we do not yet have a robust model of identification criteria for analogical dialogue acts, so we extended EA NLU's grammar to have at least one naturally occurring pattern for every ADA. As part of the translation to QRG-CE, texts are rewritten to use those patterns when we view an analogical dialogue act as being present. This allows the system to automatically classify ADAs during processing. Here our goal is to model the processing that must take place once such acts are recognized, since identifying such acts is irrelevant if they are not useful for reasoning. EA NLU's parsing system produces semantic representations used in its discourse interpretation processing. The ADA recognition rules are used along with EA NLU's standard discourse interpretation rules to generate ADA hypotheses as part of its discourse representations (Figure 1).

We believe that there are significant individual differences in processing strategies for these acts. For example, some people seem to be quite aggressive about building up mappings, whereas others appear to do minimal work. Consequently, we have started with the simplest possible approach. Here is what our simulation currently does for each of the types of acts:

Introduce Comparison: Builds initial construals of the base and the target by retrieving relevant facts from the knowledge base[2].

Extend Base/Extend Target: The understanding of the sentence is added to the base or target, as appropriate. This decision is made by keeping track of the concepts that are mentioned by statements in each domain, starting with the Introduce Comparison act.

Introduce Correspondence: A required correspondence constraint is introduced for the entities involved, to be used when SME is run for this analogy.

Introduce Candidate Inference: The information in these statements is simply treated as a fact about the target domain. We do not currently change the mapping if a candidate inference in text is not part of the mapping computed.

Block Correspondence/Candidate Inference: Not implemented currently, because examples of these did not show up in our initial corpus.

Analogical dialogue acts are identified via inference rules that are run over the discourse-level interpretation that EA NLU produces. Analogical mapping occurs only at the end of processing a text, rather than incrementally. Statements about the base and target are accepted uncritically, rather than being tested for inconsistencies against background knowledge. These simplifications represent one point in the possible space of strategies that people seem likely to use; plans to explore other strategies are discussed below.

Once the ADA hypotheses are used to construct the base and target domain and the required correspondences between them, this information is used by SME to generate candidate inferences - statements that might be true on the basis of the analogy constructed. The base and target case are expanded using dynamic case construction, which adds knowledge from the KB to fill in information that the text leaves out. For example, a text may not explicitly mention that rain falls from the sky to the earth, taking it as a given that the reader is aware of this.

Example	**#O**	**#A**
Gold mining/Collecting solar energy	8	11
Water flow/heat flow	11	12
depth of water in bucket/temperature of house	8	16
Bucket with hole/house leaking heat	4	10
Bucket/Solar collector	5	8
Earth's atmosphere/greenhouse	7	14
Mean	7.2	11.8

Table 1: Corpus Information. #O/#A = # sentences before/after translation to QRG-CE

5 Experiment

An essential test for a theory of analogy dialogue acts is whether or not it can be used to construct new knowledge from instructional analogies in text. To test this, we extracted a small corpus of 6 instructional analogies from a book on solar energy (Buckley, 1979) and a book on weather (Lehr et al

[2] We use a case constructor similar to `CaseFn` from Mostek et al 2000, but including automatic expansion of rule macro predicates and using microtheory information for filtering.

1987). We simplified the syntax of the original texts into QRG-CE, using the appropriate surface forms for the analogy dialogue acts that we perceived in the text. One of the analogies is illustrated in Figure 1, with part of its translation is shown in Figure 3. Table 1 summarizes properties of the original texts and the simplification process.

Original: Similarly, a full can of water will leak volume from a hole in the side of the can.
QRG-CE: A hot brick brick005 is like a can can001 of water water001. There is a hole hole001 in can can001. The water water001 exits can can001 through hole hole001.

Figure 3: Example of translation to QRG-CE. The specific individuals are added to factor out anaphora processing. Cues to analogical dialogue acts spread across multiple sentences in the original text are combined into single sentences during the translation process.

To test the effectiveness of knowledge capture, 12 comprehension questions similar to those found in middle-school science texts were generated by independent readers of the texts (see Figure 4 for an example). All questions were designed to require understanding the analogy in order to answer them. Moreover, some of the questions require combining information from the knowledge base with knowledge gleaned from the text.

Question: What disappears as the heat leaks from the brick?
Predicate calculus version:

```
(and
 (inputsDestroyed ?d ?ourAnswer)
 (after-Underspecified ?d ?leaving)
 (objectMoving ?leaving heat005)
 (isa ?heat ThermalEnergy)
 (isa ?leaving LeavingAPlace)
 (fromLocation ?leaving brick005))
```

Figure 4: A question for the analogy of Figure 1, in English and the hand-generated predicate calculus generated from it.

Four experimental conditions were run, based on a 2x2 design here the factors were whether or not analogy was used (+A) or not used (-A), and whether what was learned from the text was augmented with information from the knowledge base (+K) or not (-K).

Table 2 shows the results. The system was able to answer all twelve questions when it understood the analogy and combined what it learned by reading with information from the knowledge base.

Condition	# correct	%
-A, -K	0	0
+A, -K	7	58
-A, +K	0	0
+A, +K	12	100

Table 2: Results for Q/A. +/- means with/without, A means analogy, K means facts retrieved from KB

That this was due to understanding the analogy can be seen from the other conditions. The information from the text alone is insufficient to answer any of the questions (-A, -K), as is the information from the KB alone (-A, +K). Analogy by itself over what was learned by reading the passages can handle over half the questions (+A, -K), but the rest require combining facts learned by reading with facts from the KB (+A, +K).

6 Related Work

There has been very little work on modeling analogies in dialogue. One of the few efforts has been Lulis & Evans (2003), who examined the use of analogies by human tutors for potential extensions to their intelligent tutoring system for cardiac function. Recently they have begun incorporating analogies into their tutor (Lulis, Evans, & Michael, 2004), but they have not focused on understanding novel analogies presented via language.

Because EA NLU is designed to explore issues of understanding, it is focused more on semantic coverage than on syntactic coverage. The most similar system is Boeing's BLUE (Clark & Harrison, 2008), which also uses simplified syntax and focuses on integrating language with a knowledge base and reasoning.

Aside from SME, we suspect that the only other current widely tested model of analogy that might be able to handle this task is IAM (Keane & Brayshaw 1988). CAB (Larkey & Love 2003) does not model inference, and hence could not model this task. Although LISA (Hummel & Holyoak, 2003) can model some analogical inferences, the number of relations (see Table 3) in these analogies is beyond the number of relationships it can currently handle (2 or 3).

The first simulation of analogy to use natural language input was Winston's (1982, 1986), which used a simple domain-specific parser in modeling the learning of if-then rules and censors. EA NLU benefits from subsequent progress in natural language research, enabling it to handle a wider range of phenomena.

Example	#S	#BA	#BR	#TA	#TR
Gold mining/Collecting solar energy	8	26	32	4	4
Water flow/heat flow	11	14	21	13	16
depth of water in bucket/temperature of house	8	12	19	9	12
Bucket with hole/house leaking heat	4	14	20	8	6
Bucket/Solar collector	5	13	15	4	4
Earth's atmosphere/greenhouse	7	12	19	11	14
Mean	7.2	15.2	21	8.2	9.3

Table 3: Statistics of base and target domains produced by EA NLU. #S = number of sentences, B/T = Base, Target; A/T = Attributes/Relations

7 Discussion and Future Work

Modeling the roles that analogy plays in understanding language is an important problem in learning by reading. This paper is an initial exploration of how analogy can be integrated into dialogue act theories, focusing on instructional analogies in text. We presented a catalog of analogical dialogue acts, based on an analysis of how the functional constraints of analogical mapping and case construction interact with the properties of discourse. We showed that a simulation using these ideas, combined with a natural language understanding system to semi-automatically produce input representations, can indeed learn information from simplified English analogies, which is encouraging evidence for these ideas.

The next step is to expand the corpus substantially, including more examples of all the ADAs, to better test our model. We also need to implement the rest of the ADAs, and experiment with a wider range of processing strategies.

To better model how ADAs can be identified in natural texts, we plan to use a large-scale web-based corpus analysis. We have focused on text here, but we believe that these ideas apply to spoken dialogue as well. We predict more opportunities for blocking in spoken dialogue, due to opportunities for feedback.

Our goal is to incorporate these ideas into a 2nd generation learning by reading system (e.g., Forbus et al 2007; Forbus et al 2009a), along with other dialogue processing, to better interpret larger-scale texts (e.g., Lockwood & Forbus, 2009). This will be built using the Companions cognitive architecture (Forbus et al 2009b), to more easily model a wider range of processing strategies, and so that the system can learn to improve its interpretation processes.

Acknowledgments

This research was supported by the Intelligent and Autonomous Systems Program of the Office of Naval Research.

References

Allen, J.F. (1994). Natural Language Understanding. (2nd Ed.) Redwood City, CA: Benjamin/Cummings.

Allen, J. F. & C. R. Perrault (1980). Analyzing Intention in Utterances. Artificial Intelligence 15(3).

Buckley, S. (1979). From Sun Up to Sun Down. New York: McGraw-Hill.

Clark, P. & Harrison, P. (2008). Boeing's NLP system and the challenges of semantic representation

Clark, P., Harrison, P., Jenkins, T., Thompson, J. & Wojcik, R. (2005). Acquiring and using world knowledge using a restricted subset of English. 18th International FLAIRS Conference.

Falkenhainer, B., Forbus, K. & Gentner, D. (1989). The Structure-Mapping Engine: Algorithms and Examples. Artificial Intelligence, 41, 1-63.

Forbus, K., Ferguson, R. & Gentner, D. (1994) Incremental structure-mapping. Proceedings of CogSci94.

Forbus, K., Lockwood, K. & Sharma, A. (2009). Steps towards a 2nd generation learning by reading system. AAAI Spring Symposium on Learning by Reading, Spring 2009.

Forbus, K., Klenk, M., & Hinrichs, T. , (2009). Companion Cognitive Systems: Design Goals and Lessons Learned So Far. IEEE Intelligent Systems, vol. 24, no. 4, pp. 36-46, July/August.

Forbus, K., Mostek, T. & Ferguson, R. (2002). An analogy ontology for integrating analogical processing and first-principles reasoning. Proceedings of IAAI-02, July.

Forbus, K. Riesbeck, C., Birnbaum, L., Livingston, K., Sharma, A., & Ureel, L. (2007). Integrating natural language, knowledge representation and reasoning, and analogical processing to learn by reading. Proceedings of AAAI-07 Vancouver, BC.

Gentner, D. (1983). Structure-Mapping: A Theoretical Framework for Analogy. Cognitive Science, 7: 155-170.

Gentner, D., Bowdle, B., Wolff, P., & Boronat, C. (2001). Metaphor is like analogy. In Gentner, D., Holyoak, K., and Kokinov, B. (Eds.) The analogical mind: Perspective from cognitive science. pp. 199-253, Cambridge, MA: MIT Press.

Hummel, J. E., & Holyoak, K. J. (2003). A symbolic-connectionist theory of relational inference and generalization. Psychological Review, 110, 220-264.

Kamp, H. & Reyle, U. (1993). From Discourse to Logic: Introduction to Model-theoretic Semantics of Natural Language. Kluwer Academic Dordrecht: Boston.

Keane, M., and Brayshaw, M. (1988). The Incremental Analogy machine: A computational model of analogy. European Working Session on Learning.

Larkey, L. & Love, B. (2003). CAB: Connectionist Analogy Builder. Cognitive Science 27,781-794.

Lehr, P. E., Burnett, R. W., & Zim, H. S. (1987). Weather. New York, NY: Golden Books Publishing Company, Inc.

Lockwood, K. & Forbus, K. 2009. Multimodal knowledge capture from text and diagrams. Proceedings of KCAP-2009.

Lulis, E. & Evans, M. (2003). The use of analogies in human tutoring dialogues. AAAI Technical Report SS-03-06.

Lulis, E., Evans, M. & Michael, J. (2004). Implementing analogies in an electronic tutoring system. In Lecture Notes in Computer Science, Vol 3220, pp. 228-231, Springer Berlin/Heidelberg.

Macleod, C., Grisham, R., & Meyers, A. (1998). COMLEX Syntax Reference Manual, Version 3.0. Linguistic Data Consortium, University of Pennsylvania: Philadelphia, PA.

Mostek, T., Forbus, K, & Meverden, C. (2000). Dynamic case creation and expansion for analogical reasoning. Proceedings of AAAI-2000. Austin, TX.

Tomai, E. & Forbus, K. (2009). EA NLU: Practical Language Understanding for Cognitive Modeling. Proceedings of the 22nd International Florida Artificial Intelligence Research Society Conference. Sanibel Island, Florida.

Traum, David R. (2000). 20 Questions on Dialogue Act Taxonomies. Journal of Semantics, 17, 7-30.

Winston, P.H. 1982. Learning new principles from precedents and exercises. Artificial Intelligence 23(12).

Winston, P. 1986. Learning by augmenting rules and accumulating censors. In Michalski, R., Carbonell, J. and Mitchell, T. (Eds.) Machine Learning: An Artificial Intelligence Approach, Volume 2. Pp. 45-62. Morgan-Kaufman.

A Hybrid Approach to Unsupervised Relation Discovery Based on Linguistic Analysis and Semantic Typing

Zareen Syed
University of Maryland Baltimore County
1000 Hilltop Circle
Baltimore, MD 21229, USA

Evelyne Viegas
Microsoft Research
One Microsoft Way
Redmond, WA 98052, USA

Abstract

This paper describes a hybrid approach for unsupervised and unrestricted relation discovery between entities using output from linguistic analysis and semantic typing information from a knowledge base. We use Factz (encoded as subject, predicate and object triples) produced by Powerset as a result of linguistic analysis. A particular relation may be expressed in a variety of ways in text and hence have multiple facts associated with it. We present an unsupervised approach for collapsing multiple facts which represent the same kind of semantic relation between entities. Then a label is selected for the relation based on the input facts and entropy based label ranking of context words. Finally, we demonstrate relation discovery between entities at different levels of abstraction by leveraging semantic typing information from a knowledge base.

1 Introduction

There are a number of challenges involved when using facts extracted from text to enrich a knowledge base (KB) with semantic relations between entities: co-reference resolution as there are many co-referent objects; entity resolution in order to link the entities mentioned in text to the right entities in the KB; handling co-referent relations, as a particular semantic relation between entities can be expressed in a variety of ways in the text and therefore have multiple facts associated between the entities. In addition, the facts extracted from linguistic analysis are usually noisy and sparse.

Our work focuses on a recent line of exploratory work in the direction of Unrestricted Relation Discovery which is defined as: the automatic identification of different relations in text without specifying a relation or set of relations in advance (Shinyama and Sekine, 2006). We use the facts which are the output of linguistic analysis from Powerset (www.Powerset.com). Powerset is an online search engine for querying Wikipedia using Natural Language Queries. Powerset performs a linguistic analysis of the sentences within Wikipedia and outputs facts in the form of subject, predicate and object triples which can be queried through the online interface. For most entities like persons, places and things, Powerset shows a summary of facts from across Wikipedia (figure 1). In our approach we use the readily available "Factz" from Powerset as input to our system. Powerset is Wikipedia independent and can run on any corpus with well-formed sentences and hence our approach is also not limited to Wikipedia. The Factz output from Powerset may represent relations between named entities or just nouns for example,

Bank of America	<acquired>	bank
Bank of America	<acquired>	Merrill Lynch
Bank of America	<owned>	building

Linguistic analysis has been recently described as an effective technique for relation extraction (Yan et al., 2009; Kambhatla, 2004; Nguyen et al., 2007). Following that trend, we incorporate Factz, that are the output of linguistic analysis done by Powerset, to discover semantic relations between entities.

Information from existing knowledge re-

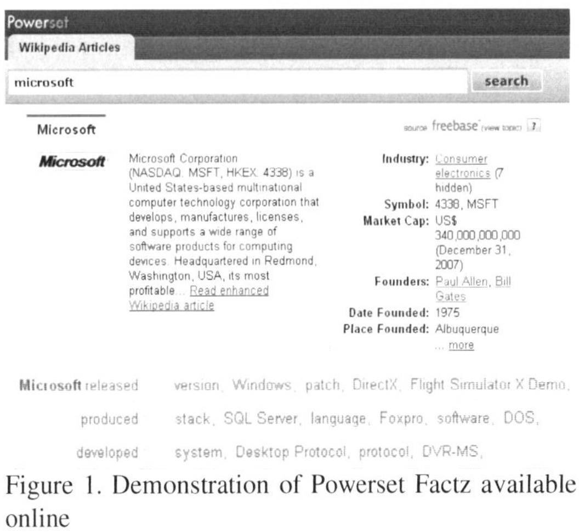

Figure 1. Demonstration of Powerset Factz available online

Proceedings of the NAACL HLT 2010 First International Workshop on Formalisms and Methodology for Learning by Reading, pages 105–113,
Los Angeles, California, June 2010.

sources can help in tasks like named entity disambiguation by providing additional context in the form of linked entities in the KB and aid in linking the entities mentioned in the text to the entities in the KB. The KB can also provide information about the entity types which can in turn be used to discover relations between entity types at different levels of abstraction and help in enriching the KB itself. This could allow ontology engineers to explore the kind of relations existing between different entity types in a corpus and then design an ontology which is representative of the entities and relations evident in the corpus.

Our overall approach to automatic relation discovery consists in a hybrid approach based on Powerset Factz that are the output of linguistic analysis, and serve as input to our system; Text based label ranking by directly considering the context words in the sentences; and, Semantic Typing information from existing knowledge resources to discover relations between Entity types at different levels of abstraction.

The paper is organized as follows. We discuss the related work in the next section. In section 3 we propose our approach and give the details of different components in our system. In section 4, we discuss preliminary experiments and results. In the last section we conclude our work and give future work directions.

2 Related Work

Hasegawa et al. (2004) developed an approach for unsupervised relation discovery by clustering pairs of entities based on intervening words represented as context vectors. They used the most frequent common word to label the cluster and hence the relation represented by the cluster.

Shinyama and Sekine (2006) developed an approach to preemptively discover relations in a corpus and present them as tables with all the entity pairs in the table having the same relations between them. For pairs of entities they generate basic patterns that are parts of text syntactically connected to the Entity and use the predicate argument structure to make the basic patterns more generalized. They generate a basic cluster from articles based on having similar basic patterns to represent the same event and then they cluster the basic clusters to get a set of events having the same relation.

Davidov et al. (2007) developed a web mining approach for discovering relations in which a specified concept participates based on clustering patterns in which the concept words and other words appear. Their system is based on the initial seed of two or more words representing the type of concept one is interested in.

Linguistic analysis has been reported as an effective technique for semantic relation extraction. Harabagiu et al. (2005) used shallow semantic parsers to enhance dependency tree kernels and to build semantic dependency structures to improve relation extraction, they reported that their method improved the quality of the extracted relations as compared to kernel-based models that used semantic class information only.

Nguyen et al. (2007) presented an approach for relation extraction from Wikipedia by extracting features from subtrees mined from the syntactic structure of text. Kambhatla (2004) developed a method for extracting relations by applying Maximum Entropy models to combine lexical, syntactic and semantic features and report that they obtain improvement in results when they combine variety of features. Most of the existing approaches have used linguistic analysis to generate features for supervised or semi-supervised relation extraction.

Recently, Yan et al. (2009) have developed an approach for unsupervised relation discovery by integrating linguistic analysis done on Wikipedia with context generated from the Web. They develop a clustering approach based on dependency patterns from dependency analysis of Wikipedia and surface patterns by querying the web to introduce redundancy. They report that dependency patterns improve the precision whereas, the surface patterns improved the coverage.

Banko et al. (2008) introduce the TextRunner system which takes a small corpus sample as input and uses a linguistic parser to generate training data which they use to train the extractor which can run at web scale. However, Kok and Domingos (2008) have reported that the triples output from the TextRunner system are noisy, sparse and contain many co-referent objects and relations which is also the case with Powerset. Their system uses the output from the TextRunner system and uses Multiple Relational Clustering model to get object clusters and relation clusters.

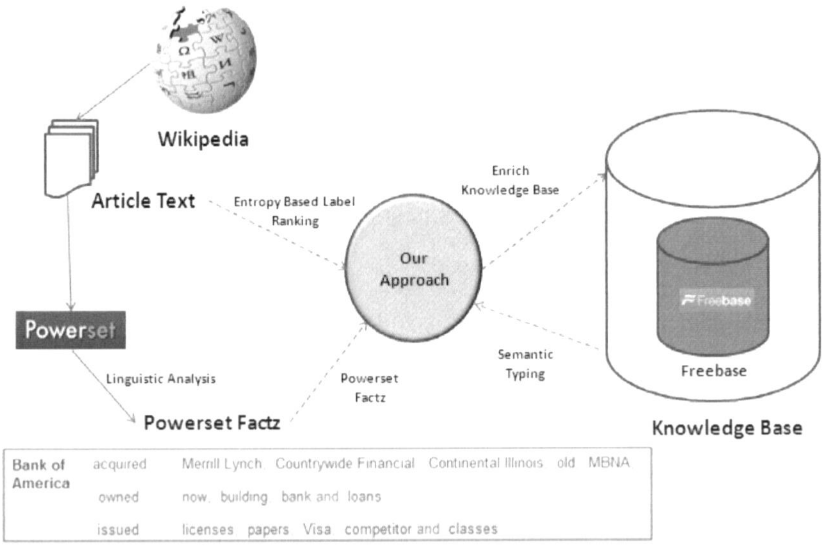

Figure 2. The Knowledge Discovery approach uses Powerset Factz which are the output from linguistic analysis, article text for entropy based label ranking and existing knowledge resources for discovering relations at different levels of abstraction and hence aiding in enriching the existing knowledge resources.

3 Approach

In this section we describe in detail the different steps in our approach involving querying Factz from Powerset, collapsing facts expressing same type of relation, Label Selection and introducing Semantic Typing information. Figure 2 gives an overview of our approach and Figure 3 shows the different components in our system. We discuss each component in detail below.

3.1 Querying Powerset and Retrieving Factz

In the first step we query Powerset API by giving as input a list of entities or list of entity pairs and retrieve all the Factz and sentences that are associated with the entities or entity pairs from the Powerset API output.

3.2 Collapsing Similar Relations

A particular semantic relationship can be expressed in different ways in sentences. For example words like "purchase", "buy" and "acquire" may represent the same semantic relation between the subject and the object. Sometimes the words might be direct synonyms in which case resources like WordNet (Miller et al., 1990) can help in identifying the same relation whereas in other cases the words might not be synonyms at all but may still imply the same semantic relation between the subject and the object. For example, we queried Powerset to get a sample of relations between companies and products. We got relations like *introduce, produce, sell, manufacture* and *make*. It is often the case that companies *introduce* and *sell* the products that they *manufacture, make* or *produce*. However, all of these words are not synonyms of each other and it may not be feasible to express the relation between a company and a product in all these different ways in a KB.

We have developed an approach for collapsing relations expressed using different words in the facts and represent it using the dominating relation between the pair of entities. We explain the different steps in our approach below.

3.2.1 Relation Clustering

We consider relations to be similar if they appear between the same subjects and the objects. We take the set of Factz that we got by querying Po-

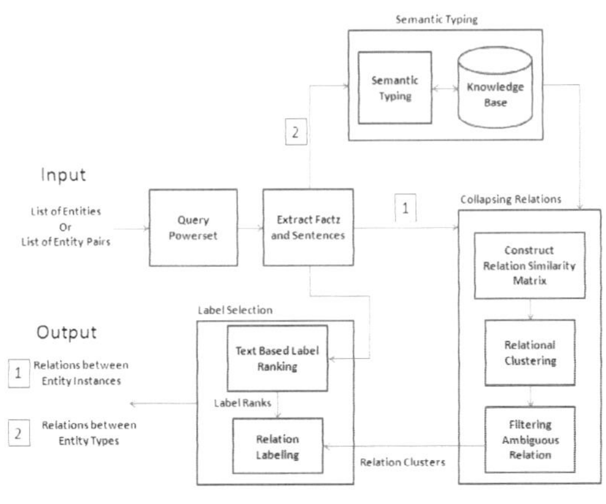

Figure 3. System Framework

werset in the previous step and based on those Factz we construct a similarity matrix to represent similarity between all pairs of relations in the data set. Each entry in the similarity matrix represents the number of times the pair of relations had the same subject and object in the Factz data set. For example, in the sample dataset in table 1, the similarity matrix entry for the pair *acquired* and *purchased* would be 3. We use that similarity matrix as input and apply average link agglomerative clustering algorithm over it.

Subject	Predicate	Object
Bank of America	acquired	Merrill Lynch
Bank of America	acquired	MBNA
Bank of America	acquired	FleetBoston
Bank of America	purchased	FleetBoston
Bank of America	purchased	Merrill Lynch
Bank of America	purchased	MBNA

Table 1. Relations between same subjects and objects in Powerset

3.2.2 Filtering Ambiguous Relations

After the clustering step we have a step for filtering ambiguous relations from the clusters. We explain the filtering procedure using an example from one of the experiments in which two clusters were produced. First cluster had *acquire, purchase, buy* and *own* relations and the second cluster had *introduce, produce, make* and *say about* relations. After clustering the relations we have the following steps:

1. We take each pair of entities and get the set of relations between the pair of entities. For example, the set of relation between "Bank of America" and "Merrill Lynch" are *acquire, purchase* and *say about* (figure 4).
2. By considering the set of relations between each pair of entities we assign it to a cluster based on the maximum number of overlapping relations between the set and the cluster members. In our example clusters, we assign it to cluster one with which there is an overlap of two relations i.e. *acquire* and *buy* instead of assigning it to cluster two with which it has an overlap of one relation i.e. *say about* (figure 4).
3. Once an entity pair is assigned to a cluster, we consider other relations in the set of relations present between that entity pair and if any of those relations exists as a member of another cluster we filter out that relation from that cluster. For example, one of the relations present between "Bank of America" and "Merill Lynch" is

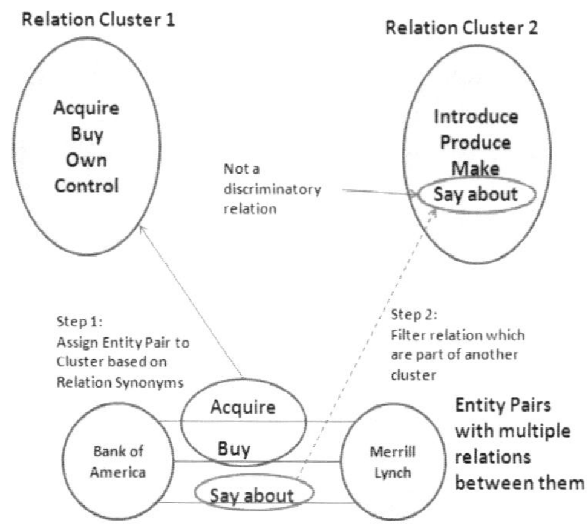

Figure 4. Filtering ambiguous relations from existing clusters

say about, and this relation is actually a member of cluster two whereas, this pair is assigned to cluster one and therefore, we filter out *say about* from cluster two. After cluster filtering, the label for the cluster is selected as the label that is the most frequent relation found in the set of entity pairs being assigned to the cluster.

3.3 Relation Label Selection

A pair of entities might have more than one fact associated with them. We select a representative label based on a hybrid approach by combining the output from entropy based label ranking (Chen et al., 2005) and clusters of similar relations found by relational clustering. We select the relation label as the cluster label of the cluster which has the maximum member overlap with the predicates in the set of facts between a pair of entities. In case there is an overlap of just one relation, we select the label that is ranked highest through entropy based label ranking approach (Chen et al., 2005). According to their algorithm, the importance of terms can be assessed using the entropy criterion, which is based on the assumption that a term is irrelevant if its presence obscures the separability of the dataset. There may be cases where there are multiple relations existing between a given pair of entities, however, in our approach we select the relation label that is evident in the majority of the facts associated with the pair.

3.4 Semantic Typing

For certain applications there might be the need of discovering relations between specific types of entities rather than instances of entities. For example, for ontology engineering, the ontology engineer might want to explore the kind of relations that exist between different entity types based on the data set and then develop an ontology representing those relations. Therefore, we have a component in our system that incorporates semantic type information into the Factz before collapsing the relations present in the facts. The semantic type module queries a knowledge base for the entity type and replaces the entity instance names with entity types in the Factz data set. We have used the Freebase (Metaweb Technologies, 2009) Knowledge base to associate the entity types for the entities that we experimented with. When this modified version of the Factz dataset is given as input to the next component of the system i.e. Collapse Relations, the similarity between relations is computed based on having the same subject and object entity types rather than entity instances. Following the Semantic Typing path in the system would output the relations discovered between types of entities. Introducing Semantic Typing information can also help in creating redundancy in the dataset and overcome the data sparseness problem. For example in case of relations such as *acquire* and *purchase* if we cannot get evidence of overlap in the subject and object in the Factz dataset then we cannot assign them any similarity score in the similarity matrix however, if we replace the instance names with instance types and consider the overlap between the instance types we can get more evidence about their similarity.

4 Experiments and Results

In this section, we present the preliminary experiments we conducted to evaluate the approach. We start by an initial evaluation of Powerset Factz by comparing them with ground truth and text based label ranking (Chen et al., 2005). We then use our approach to discover relations between different entity types. The details of the experiments and results are discussed below.

4.1 Preliminary Evaluation of Powerset Factz

Our first experiment was targeted towards a preliminary evaluation of the accuracy of Powerset Factz themselves and their performance when compared with ground truth and with Entropy based label ranking approach which does not use any linguistic analysis. To achieve this we took the "acquisitions" table from Freebase. The "acquisitions" table has a list of companies and their acquisitions. We considered the acquisitions table as ground truth as this information is either entered manually by contributors or imported from Wikipedia via DBpedia. We queried Powerset by giving the entity pairs as input and were able to retrieve Factz for 170 pairs out of 1107 entity pairs present in Freebase table. The number of pairs for which Powerset returned Factz is low because Powerset currently extracts Factz from well formed sentences and not semi-structured or structured information such as tables or info-boxes in Wikipedia and the *acquisition* relation is mostly expressed in the form of tables or lists in Wikipedia articles. We applied relational clustering and stopped clustering when the similarity between the clusters was less than 4. We identified one cluster (*acquire, purchase, buy*) having more than one member and got 146 relations labeled accurately i.e. 85% accuracy through our approach. We repeated the experiment using Entropy based label ranking approach (Chen et al., 2005). We were mainly focusing on relations that were expressed by verbs. We took all sentences between a pair of entities from which Powerset had extracted Factz. We extracted verbs from those sentences and ranked those verbs based on the entropy based label ranking approach and considered any of the labels matching with the cluster members (*acquire, purchase, buy*) as correct prediction. We compared the results with the ground truth and got the accuracy of 72% (table 2). Our preliminary experiment on the sample dataset demonstrated that the relation labels assigned by Powerset have reasonably high accuracy when compared with ground truth i.e. 85% and also give higher accuracy as compared to the entropy based label ranking approach for the sample data set.

Approach	Accuracy
Powerset Factz based approach	85%
Entropy based Label ranking	72%

Table 2. Comparison of Powerset Factz based approach and Entropy based label ranking

4.2 Discovering Relations between Different Types of Entity Pairs

In this experiment we wanted to explore if our approach was successful in discovering relations existing between different types of entity pairs and clusters the pairs into separate clusters.

We constructed two datasets using Wikipedia page links between articles on entities namely Persons and Organizations. Using "person" type and "organization" type specified in Freebase, we were able to construct a list of Wikipedia articles that were on Persons and Organizations. The Wikipedia article links served the purpose of finding out which organizations are related to which other organizations and which persons are related to which organizations. The first dataset represented relations between Organizations whereas the second dataset represented relations between Persons and Organizations. We applied relational clustering for collapsing similar relations and evaluated the output clusters at different thresholds to see if they represented relations between different types of entities. At stopping with a threshold of 2 we found the following two clusters having more than one member: one of the clusters represented the relations present between a pair of Organizations (*acquire, purchase, buy, own, say about, take over*) and the other cluster represented the relations between Persons and Organizations (*formed, found, lead*) (table 3). The experiment confirmed the effectiveness of clustering approach as it clusters relations between different kinds of entity pairs into different clusters.

Relations	Clusters
Org-Org	Cluster 1: acquire, purchase, buy, own, say about, take over over
Pers-Org	Cluster 2: found, lead, form

Table 3. Relations between different types of entity pairs are clustered into different clusters

4.3 Improving Recall

In this experiment we were interested in finding if Factz from Powerset can help in discovering relations between entities that are not present in resources like DBpedia and Freebase. We took a list of organization (with > 28,000 organization names from Freebase and an internal Knowledge Base) and retrieved Powerset Factz having those organizations as subjects. We performed relation clustering and output clusters at different thresholds. We selected the minimum threshold for which there were at least two clusters with more than one member. From the two clusters, one cluster had *manufacture, produce* and *make* relations and the second had *acquire, purchase, own, operate* and *buy* relations (table 4). Our intuition was that the first cluster represented relations between organizations and products. Therefore, we took the "company-products" table from Freebase and compared it with our dataset. However, we could only find an overlap of 3 subject object pairs. The second cluster had relations that we earlier found to exist between organizations having the *acquisition* relation between them, therefore, we took the "acquisitions" table from Freebase and compared it against our dataset. Comparing the pairs with our list of organizations, we found 104 pairs that had an organization as a subject and an object. Out of those 104 pairs 97 pairs were assigned to cluster 2 and 7 pairs were assigned to cluster 1. When we compared those 97 pairs with Freebase "acquisition" table (which had 73 pairs of organizations that overlapped with our dataset) we found that 66 existed in the set and were therefore predicted correctly. We then inspected the rest of the pairs manually and found that there were 16 additional pairs that were predicted to have the *acquire* relation and which were not present in the Freebase table. Therefore, this approach helped in identifying 16 additional organization pairs having *acquisition* relation between them correctly.

Cluster	Cluster Members
1	manufacture, produce, make
2	acquire, purchase, own, operate, buy

Table 4. Clustering results for Relations having Organizations as subjects

Statistics	
No. of pairs in Freebase table	73
No. of discovered pairs matching Freebase	66
No. of additional pairs discovered	16
Total no. of correctly discovered pairs	82/104
Accurate Predictions %age	78%

Table 5. Evaluation results for improving recall by discovering additional entity pairs having the *acquisition* relation

Another observation worth mentioning is that the *acquisition* relation is represented mostly in the form of tables in Wikipedia whereas Powerset only processes information that is present in sentences. In spite of that, our approach was able to find new entity pairs from text that did not already exist in information extracted by other sources (table 5).

4.4 Discovering Relations at Different Levels of Abstraction

In this experiment we introduced Semantic Type information in the Factz data set to discover relations at different levels of abstraction i.e. between Entity Types at different levels (For example School or Organization, where School is a type of Organization).

We took a list of 13000 organizations for which we had their Organization Types available from an internal KB and queried Powerset for Factz between all pairs of organizations and were able to retrieve more than 88,000 Factz. We passed on the Factz to the Semantic Typing module to replace the Organization names with their types. The Factz dataset with Semantic Type information was given as input for collapsing relations, where the similarity matrix was constructed based on the same subject and object types (rather than same subject and object instances), after which the clustering was performed. We evaluated the clusters at different stopping thresholds but the system did not generate any meaningful clusters. We then looked into the dataset and realized that a lot of noise was introduced into the system due to various organization names which were very ambiguous and replacing the ambiguous organization names with organization types had magnified the noise. For example, in our organizations list there is an organization with the name "Systems" which is of type "Medical Instrument Supplies". It had the following fact related to it: <3d systems> <manufacture> <systems>. Replacing the organization name with the type resulted in the following fact i.e., <multimedia graphics software> <manufacture> <medical instruments supplies>. Such ambiguous names when replaced with wrong types further magnified the noise.

4.4.1 Resolving Ambiguity

As discussed, ambiguous organization names introduced noise and replacing them with organization types magnified the noise. Therefore, it was important to resolve the ambiguity in the names of entities before applying Semantic Typing. There are different approaches than can be used to recognize and disambiguate Named Entities, which we discuss below.

4.4.1.1 Named Entity Recognition

Powerset has Factz that are extracted from sentences. The Factz may be present between Named Entities or even just words in sentences. For example "Accord" is a name of a trade union and is also a word. Running Named Entity Recognition systems over the sentences from which the Factz have been extracted can help in identifying named entities and in eliminating such factz which are not between named entities. In general, the relation extraction systems have an initial step where they identify entities in sentences through NER systems and then discover relations between those entities.

Most of Named Entity Recognition and Disambiguation systems use the contextual information to disambiguate between entities. The contextual information could be words in the sentences or other entities in the sentences where the entity is mentioned. Having some evidence that two entities are related in some way can also help in eliminating much of the ambiguity. In general, the relation extraction systems have an initial step where they find related entity pairs based on Co-occurrences and then discover relations between those pairs of entities which frequently co-occur with each other in sentences.

We followed the approach of getting additional context by using entity pairs for querying Powerset for which we have background knowledge that the pairs are related through some relation and only retrieved the Factz that were between those entity pairs. We repeated the same experiment. However, this time we gave as input pairs of entity names for which we have evidence that the entities are related and then ran the experiment with and without semantic typing information to validate if introducing semantic typing can give us some additional advantage. We discuss the details of our experiment below.

Relations between Entity Types	Freebase Source
person - organization	PersonEmployment table
person- school	Education table
organization-organization	Acquisitions table

Table 6. Data Set with relations between different types of entities extracted from Freebase tables

Using Freebase tables we extracted datasets for relations present between three different kinds of entity pairs i.e persons and organizations (e.g. Person-join-Organization), persons and school (e.g. Person-attend-School) and Organizations and Organizations (e.g. Organization- acquire-Organization) (table 6). We used the pairs of entities (Persons - Organizations, Persons - Schools and Organizations - Organizations) to query Powerset and extracted the Factz that corresponded to those pairs. Table 7 gives an example of the predicates in the Factz found between the different types of entity pairs.

After clustering we evaluated the clusters and were expecting to get the relations between three different kinds of entity pairs namely Person - Organization, Person - School, Organization - Organization into three separate clusters. We evaluated the output clusters at different stopping thresholds but were not able to get three clusters using any threshold. Table 8 shows the clusters found at threshold of 2. There were two possible reasons for this outcome, one reason was that we did not have enough redundancy in the data set to get meaningful clusters and secondly, "school" is a type of "organization" which could have introduced ambiguity. In order to introduce redundancy we replaced all the entity names with their types (i.e., Person, Organization, School) in the Factz and repeated the experiment with Entity Type information rather than Entity names. We evaluated the clusters at different thresholds and were able to separate the relation sets into three clusters with greater than one member. Table 9 gives the results of clustering where we got three clusters with more than one member at minimum threshold.

The clusters represented the relations present between the three different types of entity pairs i.e., person and school, organization and organization and person and organization (table 9).

Wikipedia is a very non-redundant resource and redundancy helps in getting more evidence about the similarity between relations. Other approaches (Yan et al., 2009) have used the web for getting redundant information and improving recall. In addition, there are many sentences in Wikipedia for which Powerset has no corresponding Factz associated (it might be due to some strong filtering heuristics). Using semantic typing helped in introducing redundancy, without which we were not able to cluster the relations between different types of entity pairs into separate clusters. Semantic Typing also helped in identifying the relations present between entities at different levels of abstraction. This can help in suggesting relations between different entity types evident in the corpus during the Ontology engineering process.

Relation	Example of Powerset Factz Predicates
Person- Organization	join, leave, found, form, start, create
Person – School	attend, enter, return to, enroll at, study at
Organization - Organization	acquire, purchase, buy, own

Table 7. Example of Predicates in Powerset Factz representing relations between different types of entity pairs

No.	Cluster Members	Semantic Types
1	enroll at, return to	Person-School
2	found, purchase, buy, acquire, create, say about, own	Organization- Organization, Person-Organization

Table 8. Results of Clustering Relations between Entity Pairs without using Semantic Typing

No.	Cluster Members	Semantic Relation
1	lead, prep at, play for, enter, study, play, graduate, transfer to, play at, enroll in, go to, remain at, enroll at, teach at, move to, attend, join, leave, teach, study at, return to, work at	Person- School
2	acquire, purchase, buy, own, say about	Organization - Organization
3	found, create	Person - Organization

Table 9. Results of Clustering Relations with Semantic Typing

5 Conclusions

We have developed a hybrid approach for unsupervised and unrestricted relation discovery between entities using linguistic analysis via Powerset, entropy based label ranking and semantic typing information from a Knowledge base. We initially compared the accuracy of Powerset Factz with ground truth and with entropy based label ranking approach on a sample dataset and observed that the relations discovered through Powerset Factz gave higher accuracy than the entropy based approach for the sample dataset. We also developed an approach to collapse a set of relations represented in facts as a single dominating relation and introduced a hybrid approach for label selection based on relation clustering and entropy based label ranking. Our experiments showed that the relational clustering approach was able to cluster different kinds of entity pairs into different clusters. For the case where the kinds of entity pairs were at different levels of abstraction, introducing Semantic Typing information helped in introducing redundancy and also in clustering relations between different kinds of entity pairs whereas, the direct approach was not able to identify meaningful clusters. We plan to further test our approach on a greater variety of relations and on a larger scale.

References

Dat P. T. Nguyen, Yutaka Matsuo, and Mitsuru Ishizuka. 2007. Subtree mining for relation extraction from Wikipedia. In Proc. of NAACL '07: pages 125–128.

Dmitry Davidov, Ari Rappoport and Moshe Koppel. 2007. Fully unsupervised discovery of concept-specific relationships by Web mining. Proceedings of the 45th Annual Meeting of the Association of Computational Linguistics, pp. 232–239.

George A. Miller , Richard Beckwith , Christiane Fellbaum , Derek Gross , Katherine Miller. 1990. Wordnet: An on-line lexical database. International Journal of Lexicography, 3(4):235-312.

Jinxiu Chen, Donghong Ji, Chew Lim Tan and Zhengyu Niu. Unsupervised Feature Selection for Relation Extraction. In Proc. of IJCNLP-2005.

Metaweb Technologies, Freebase Data Dumps, http://download.freebase.com/datadumps/ July, 2009

Michele Banko , Michael J Cafarella , Stephen Soderl , Matt Broadhead , Oren Etzioni. 2008. Open information extraction from the web. Commun. ACM 51, 12 (Dec. 2008), 68-74.

Nanda Kambhatla. 2004. Combining lexical, syntactic and semantic features with maximum entropy models. In Proceedings of the ACL 2004 on Interactive poster and demonstration sessions.

Sanda Harabagiu, Cosmin Andrian Bejan, and Paul Morarescu. 2005. Shallow semantics for relation extraction. In Proc. of IJCAI 2005.

Soren Auer, Christian Bizer, Georgi Kobilarov, Jens Lehmann, Richard Cyganiak, and Zachary Ives. 2007. Dbpedia: A nucleus for a web of open data. In Proc. of ISWC 2007.

Stanley Kok and Pedro Domingos. 2008. Extracting Semantic Networks from Text Via Relational Clustering. In Proc. of the ECML-2008.

Takaaki Hasegawa, Satoshi Sekine and Ralph Grishman. 2004. Discovering Relations among Named Entities from Large Corpora. In Proc. of ACL-04.

Powerset. www.Powerset.com

Yulan Yan, Naoaki Okazaki, Yutaka Matsuo, Zhenglu Yang, and Mitsuru Ishizuka. 2009. Unsupervised relation extraction by mining Wikipedia texts using information from the web. In ACL-IJCNLP '09: Volume 2, pages 1021–1029.

Yusuke Shinyama and Satoshi Sekine. 2006. Preemptive information extraction using unrestricted relation discovery. In HLT/NAACL-2006.

Supporting rule-based representations with corpus-derived lexical information.

Annie Zaenen
Cleo Condoravdi
Daniel G. Bobrow
PARC
3333, Coyote Hill Road
Palo Alto, CA, 94304, USA
{zaenen,condorav,bobrow}@parc.com

Raphael Hoffmann
University of Washington
Box 352350
Seattle, WA, 98195, USA
raphaelh@cs.washington.edu

Abstract

The pervasive ambiguity of language allows sentences that differ in just one lexical item to have rather different inference patterns. This would be no problem if the different lexical items fell into clearly definable and easy to represent classes. But this is not the case. To draw the correct inferences we need to look how the referents of the lexical items in the sentence (or broader context) interact in the described situation. Given that the knowledge our systems have of the represented situation will typically be incomplete, the classifications we come up with can only be probabilistic. We illustrate this problem with an investigation of various inference patterns associated with predications of the form 'Verb from X to Y', especially 'go from X to Y'. We characterize the various readings and make an initial proposal about how to create the lexical classes that will allow us to draw the correct inferences in the different cases.

1 Introduction

Machine Reading requires a level of Natural Language Processing that allows direct inferences to be drawn from the processed texts. Most heavy duty inferencing will be done by a reasoning engine working on the output of the linguistic analysis (with possible loops between the two) but for this to be possible, the linguistic analysis should deliver representations where a certain level of disambiguation and content specification has been done. For instance, a human will draw different conclusions from the following two sentences about the position of the referent of the subject: 'Eric went from Paris to Lyon' and 'The road went from Paris to Lyon'. The first sentence implies that a person named Eric was in Paris at some time and in Lyon at a later time, whereas the second sentence implies that a part of the road was in Paris and a part of it was in Lyon at the same time. For the reasoner to draw such conclusions, the linguistic analysis should assign appropriate roles to the subject argument and the *from-to* adjunct or argument phrases of the verbal predicate *go* so as to convey that the first sentence involves movement, while the second involves spatial extent.

In this paper we look at a range of such inferences associated with *from-to* phrases. We limit ourselves to rather simple cases of the use of *from-to* phrases: those that describe no change or gradual changes in the physical world. We show that beyond inferences about time-dependent locations and spatial extent of particular entities, *from-to* phrases give rise to inferences about change of an entity in some dimension (e.g. temperature or width) either through time or through space. We first discuss the inferences we would like to be able to draw, and describe features of a representation that captures enough distinctions to enable these inferences to be drawn. This allows us to isolate the factors leading to such inferences. Finally, we give a preliminary sketch of a corpus analysis that would help make the required distinctions

Proceedings of the NAACL HLT 2010 First International Workshop on Formalisms and Methodology for Learning by Reading, pages 114–121,
Los Angeles, California, June 2010.

and characterize appropriate lexical classes.

2 Some simple inferences

Consider the following sentences:

1. Eric went from Paris to Lyon.
2. The road went from Paris to Lyon.
3. The meeting went from 3 p.m. to 5 p.m.
4. The temperature in the room went from 20 degrees to 30 degrees from 10 to 11 a.m.
5. The temperature went from 20 to 30 degrees from the front to the back of the room
6. The temperature went from 20 degrees to 30 degrees.
7. The room went from 20 to 30 degrees.

As indicated above, we would like the system to be able to conclude from (1) that Eric was in Paris before being in Lyon, and from (2) that one part of the road is in Paris whereas another part is in Lyon at the same time. From (3) the system should infer that the mentioned event, the meeting, started at 3 p.m. (or no later than 3 p.m.) and ended at 5 p.m. (or no earlier than 5 p.m.). From (4) the system should infer that the value of the function *temperature* as it applies to the room increases over the given temporal span. It is worth noting at this point that the two sets of *from-to* phrases in (4) play different roles. The temporal *from-to* phrases specify the relevant domain of the temporal argument of the function, while the measure *from-to* phrases specify the range of the function on the given domain. (5) has a similar implication to that of (4), that the temperature changes, but this time over a spatial dimension: the temperature is implied to vary in different parts of the room, being 20 degrees in the front of the room and 30 degrees in the back. Again the two sets of *from-to* phrases in (5) play different roles. The spatial *from-to* phrases specify the relevant domain of the spatial argument of the function and the measure *from-to* phrases specify the range of the function on the given domain. (6) and (7) have similar implications to those of (4) and, in the right context, to those of (5) but they present challenges of their own. In (6) the temporal (or spatial) dimension is implicit and needs to be inferred. (7) requires the inference that a change of the values of the function *temperature* is involved.[1]

These examples show that sentences that have substantially the same syntax and even use the same main verb can exhibit very different relations between their parts. The first question we want to address is how to explicate these differences and the second question is how to get from the words used in these sentences to the information needed about their type of referent to ensure the right interpretation in each case.

The verb 'to go' is, of course, not the only one that exhibits this behavior. The difference in interpretation between examples (1) and (2) can also be found with manner-of-motion verbs such as 'run' and 'zigzag'. Some verbs do lexically encode a particular functional dimension, such as temperature or width. These are known as degree achievements (Dowty, 1979; Abusch, 1986).[2] Examples of degree achievements include 'widen', 'lengthen', 'shorten', 'cool', 'age'. They exhibit similar patterns of modification with *from-to* phrases as we saw above:

8. The road widens from Palo Alto to Menlo Park.
9. The road widens from 12 to 24 feet.

Here 'widen' is interpreted statively, like 'go' in (2), and the two sentences imply spatial change in width, over subparts of the road. The two *from-to* phrases, however, have a different function giving rise to different implications. (8) implies that the road is wider in Menlo Park than it is in Palo Alto. (9) specifies the relation between the measures of width at two different subparts of the road. The *from-to* phrases in (8) specify

[1] It is not clear that the change has to be in one directional in all cases:

> This summer, the temperature went from 20 degrees to 30 degrees.

In this example, it seems that the temperature varied from 20 to 30 degrees, not necessarily that 20 degrees was a starting point or 30 degrees an end point. See section 4.1 for some further discussion.

[2] In English most degree achievements are derived from gradable adjectives. When this is the case, the meaning of degree achievements and underlying adjectives is systematically related, as argued in (Hay et al., 1999).

the domain of the spatial argument of the function *width* as it applies to the referent of 'the road'. Those in (9) specify the range of the values of the function *width* as it applies to different parts of the referent of 'the road'.

In what follows we will distinguish between *extent readings* and *change readings*. Extent readings specify, in full or in part, the temporal or spatial extent of a temporal or spatial entity, as seen in (3) and (2). Change readings specify the values of a function as applied to a given entity through a temporal or spatial span. The function is either determined directly by the verb, as in (8) and (9), or by the verb in combination with one of its arguments, as in (4) – (6), or it has to be inferred, as in (1) and (7).

3 Representing the different readings

For the sake of concreteness, in this section we show how the distinctions discussed above are represented and implemented in AKR, an abstract knowledge representation language into which sentences are mapped after they are parsed in the NL system developed at PARC (Bobrow et al., 2007). The idea behind AKR is to canonicalize many variations of an input text with the same underlying meaning into a more uniform representation. This ought to make the task of interfacing with reasoners easier.

The AKR of a sentence consists of a list of assertions. Terms are generated for each of the content words of a sentence, such as verbs and nouns, and are associated with assertions about the types of events and objects their corresponding words refer to. Predicates and their arguments or modifiers are related via role relations. The inventory of roles we use extends the set of semantic or thematic roles often assumed in linguistic analyses and found in resources such VerbNet or FrameNet. It includes among other things temporal or spatial relations of inclusion, precedence, etc.

We assume that sentences with *from-to* phrases imply the existence of a path and that the further information about the path specified is about the "location" of its initial and final points. In representing such sentences a term is created to represent a path and the path term is linked by a role *initial* to the term for the complement of *from*, and by a role *final* to the term for the complement of *to*. On our analysis then the *from-to* phrases are used to specify restrictions on the path term and do not translate into thematic roles relating the verbal predicate and the complement NP, such SOURCE or GOAL. The path term is related to the verbal term via different roles, depending on the type of interpretation. Below is an example that shows the role relations in AKR for sentence (1).

role(theme, go:13, Eric:7)
role(mpath, go:13, path:23)
role(initial,path:23,loc(-at-,Paris:4))
role(final,path:23,loc(-at-,Lyon:6))
role(dimension,path:23,loc)

3.1 Extent interpretations

In extent readings the subject argument denotes an entity extended in space, as seen in (2), or a non-punctual event, as seen in (3). The verb itself does little work other than to signal that the *from-to* phrases give information about the spatial or temporal extent of its subject argument. The way they do that is by saying that the given path is a spatial or temporal part of the entity that is the referent of the subject argument. Let us start with the representation of (3), as the representation of its meaning in our terms is quite intuitive. Temporal paths, such as from-to-span:11, correspond to time periods.

role(initial,time-span:11,timepoint(-at-,3pm))
role(final,time-span:11,timepoint(-at-,5pm))
role(temporalWithin,time-span:11,meeting:1)

It should now be clear that the representation for the spatial extent reading would differ minimally from that of the temporal extent reading: the relation between the path and the road terms would be that of spatial inclusion and the dimension of the path is locational.

role(initial,path:23,loc(-at-,Paris:4))
role(final,path:23,loc(-at-,Lyon:6))
role(spatialWithin,path:23,road:10)

3.2 Change interpretations

As discussed in section 2, change interpretations establish a dependency between two paths which should be represented explicitly. The paths themselves may be specified overtly by *from-to* phrases or they may be implicit. Functionally relating two paths of this type was first discussed, to our knowledge, in (Jackendoff, 1996) and further developed in (Gawron, 2005) and (Gawron, 2009).

Let us consider first example (4), where the two paths are given explicitly. (4) implies a change in the temperature of the room over time so the function *temperature* should be construed as time-dependent. The temporal path specifies the time period over which the given change in temperature takes place; the scalar path *partially* specifies the range of the function over the given temporal domain. What we can conclude for certain from (4) is that the temperature in the room was 20 degrees at 10 a.m. and 30 degrees at 11 a.m. The sentence gives no specific information about the temperature of the room in between 10 and 11 a.m. though in this case, given that change in temperature is continuous, we can conclude that every degree between 20 and 30 was the temperature of the room at some point within the relevant time period.

In order to represent the dependency between the two paths we use a higher order predicate *path-map* that specifies a function, that varies over a range (in this case the scalar path from 20 degrees to 30 degrees) with a domain (in this case the temporal path from 10 a.m. to 11 a.m.). More generally: the higher-order predicate, **path-map(F,D,R)**, relates a function F and two posets D and R. The path-map relation expresses that the image of D under F is equal to R.[3] For (4) we end up with the following representation.

role(scale,go:5,path:4)
role(dimension, path:4,temperature)
role(initial,path:4,temperature(-at-,20 deg))
role(final,path:4,temperature(-at-,30 deg))
role(initial,time-span:11,timepoint(-at-,10am))
role(final,time-span:11,timepoint(-at-,11am))
path-map(function(temperature,room:2),
time-span:11,path:4)

The fact that path:4 is a scalar path is marked by relating it to the verbal term via the role *scale*.

The other examples discussed in section 2 receive representations based on this model. (5) implies a change in the temperature of the room over its spatial extent oriented from the front to the back, so the function *temperature* should be construed as location-dependent. Below we give the assertions for the representation of (5) that differ from those of (4). Note the additional assertion relating the spatial path term to the room term.

role(initial,path:11,loc(-at-,front:10))
role(final,path:11,loc(-at-,back:12))
role(spatialWithin,,path:11,room:2)
path-map(function(temperature,room:2),
path:11,path:4)

The representation of sentences with degree achievements, such as *The road widens from 12 to 24 feet from Palo Alto to Menlo Park*, would the same in all relevant respects except that the dimension of the scalar path would be determined by the verb, in this case being *width*.

To derive full representations for (6) and (7) we need to be able to infer the second and the first argument of *function*, respectively. Moreover, we need to fix the dimension of the implicit path. Generally, when only one path is specified overtly, as in (6), (7) and (8) and (9) the existence of the other type of path is understood. When only the range path is given, the understood domain path can be either temporal or locational.

We come now to the prototypical use of a *from-to* phrase with verbs like 'go' to describe movement whose origin is specified by the *from* phrase and whose destination is specified by the *to* phrase. We gave a preliminary representation for (1) at the beginning of section 3. Missing from that representation is the explicit link between the location of the theme argument during

[3] Depending on what F, D and R are, this mapping may also be order preserving, i.e. for all elements x, y in D, if x precedes y then F(x) precedes F(y).

the time of the movement. This link, of course, can now be given in terms of the following path-map assertion:

path-map(function(location,Eric:7),
    time(go:13),path:23)

4 Which elements in the sentence guide interpretation?

In our system roles and dimensions are introduced by rules that take the output of the syntactic parse of the sentence as input. The exact form of these rules need not to concern us here. But an important question for NLP is where the information comes from that allows us to determine which role and dimension a path has. As the examples show, the verb is not necessarily the place to look: most of the examples use the verb 'to go'.

In fact, the information can come from various places in the sentence (or the broader textual context: ellipsis and anaphoric relations play their usual roles here). Moreover in some cases information about, say, the dimension can come from the arguments of *from* and *to* whereas in other cases this information can come from the verb. 'Widen' for instance imposes the width-dimension but if we use the verb 'to go' to describe a widening event, the information about the dimension has to come from the arguments of *from* and *to* and the subject.

Similar problems arise with respect to the determination of the roles. Example 1 and 2 seem to have straightforward interpretations where the path role in the first case is clearly a movement path whereas in the second case we have to do with a stative interpretation. At first blush, it seems that this information could be straightforwardly lexically encoded: people move and roads don't. But further reflection shows that this will not do. Take the following example:

10. The train went from one end of the station to the other.

In this case we can have two interpretations: either the length of the train is such that it covers that of the whole station or the train moved from one end of the station to the other. What is important is not an intrinsic characteristic of the lexical item but whether it is appropriate for the extent (length) of its referent to be measured by the *from-to* phrase.

Some more or less stable relations between syntax and semantics can help us determine which analysis to give. For instance, the starting and end points of movement paths and stative locational paths are referential (in contradistinction to those of scalar paths). As such, they tend to be expressed by proper names or by a noun phrase with a determiner.[4]

Manner of motion verbs are surprisingly uninformative: many of them can have a moving object or a stationary object or a function such as the temperature as their subject. The combinations summarized in the following are all possible:

11. Liz/the road/the temperature
    went/crawled/moved/meandered
    from X to Y.

With verbs of inherent directed motion, the verb contributes a polarity for the direction but very little else, as example 12 illustrates:

12. Liz/the road/the temperature
    descended/climbed/ascended/fell/tumbled
    from X to Y.

Again whatever information there is about the type of path or the dimension it has to come from the subject or from the *from-to* arguments. *From-to* arguments can give the necessary information about the dimension (locations, money, time, degrees) but when they are scalar or temporal, the measurement units will often be omitted and the theme will indicate the dimension.

Degree achievements tend to be more specialized. They indicate the dimension (width, temperature). Lexicons can contain many of the function names but will not help with the cases of metonymy (where an argument is given instead of the name of the function itself).

[4]There are, however, exceptions:

He ran from where Bill was to where the field ends.
His tattoo goes from head to toe.
The path meanders from mountain to mountain.

4.1 Characterizing components of the representations

In the previous subsection we have discussed different types of *from-to* phrases, and the roles that link the elements of the representations of these types. The question we address now is how we can provide our system with the necessary information to make these distinctions. This is a preliminary investigation as yet without implementation.

Ideally, we would have ontologies to give us the right characteristics of the entities underlying our lexical items and we would have adequate mappings from the lexical items to these ontologies. These ontologies and these mappings are currently not available. Natural language processing applications, however, have taught us that even if humans can do surprising things and language can express surprising thoughts, most of the time, the reality that human language expresses is rather predictable, so that the mapping to ontologies can up to a certain point be mimicked by probabilistic feature assignments to lexical items. For 'Eric' we can assume that with a high probability it will be the theme of a movement path and whereas for 'the road' a high probability assigns it as the theme of a stative path. In other cases, however, we need concrete co-occurrence statistics to assign the right representations. Next, we sketch a preliminary investigation of some Wikipedia data that can be brought to bear on this issue. We indicate how the data might help and point out some of the new problems it brings up.

A first question that arises is of how much practical relevance the different types that we have discussed are. We looked at the first 100 'went from X to Y' sentences pulled out of Wikipedia parsed with the Stanford dependency parser, that had the required syntactic pattern and found that 61 fell into the categories described in the previous sections (gradual change or no change in the physical domain) whereas about 39 are clearly transformational *from-to*'s (for instance 'The SU-152 went from design concept to field trials in a record twenty-five days'). Of these 61, 4 had temporal *from-to* modifiers, 19 had various scales or numeric *from-to* modifiers and 38 were locational. Of the locational ones, 11 had a stationary reading and 17 had a movement reading. So all the cases under discussion are well represented in naturally occurring text.

A second question is how we can obtain the relevant features from the data. We see four potential methods: (1) the characterization of words within existing ontologies like WordNet (Miller, 1995), (2) the combination of stated facts through reasoning, (3) co-occurrence statistics of words in text, and (4) solicitation of novel features from human annotators. We illustrate these methods based on Wikipedia examples.

A first idea might be that there is at least a straightforward ontological characterization for difference between the movement and the stative reading: for the movement reading we require living beings and for the stative reading we require long stationary entities. These impressions are, of course, not completely wrong but in the first case, we have to include in the living beings not only groups such as brigades but also ships (as in 'She went from the Red Sea to the Mediterranean to relieve USS Coral Sea ...'), flights (as in 'This flight went from Spitsbergen (Svalbard) to Alaska nonstop, so there is little doubt that they went over the North Pole.') and messages (as in 'The message went from the Palace in Stockholm to the King at Drottningholm.'). And in the second categories we have not only roads and various transportation lines but also borders (as in 'The boundary of Manila province went from northeast to southwest, ...') and trade routes and things such as (rifle) suppressors as in 'The suppressor, 2 inches in diameter, went all the way from the back of the barrel to well beyond the muzzle ...'). A quick inspection of WordNet shows that there is no interesting ancestor node that covers all the movement cases but it also suggests that a great number of the cases can be covered with 'conveyance, transport' together with 'motion, movement, move' as well as 'organism, being'. But 'organism, being' also covers 'plants' and 'sitter' and 'stander' and other subclasses that don't seem to be plausible candidates for the movement analysis. There is no interesting hypernym for both 'road' and 'border' before we get to the useless level of 'object, physical object' and no already existing ontology will help with the suppressor case. Thus we might get some data by using the first method but most likely not everything we want.

As far as the arguments of the *from-to* phrases themselves, locations can be indicated by place names, institution names, nouns referring to locations, but also nouns referring to spatial located entities that we do not think of as locations, such as parts of pieces of equipment. The very limited inspection of data we have done up to now does not lead us to expect that the nature of the *from-to* arguments occurring with movement readings is very different from that found with stationary readings. In the current state of affairs, many of the arguments of the *from-to* phrases can be found either in gazetteers or through the analysis of a reasonably well-circumscribed spatial vocabulary.[5]

Some cases, however, fall outside of these resources. The most interesting problem is presented by the reference to spatial entities that are not clearly flagged as locations in ontologies, such as those found in the suppressor-sentence ('The suppressor, 2 inches in diameter, went all the way from the back of the barrel to well beyond the muzzle ...') above. We admit that his type of sentence seems to be rather rare in the Wikipedia corpus but it is problematic because detailed ontological representations of even common objects are not readily available. Wikipedia, however, has some information that might help one to formulate reasonable hypotheses about parts. For instance, the article that contains the suppressor-sentence, also contains a structured specification of the carbine under description mentioning the barrel and the muzzle. Here we need to use the second method, reasoning. The question then becomes whether we can find reasoning patterns that are general enough to give interesting results.

[5]Whereas it is possible to enumerate an extensive part of the relevant vocabulary, there is no extensive description of meaning contribution of these elements.

The third method, already demonstrated in the context of semantic parsing (Poon and Domingos, 2009), seems also to be promising. For instance, even staying within the class of movement verbs, different verbs have different signatures that might help us with the classification of their subjects and their *from-to* arguments. While 'go' has indeed the wide range of meanings that we expected, 'run' is rather different: apart from three examples where 'run' refers to the movement of living beings and three referring to vehicles moving, the other examples of the combination of 'run' with *from-to* fall in two classes: indications of the spatial extent of roads, railways and the like (27) and temporal extensions of shows, games or strips running (16). The nature of the corpus has certainly an influence here (Wikipedia does not contain narrative texts) but this type of information might be valuable to disambiguate parses: if we can distinguish the cases where 'run' occurs with spatial extent readings and the cases where it occurs with temporal extent meanings, we can harvest a set of possible subjects that are also possible subjects for the spatial extent meaning of 'go'. The distinction between the two readings of 'run' is not very difficult to make as most of the temporal extent readings of 'run' have a temporal *from-to* phrase.[6]

A different way in which the characteristics of specific verbs or verb argument combinations might at least probabilistically disambiguate possible readings is illustrated with a difference between 'go' and 'range' with scalars. In section 3.2, we observed that scalar 'go' does not always imply that there is a steady increase or decrease over time or space. However in all the numerical or scalar examples except for one in our first sample, the interpretation implies such

[6]But those readings themselves bring up a new classificatory problem: most of the time the subject is an event, a show, or a game. However, in most cases the meaning is not that one performance of the show ran for several months or year but that several successive performances ran. Moreover, the construction cannot only be used with event-referring expressions but also with entities such as 'strips'. Here we get into problems of regular polysemy. The treatment we have given above needs to be complicated to take these into account.

a steady increase or decrease. We also examined the sentences with 'price ranged' and 'price went' in the whole of Wikipedia. Unfortunately there are very few examples but for these, the difference in interpretation for 'range' and 'go' seems to hold up: all 4 examples with 'go' had the interpretation of steady increase or decrease. So 'the price ranged ...' and 'the price went ...' statistically might get a different interpretation even if in some cases 'go' can be synonymous with 'range'.

Finally, there is a possibility that due to sparseness some required features can neither be derived from existing ontologies nor from natural language text itself. For example, in 'The 2006 Trek the Trail event was organised on the Railway Reserve Heritage Trail and went from Mundaring to Darlington' we assume an extent interpretation, and may thus be inclined to classify all events that way. However, in 'The case Arklow vs MacLean went all the way from the New Zealand High Court to the Privy Council in London.' we assume a change interpretation (movement), although WordNet sees 'event' as a hypernym of 'case'. Interestingly, it is not the arguments that determine the right interpretation here, but rather our distinction between different kinds of events: those for which spatial extent is important (street festivals) and those for which not (lawsuits). More generally, in cases where we are unable to make such fine distinctions based on features derived from available corpora, we can use our fourth method, soliciting additional features from human annotators, to group concepts in novel ways.

5 Conclusion

In this paper we first described the distinctions that need to be made to allow a correct interpretation of a subclass of *from-to* sentences. We then looked at the resources that are available to help us guide to the correct interpretation. We distinguished four different ways to obtain the information needed: features in an existing ontology, features statistically derived for the relations used with a concept, features computed through reasoning and features obtained through human annotation. We saw that a small, very preliminary examination of the data suggests that the three first methods will allow us to make the right distinctions in an important number of cases but that there will be cases in which the fourth method, human annotation, will be necessary.

Acknowledgments

This material is based in part upon work supported by the Air Force Research Laboratory (AFRL) under prime contract no. FA8750-09-C-0181. Any opinions, findings, and conclusion or recommendations expressed in this material are those of the author(s) and do not necessarily reflect the view of the Air Force Research Laboratory (AFRL).

References

Dorit Abusch. 1986. *Verbs of Change, Causation, and Time.* Report CSLI, Stanford University.

Daniel Bobrow, Robert Cheslow, Cleo Condoravdi, Lauri Karttunen, Tracy, Rowan Nairn, Valeria de Paiva, Lotti Price, and Annie Zaenen. 2007. PARC's Bridge question answering system. In *Proceedings of the GEAF (Grammar Engineering Across Frameworks) 2007 Workshop.* Stanford, CA.

David Dowty. 1979. *Word Meaning and Montague Grammar: The Semantics of Verbs and Times in Generative Semantics and in Montague's PTQ.* Springer.

Jean Mark Gawron. 2005. Generalized Paths. *SALT 17.*

Jean Mark Gawron. 2009. The Lexical Semantics of Extent Verbs.

Jennifer Hay, Christopher Kennedy, and Beth Levin. 1999. Scale structure underlies telicity in 'degree achievements'. pages 127–144.

Ray Jackendoff. 1996. The Proper Treatment of Measuring Out, Telicity, and Perhaps Even Quantification in English. *Natural Language and Linguistic Theory 14*, pages 305–354.

George A. Miller. 1995. Wordnet: A lexical database for english. *Communications of the ACM*, 38(11):39–41.

Hoifung Poon and Pedro Domingos. 2009. Unsupervised semantic parsing. In *EMNLP*.

PRISMATIC: Inducing Knowledge from a Large Scale Lexicalized Relation Resource*

James Fan and **David Ferrucci** and **David Gondek** and **Aditya Kalyanpur**
IBM Watson Research Lab
19 Skyline Dr
Hawthorne, NY 10532
{fanj, ferrucci, gondek, adityakal}@us.ibm.com

Abstract

One of the main bottlenecks in natural language processing is the lack of a comprehensive lexicalized relation resource that contains fine grained knowledge on predicates. In this paper, we present PRISMATIC, a large scale lexicalized relation resource that is automatically created over 30 gb of text. Specifically, we describe what kind of information is collected in PRISMATIC and how it compares with existing lexical resources. Our main focus has been on building the infrastructure and gathering the data. Although we are still in the early stages of applying PRISMATIC to a wide variety of applications, we believe the resource will be of tremendous value for AI researchers, and we discuss some of potential applications in this paper.

1 Introduction

Many natural language processing and understanding applications benefit from the interpretation of lexical relations in text (e.g. selectional preferences for verbs and nouns). For example, if one knows that things being annexed are typically geopolitical entities, then given the phrase *Napoleon's annexation of Piedmont*, we can infer *Piedmont* is a geopolitical entity. Existing linguistic resources such as VerbNet and FrameNet provide some argument type information for verbs and frames. However, since they are manually built, they tend to specify type constraints at a very high level (e.g, Solid, Animate), consequently they do not suffice for cases such as the previous example.

We would like to infer more fine grained knowledge for predicates automatically from a large amount of data. In addition, we do not want to restrict ourselves to only verbs, binary relations, or to a specific type hierarchy.

In this paper, we present PRISMATIC, a large scale lexicalized relation resource mined from over 30 gb of text. PRISMATIC is built using a suite of NLP tools that includes a dependency parser, a rule based named entity recognizer and a coreference resolution component. PRISMATIC is composed of frames which are the basic semantic representation of lexicalized relation and surrounding context. There are approximately 1 billion frames in our current version of PRISMATIC. To induce knowledge from PRISMATIC, we define the notion of frame-cuts, which basically specify a cut or slice operation on a frame. In the case of the previous Napoleon annexation example, we would use a noun-phrase $\rightarrow$ object type cut to learn the most frequent type of things being annexed. We believe there are many potential applications that can utilize PRISMATIC, such as type inference, relation extraction textual entailment, etc. We discuss some of these applications in details in section 8.

2 Related Work

2.1 Manually Created Resources

Several lexical resources have been built manually, most notably WordNet (Fellbaum, 1998), FrameNet(Baker et al., 1998) and VerbNet(Baker et

*Research supported in part by Air Force Contract FA8750-09-C-0172 under the DARPA Machine Reading Program

Proceedings of the NAACL HLT 2010 First International Workshop on Formalisms and Methodology for Learning by Reading, pages 122–127,
Los Angeles, California, June 2010.

al., 1998). WordNet is a lexical resource that contains individual word synset information, such as definition, synonyms, antonyms, etc. However, the amount of predicate knowledge in WordNet is limited.

FrameNet is a lexical database that describes the frame structure of selected words. Each frame represents a predicate (e.g. eat, remove) with a list of frame elements that constitutes the semantic arguments of the predicate. Different words may map to the same frame, and one word may map to multiple frames based on different word senses. Frame elements are often specific to a particular frame, and even if two frame elements with the same name, such as "Agent", may have subtle semantic meanings in different frames.

VerbNet is a lexical database that maps verbs to their corresponding Levin (Levin, 1993) classes, and it includes syntactic and semantic information of the verbs, such as the syntactic sequences of a frame (e.g. *NP V NP PP*) and the selectional restriction of a frame argument value *must be ANIMATE*,

Compared to these resources, in addition to being an automatic process, PRISMATIC has three major differences. First, unlike the descriptive knowledge in WordNet, VerbNet or FrameNet, PRISMATIC offers only numeric knowledge of the frequencies of how different predicates and their argument values through out a corpus. The statistical profiles are easily to produce automatically, and they allow additional knowledge, such as type restriction (see 8.1), to be inferred from PRISMATIC easily.

Second, the frames are defined differently. The frames in PRISMATIC are not abstract concepts generalized over a set of words. They are defined by the words in a sentence and the relations between them. Two frames with different slot values are considered different even though they may be semantically similar. For example, the two sentences "John loves Mary" and "John adores Mary" result in two different frame even though semantically they are very close. By choosing not to use frame concepts generalized over words, we avoid the problem of determining which frame a word belongs to when processing text automatically. We believe there will be enough redundancy in a large corpus to produce valid values for different synonyms and variations.

Third, PRISMATIC only uses a very small set of slots (see table 1) defined by parser and relation annotators to link a frame and its arguments. By using these slots directly, we avoid the problem of mapping parser relations to frame elements.

2.2 Automatically Created Resources

TextRunner (Banko et al., 2007) is an information extraction system which automatically extracts relation tuples over massive web data in an unsupervised manner. TextRunner contains over 800 million extractions (Lin et al., 2009) and has proven to be a useful resource in a number of important tasks in machine reading such as hypernym discovery (Alan Ritter and Etzioni, 2009), and scoring interesting assertions (Lin et al., 2009). TextRunner works by automatically identifying and extracting relationships using a conditional random field (CRF) model over natural language text. As this is a relatively inexpensive technique, it allows rapid application to web-scale data.

DIRT (Discovering Inference Rules from Text) (Lin and Pantel, 2001) automatically identifies inference rules over dependency paths which tend to link the same arguments. The technique consists of applying a dependency parser over 1 gb of text, collecting the paths between arguments and then calculating a path similarity between paths. DIRT has been used extensively in recognizing textual entailment (RTE).

PRISMATIC is similar to TextRunner and DIRT in that it may be applied automatically over massive corpora. At a representational level it differs from both TextRunner and DIRT by storing full frames from which n-ary relations may be indexed and queried. PRISMATIC differs from TextRunner as it applies a full dependency parser in order to identify dependency relationships between terms. In contrast to DIRT and TextRunner, PRISMATIC also performs co-reference resolution in order to increase coverage for sparsely-occurring entities and employs a named entity recognizer (NER) and relation extractor on all of its extractions to better represent intensional information.

3 System Overview

The PRISMATIC pipeline consists of three phases:

1. **Corpus Processing** Documents are annotated

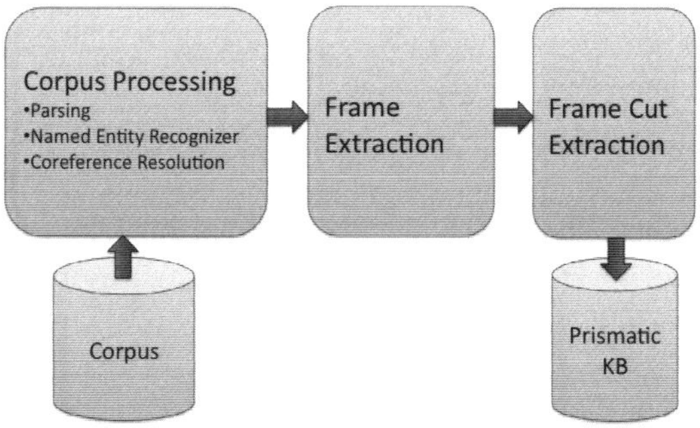

Figure 1: System Overview

by a suite of components which perform dependency parsing, co-reference resolution, named entity recognition and relation detection.

2. **Frame Extraction** Frames are extracted based on the dependency parses and associated annotations.

3. **Frame-Cut Extraction** Frame-cuts of interest (e.g. S-V-O cuts) are identified over all frames and frequency information for each cut is tabulated.

4 Corpus Processing

The key step in the Corpus Processing stage is the application of a dependency parser which is used to identify the frame slots (as listed in Table 1) for the Frame Extraction stage. We use ESG (McCord, 1990), a slot-grammar based parser in order to fill in the frame slots. Sentences frequently require co-reference in order to precisely identify the participating entity, and so in order to not lose that information, we apply a simple rule based co-reference resolution component in this phase. The co-reference information helps enhance the coverage of the frame-cuts, which is especially valuable in cases of sparse data and for use with complex frame-cuts.

A rule based Named Entity Recognizer (NER) is used to identify the types of arguments in all frame slot values. This type information is then registered in the Frame Extraction stage to construct intentional frames.

5 Frame Extraction

Relation	Description/Example
subj	subject
obj	direct object
iobj	indirect object
comp	complement
pred	predicate complement
objprep	object of the preposition
mod_nprep	*Bat Cave in Toronto is a tourist attraction.*
mod_vprep	*He made it to Broadway.*
mod_nobj	the object of a nominalized verb
mod_ndet	*City's budget was passed.*
mod_ncomp	*Tweet is a word for microblogging.*
mod_nsubj	*A poem by Byron*
mod_aobj	*John is similar to Steve.*
isa	subsumption relation
subtypeOf	subsumption relation

Table 1: Relations used in a frame and their descriptions

The next step of PRISMATIC is to extract a set of frames from the parsed corpus. A frame is the basic semantic unit representing a set of entities and their relations in a text snippet. A frame is made of a set of slot value pairs where the slots are dependency relations extracted from the parse and the values are the terms from the sentences or annotated types. Table 2 shows the extracted frame based on the parse tree in figure 2.

In order to capture the relationship we are interested in, frame elements are limited to those that represent the participant information of a predicate. Slots consist of the ones listed in table 1. Furthermore, each frame is restricted to be two levels deep at the most, therefore, a large parse tree may result in multiple frames. Table 2 shows how two frames are extracted from the complex parse tree in figure 2. The depth restriction is needed for two reasons. First, despite the best efforts from parser researchers, no parser is perfect, and big complex parse trees tend to have more wrong parses. By limiting a frame to be only a small subset of a complex parse tree, we reduce the chance of error parse in each frame. Second, by isolating a subtree, each frame focuses on the immediate participants of a predicate.

Non-parser information may also be included in a frame. For example, the type annotations of a word from a named entity recognizer are included, and such type information is useful for the various ap-

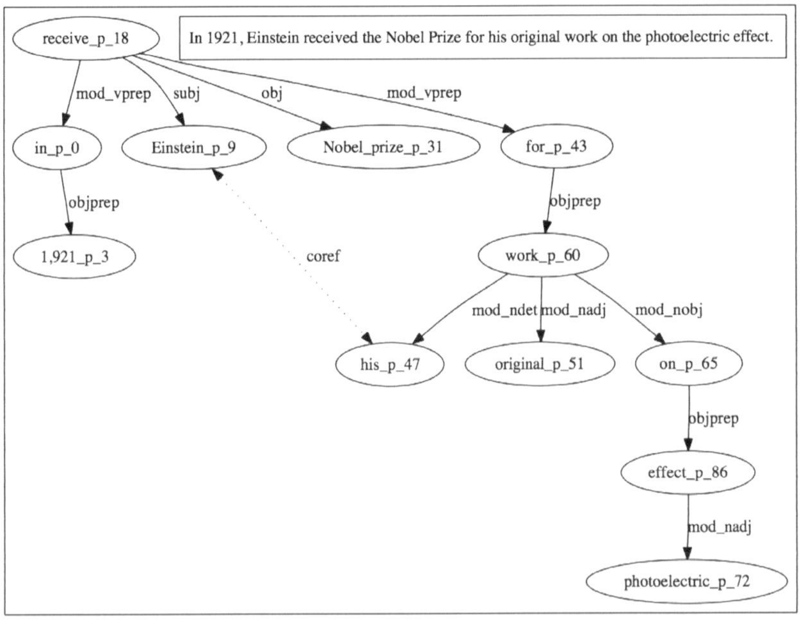

Figure 2: The parse tree of the sentence *In 1921, Einstein received the Nobel Prize for his original work on the photoelectric effect.*

Frame01	
verb	receive
subj	Einstein
type	PERSON / SCIENTIST
obj	Nobel prize
mod_vprep	in
objprep	1921
type	YEAR
mod_vprep	for
objprep	Frame02

Frame02	
noun	work
mod_ndet	his / Einstein
mod_nobj	on
objprep	effect

Table 2: Frames extracted from Dependency Parse in Figure 2

plications described in section 8. We also include a flag to indicate whether a word is proper noun. These two kinds of information allow us to easily separate the intensional and the extensional parts of PRISMATIC.

6 Frame Cut

One of the main reasons for extracting a large amount of frame data from a corpus is to induce interesting knowledge patterns by exploiting redundancy in the data. For example, we would like to learn that things that are annexed are typically regions, i.e., a predominant object-type for the noun-phrase "annexation of" is "Region" where "Region" is annotated by a NER. To do this kind of knowledge induction, we first need to abstract out specific portions of the frame - in this particular case, we need to isolate and analyze the noun-phrase $\rightarrow$ object-type relationship. Then, given a lot of data, and frames containing only the above relationship, we hope to see the frame [noun="annexation", preposition="of", object-type="Region"] occur very frequently.

To enable this induction analysis, we define frame-cuts, which basically specify a cut or slice operation on a frame. For example, we define an N-P-OT frame cut, which when applied to a frame only keeps the noun (N), preposition (P) and object-type (OT) slots, and discards the rest. Similarly, we define frame-cuts such as S-V-O, S-V-O-IO, S-V-P-O etc. (where S - subject, V - verb, O - object, IO - indirect object) which all dissect frames along different dimensions. Continuing with the annexation example, we can use the V-OT frame cut to learn that a predominant object-type for the verb "annex" is also "Region", by seeing lots of frames of the form [verb="annex", object-type="Region"] in our data.

To make frame-cuts more flexible, we allow them to specify optional value constraints for slots. For example, we can define an S-V-O frame cut, where both the subject (S) and object (O) slot values are constrained to be proper nouns, thereby creating strictly extensional frames, i.e. frames containing data about instances, e.g., [subject="United States" verb="annex" object="Texas"]. The opposite effect is achieved by constraining S and O slot values to common nouns, creating intensional frames such as [subject="Political-Entity" verb="annex" object="Region"]. The separation of extensional from intensional frame information is desirable, both from a knowledge understanding and an applications perspective, e.g. the former can be used to provide factual evidence in tasks such as question answering, while the latter can be used to learn entailment rules as seen in the annexation case.

7 Data

The corpora we used to produce the initial PRISMATIC are based on a selected set of sources, such as the complete Wikipedia, New York Times archive and web page snippets that are on the topics listed in wikipedia. After cleaning and html detagging, there are a total of 30 GB of text. From these sources, we extracted approximately 1 billion frames, and from these frames, we produce the most commonly used cuts such as S-V-O, S-V-P-O and S-V-O-IO.

8 Potential Applications

8.1 Type Inference and Its Related Uses

As noted in Section 6, we use frame-cuts to dissect frames along different slot dimensions, and then aggregate statistics for the resultant frames across the entire dataset, in order to induce relationships among the various frame slots, e.g., learn the predominant types for subject/object slots in verb and noun phrases. Given a new piece of text, we can apply this knowledge to infer types for named entities. For example, since the aggregate statistics shows the most common type for the object of the verb "annex" is Region, we can infer from the sentence "Napoleon annexed Piedmont in 1859", that "Piedmont" is most likely to be a Region. Similarly, consider the sentence: "He ordered a Napoleon at the restaurant". A dictionary based NER is very likely to label "Napoleon" as a Person. However, we can learn from a large amount of data, that in the frame: [subject_type="Person" verb="order" object_type=[?] verb_prep="at" object_prep="restaurant"], the object_type typically denotes a Dish, and thus correctly infer the type for "Napoleon" in this context. Learning this kind of fine-grained type information for a particular context is not possible using traditional hand-crafted resources like VerbNet or FrameNet. Unlike previous work in selectional restriction (Carroll and McCarthy, 2000; Resnik, 1993), PRISMATIC based type inference does not dependent on a particular taxonomy or previously annotated training data: it works with any NER and its type system.

The automatically induced-type information can also be used for co-reference resolution. For example, given the sentence: "Netherlands was ruled by the UTP party before Napolean annexed it", we can use the inferred type constraint on "it" (Region) to resolve it to "Netherlands" (instead of the "UTP Party").

Finally, typing knowledge can be used for word sense disambiguation. In the sentence, "Tom Cruise is one of the biggest stars in American Cinema", we can infer using our frame induced type knowledge base, that the word "stars" in this context refers to a Person/Actor type, and not the sense of "star" as an astronomical object.

8.2 Factual Evidence

Frame data, especially extensional data involving named entities, captured over a large corpus can be used as factual evidence in tasks such as question answering.

8.3 Relation Extraction

Traditional relation extraction approach (Zelenko et al., 2003; Bunescu and Mooney, 2005) relies on the correct identification of the types of the argument. For example, to identify "employs" relation between "John Doe" and "XYZ Corporation", a relation extractor heavily relies on "John Doe" being annotated as a "PERSON" and "XYZ Corporation" an "ORGANIZATION" since the "employs" relation is defined between a "PERSON" and an "ORGANIZATION".

We envision PRISMATIC to be applied to relation extraction in two ways. First, as described in section 8.1, PRISMATIC can complement a named entity recognizer (NER) for type annotation. This is especially useful for the cases when NER fails. Second, since PRISMATIC has broad coverage of named entities, it can be used as a database to check to see if the given argument exist in related frame. For example, in order to determine if "employs" relation exists between "Jack Welch" and "GE" in a sentence, we can look up the SVO cut of PRISMATIC to see if we have any frame that has "Jack Welch" as the subject, "GE" as the object and "work" as the verb, or frame that has "Jack Welch" as the object, "GE" as the subject and "employs" as the verb. This information can be passed on as an feature along with other syntactic and semantic features to th relation extractor.

9 Conclusion and Future Work

In this paper, we presented PRISMATIC, a large scale lexicalized relation resource that is built automatically over massive amount of text. It provides users with knowledge about predicates and their arguments. We have focused on building the infrastructure and gathering the data. Although we are still in the early stages of applying PRISMATIC, we believe it will be useful for a wide variety of AI applications as discussed in section 8, and will pursue them in the near future.

References

Stephen Soderland Alan Ritter and Oren Etzioni. 2009. What is this, anyway: Automatic hypernym discovery. In *Proceedings of the 2009 AAAI Spring Symposium on Learning by Reading and Learning to Read.*

Collin F. Baker, Charles J. Fillmore, and John B. Lowe. 1998. The berkeley framenet project. In *Proceedings of the 17th international conference on Computational linguistics*, pages 86–90, Morristown, NJ, USA. Association for Computational Linguistics.

Michele Banko, Michael J Cafarella, Stephen Soderl, Matt Broadhead, and Oren Etzioni. 2007. Open information extraction from the web. In *In International Joint Conference on Artificial Intelligence*, pages 2670–2676.

Razvan C. Bunescu and Raymond J. Mooney. 2005. A shortest path dependency kernel for relation extraction. In *HLT '05: Proceedings of the conference on Human Language Technology and Empirical Methods in Natural Language Processing*, pages 724–731, Morristown, NJ, USA. Association for Computational Linguistics.

John Carroll and Diana McCarthy. 2000. Word sense disambiguation using automatically acquired verbal preferences. *Computers and the Humanities Senseval Special Issue*, 34.

Christiane Fellbaum, 1998. *WordNet: An Electronic Lexical Database.*

Beth Levin, 1993. *English Verb Classes and Alternations: A Preliminary Investigation.*

Dekang Lin and Patrick Pantel. 2001. Dirt - discovery of inference rules from text. In *In Proceedings of the ACM SIGKDD Conference on Knowledge Discovery and Data Mining*, pages 323–328.

Thomas Lin, Oren Etzioni, and James Fogarty. 2009. Identifying interesting assertions from the web. In *CIKM '09: Proceeding of the 18th ACM conference on Information and knowledge management*, pages 1787–1790, New York, NY, USA. ACM.

Michael C. McCord. 1990. Slot grammar: A system for simpler construction of practical natural language grammars. In *Proceedings of the International Symposium on Natural Language and Logic*, pages 118–145, London, UK. Springer-Verlag.

Philip Resnik. 1993. *Selection and Information: A Class-Based Approach to Lexical Relationships.* Ph.D. thesis, University of Pennsylvania.

Dmitry Zelenko, Chinatsu Aone, and Anthony Richardella. 2003. Kernel methods for relation extraction. *J. Mach. Learn. Res.*, 3:1083–1106.

Author Index

Association for Computational Linguistics
209 N. Eighth Street
Stroudsburg, Pennsylvania 18360

RLTLN 2014: Reseaux Lexicaux pour le TAL

(RLTLN 2014: Lexical Networks for NLP)

TALN-RECITAL 2014 Workshop

Marseille, France
1 July 2014

ISBN: 978-1-63439-520-5